WHAT'S WRONG WITH ECONOMICS?

WHAT'S WRONG WITH ECONOMICS?

A PRIMER FOR THE PERPLEXED

ROBERT SKIDELSKY

YALE UNIVERSITY PRESS
NEW HAVEN AND LONDON

For information about this and other Yale University Press publications, please contact:
U.S. Office: sales.press@yale.edu   yalebooks.com
Europe Office: sales@yaleup.co.uk   yalebooks.co.uk

Set in Minion Pro by IDSUK (DataConnection) Ltd
Printed in Great Britain by TJ International Ltd, Padstow, Cornwall

Library of Congress Control Number: 2019956878

ISBN 978-0-300-24987-3

A catalogue record for this book is available from the British Library.

10 9 8 7 6 5 4 3 2 1

To students and teachers of economics

CONTENTS

FIGURES

PREFACE

Many students want to study economics to learn how to make the world better. They soon discover that studying economics is studying what economists do. The question is whether what economists do is fit for purpose. This book tries to address this question.

The question arises because of the complicity of mainstream economics in much of what has gone wrong with economic life in the last thirty years, starting with the dismantling of labour protections and proceeding, via the explosion of inequality, to the crash of the global financial system in 2007–2008. Free competition was 'set loose to run, like a huge untrained monster, its wayward course, indifferent to the fate of humanity'.[1] This quotation from Alfred Marshall's *Principles of Economics* is an apt depiction of what was allowed to happen in our own times.

Anyone with a historical sense would have realised that the hubristic attempt to make the world into a frontier- and culture-free single market would end in tears. But to the dominant tendency in economics, market-led globalisation has been a kind of coming of age, when humankind, for the first time in history, shed its irrational resistance to unlimited buying and selling. I was led to ponder the state of mind of a profession which could offer such a prospectus and call it progress. Moreover, I became convinced that the tendency to 'unleash the market' was inherent in economics from its earliest times: mainstream economics today is largely a return to the roots. The more I thought about it the more I became convinced that the cardinal fault of economics lies not in specific doctrines, but the methods it uses to reach its conclusions.

What I hope to provide is an insight into the mind of the econo-mist, into a style of thinking about economic behaviour which is characteristic of economists. I am not claiming that all economists think like this. It is a 'model' which aims to explain salient features of the *way* economists think. What I found in the mind of the economist is a picture of the human being as a utility maximiser. To economists, coherent purposes and reliable calculations of the consequences of action are the magic keys which unlock the secrets of human behaviour. This conception of *homo economicus* under-pins their policy advice: individuals will respond to interventions in a predictable way. The reason their advice is so often wrong is that their picture of human motives is incomplete. Quite simply, it leaves out all the motives for choice and action which fall outside the calculus of behaviour they have set up. As a consequence it fails to predict many outcomes accurately.

The main target of my attack is 'neoclassical' or 'marginalist' or 'mainstream' economics (I use the terms interchangeably) because this has been so dominant in the textbooks and gives a distinctive flavour to the way all economics is done today. I distinguish it from 'classical' economics which was a much broader church than its neo-classical successor, both in its view of what social matter consists of and in its view of how knowledge is attained. Neoclassical economics narrowed the discipline considerably by claiming that only individu-als *really* exist – organisations are simply constructions of individu-als – and that their rationality makes their behaviour predictable. I call this mainstream, because ever since Lionel Robbins defined the neoclassical position in a famous essay of 1932, it has been dominant in the profession. My own critical stance necessarily brings out the weaknesses rather than strengths of this method: but in view of its extravagant claims to knowledge, it is the weaknesses not strengths which need exposing. The great strength of economics lies in its power of generalisation; its weakness is to generalise from over-simple premises. It is this flaw which will be the focus of my attack.

Neoclassical economics claims to be more like physics than any other social science does, able to make 'hard' predictions. In its own estimation, this gives it unique authority. To which one may reply:

you can put on the uniform of a policeman but that does not give you the authority of a policeman. The uniform of economics is very impressive. It is replete with models, equations, regressions, statistics: the claims to authority we associate with science, and whose absence condemns studies like sociology and politics to the status of inferior, in other words palpably non-authoritative, musings. How has economics managed to pull off a feat of authority which has eluded all the other social sciences? Because it is undoubtedly the most influential of them, the discipline to which governments and administrators pay greatest homage.

No small part of the answer, as we shall see, lies in the magic of numbers. It is the ability to attach numbers to mathematical symbols which gives economics its unique selling power. It enables economists to make quantitative predictions. No other social science counts and measures its material so energetically. Many eminent economists have complained of the overuse of maths in economics, but few have explained clearly that this overuse is inherent in its restriction of economic behaviour to what can be measured. No one would have much interest in mathematical models of the economy unless they could be resolved into quantities of people and things.

As I tell it, mathematical language must be seen as part of the art of persuasion, not of demonstration, because economists cannot demonstrate the truth of what they are saying, only persuade you to see the world as they do.

An easy, and to some extent valid, attack on the way I depict neoclassical economics is to say that it is caricature. Some readers may feel that I distort what goes on in the mind of the economist. But it is the caricature which rules the textbooks. The method of stating a hypothesis in a 'silly' form (Paul Krugman's phrase) and then 'relaxing the assumptions' to bring it into closer touch with reality exerts a gravitational pull towards over-simple reasoning. And it is the 'toy' models which often pass for gospel among financial journalists, business lobbyists, and politicians. Abstracting from money in the toy model, and then adding it into the more complicated model, is a good example of a method which failed to understand the crucial role of the financial system as 'mover and shaker' in the events leading up to the crash of 2008. The toy models exclude the all-pervasive influence of power and uncertainty in shaping outcomes.

Another criticism would be that my account ignores developments in the mainstream since the 1980s. The crash of the global economy in 2008 was undoubtedly a shock, and it led to genuine soul-searching. 'Behavioural economics' has been its main fruit so far; and beside behavioural economics, there have been hundreds of papers in the specialist journals explaining how cascades, crashes, and fads can happen. All this is to be welcomed, if only as a belated discovery of behaviours which have long been obvious to non-economists. My criticism of these new approaches to realism is that they start life crippled by the attempt to render them consistent with a method which has as its root the *contrary* hypothesis of rational calculation. Indeed, in these models, it is impossible for people *not* to behave rationally (maximising, optimising) even though the results may turn out to be far from what they expect. As Nobel Laureate Thomas Sargent (b.1943), an inexhaustible source of pithy summary of mainstream positions, puts it: 'irrationality is a special case of rationality'.

In my account of how economics is done, I have tried hard to cite only the best in the field. Many of them are Nobel Laureates. Equally, it is not out of the mouths of babes and sucklings that the most incisive attacks on mainstream economics have come, but from some of the finest minds in the history of economic thought.

This is in no way a textbook, but it refers to matter which is found in textbooks. It is aimed at students of economics, and written in a way intended to catch the interest of economists and non-economists who wonder where economics is leading us. My aim is to ask economists to interrogate their *implicit* premises and, by bringing them into the light of day, consider how far they really believe what their models assert. The language is as simple as I can make it, but the ideas are complicated and often deep. The book is based on the set of lectures which I was invited to deliver for the Institute of New Economic Thinking in 2018, in London and New

York. I have taken advantage of writing the book to repair omissions from the much shorter lectures, and also to reconsider some of the things I said, following comments and criticisms the lectures received.

In what way am I qualified to talk about these matters? My first degree was in history; my Ph.D was in politics. I was always interested in the economic aspects of history and politics, but when I decided to write about the great economist John Maynard Keynes, I quickly realised that it was not enough to have a nodding acquaintance with economics. So I studied the subject seriously, wrote three volumes on Keynes, and ended up with a chair in political economy in the economics department of Warwick University.

These personal facts have a bearing on what follows, in two related ways. First, I come to economics with a strong historical bias – the bias, that is, to see economic doctrines in context. Secondly, economics not being my first discipline, I came to it as an outsider, setting myself to learn its methods, habits, and rituals, rather like an anthropologist studying a tribe, or a migrant trying to master the customs of his or her host community. I have looked into the mind of the economist from the outside, and learned a lot from it. But I speak the language of economics with an accent.

A word needs to be said about the relationship of this book to 'heterodox economics', which is also highly critical of the mainstream approach. According to Geoffrey Hodgson, a leading heterodox economist, what heterodox economics should aim to do is to establish a unified discipline which includes but transcends neoclassical economics, so as to maintain what he calls the 'cumulative advance' in economic knowledge. I don't think we are anywhere near a unified discipline, or even that a new orthodoxy is desirable.

As I see it, the right development in economics would be towards what John Kay has called a 'horses for courses' approach – that is, one which relates economic theory to the different situations in which it needs to be applied. In short, economics should abandon the attempt to construct a set of universal laws applicable to all situations and problems. Specifically, it should abandon the attempt to 'microfound' macroeconomics – in other words, to insist that all general outcomes need to be explained in terms of the rational choices of isolated individuals. This leads, for example, to the absurd, and inhumane, conclusion that mass unemployment is the sum of individual choices to work less. I prefer the label 'pluralism' to 'heterodoxy'. Pluralism involves explicitly taking into account the insights of other disciplines. In addition to this, I am far from convinced that there has been a 'cumulative advance' in economic knowledge of the kind Professor Hodgson supposes. The main reason is that, unlike in most natural sciences, there is no secure method of bringing any generalising economic proposition to the test.

There are too many fine economists and schools of thought outside the mainstream tradition to come even close to doing them justice within this book: ecological economics, feminist economics, econophysics, biophysical economics and modern monetary theory is an incomplete list of doctrines that are mostly set aside here. The only defence against their exclusion is that this book is not intended as a summary of the alternative schools or approaches. Excellent works in that vein include John T. Harvey's *Contending Perspectives in Economics* and *Rethinking Economics: An Introduction to Pluralist Economics*, an edited volume produced by members of the student movement Rethinking Economics.[2]

If the presentation of the book suggests that those outside the mainstream have the status of mere dissidents to the dominant tradition, that is entirely unintended. The focus of the book is on how and why mainstream economics has come to be the way it is. In light of its serious flaws, it might be tempting simply to dismiss the mainstream out of hand and focus on the construction of alternatives. But if we do not understand the roots of its dominance, we leave ourselves poorly placed to dislodge it.

The authority of economics derives in no small measure from its opacity. I want to insist, on the contrary, on the absolute need for the core ideas in economics (and more generally in the social sciences) to be transparent, essentially not to be buried in technical jargon. This is for two reasons. First, it is important that people should understand what is being *claimed* about their own behaviour. The language of social theory should always be open enough to make possible an argument over interpretation between the observer and the observed. Opacity is a way of disguising power.

Second, the disciplines must be able to talk to each other. Specialised language is necessary, but is also a form of blindness – blinding its users to anything being said outside their own theoretical enclaves. It is the classic form of exclusion. All the great economists of the past tried to communicate their insights in ordinary language: Alfred Marshall famously confined diagrams to appendices. But today economists normally talk maths to each other, and few bother to talk or listen to anyone else. In fact the division of labour has gone even further: the subsets of economists don't talk to each other either; and the mainstream never talks to the 'heterodox'. This fault of over-specialisation applies to all the social sciences. They hardly ever read each other's literature, even though the literatures deal with the same topics. But the fault of economists is greater because their language is more impenetrable.

I am grateful to the Institute of New Economic Thinking for making it possible for me to pursue my interest in reforming the economics curriculum; and to the many students who encouraged me on my way. I would also like to thank the following for reading earlier versions of this manuscript: James Kenneth Galbraith, Rodion Garshin, Anthony Giddens, Geoffrey Hodgson, Tony Lawson, Vladimir Masch, and Edward Skidelsky. Their incisive comments on the draft manuscript have greatly improved both the argument and its presentation. It is perhaps even more necessary to affirm that the faults are mine.

A special word of thanks goes to Sam Wheldon-Bayes, a recent economics graduate, without whose help this book could not have been written. Sam worked on the book with me for a year altogether, and I owe important arguments and examples to him. Of his own experience in studying economics at a British university he writes:

> Despite the battering it has taken since the 2008 financial crisis, both externally and from dissenters within the ranks, economics retains a privileged position in public life. Neoliberalism, the

dominant public policy paradigm of our times is, in effect, the view that essentially all social problems have economic solutions: the market knows best.

Many economists might take issue with the claim that they have so much influence, arguing that too few politicians pay them sufficient heed. It is tempting, in the era of Trump and Brexit, to go along with this view, since the rhetoric of both of these so-called 'populist revolts' might cut against economists' prescriptions of free trade. However, lurking behind both is a strain of pro-business market fundamentalism that draws its intellectual credibility almost entirely from a particular view of economics, one that bears striking resemblance to the picture of the subject offered by the standard curriculum: everything will work out just fine, so long as the government keeps its nose out.

Many professional economists have substantially more nuanced views about the role of government in economies, and argued forcefully against the election of Donald Trump, and in particular against Britain's proposed exit from the European Union. This, however, raises the important question of what we really mean when we talk of economics. Do we mean the professional views and research output of economists in academia, government, and the private sector? Or do we mean the picture of the subject that students are taught in university courses?

In other words, is it *Econometrica* or *Economics 101*, the journal or the textbook? In few subjects is the gulf between what students are taught and what researchers practise as wide as it is in economics. It is quite possible for capable, hardworking students to study economics for three years, receive an excellent mark for their degree and still not really have the faintest idea of what professional economists do. At that point, they may go forth into the world and, quite reasonably, label themselves economists.

So, the protestations that economics has reformed in the years since the crash are not as convincing as they might be. It is not enough that unreadable articles in barely accessible journals have made some minor modifications to the way they do things. The core of what the economics profession passes on to the next generation, the undergraduate curriculum, remains unchanged. One of the basic premises of academic study is that each generation should be able to absorb the lessons of their predecessors and build upon them. In economics, all too often, the next generation must dismantle the intellectual walls the previous generation has constructed for them before any progress can be made.

1

WHY METHODOLOGY?

A man is not likely to be a good economist
if he is nothing else.

John Stuart Mill[1]

The need for economists to think about economics became apparent after the global financial crisis of 2007–2008. Few economists predicted the crash; more damningly, few envisaged the possibility that such a collapse could occur, any more than the crash of an algorithmic system. Students of economics asked: what is the point of studying economics if it can't tell you what is going on, or offer policies to prevent bad things from happening? For what happened was the worst economic crisis since the Second World War. Terms to describe it go from the Lesser Depression to the Great Recession.

The roots of this failure do not lie with the incompetence or inattention of individual economists, but deep within the way economics is done – its methodology. This may sound dry and boring, but the methods of economists are key to understanding how and why economics goes wrong. Neoclassical economics has developed a peculiar method for studying the economy, and the use of any other method is not regarded as economics. In other words, the subject matter of economics is defined by the neoclassical method. Models based on this method allow for only a limited range of possibilities. Events which might occur outside this range are not picked up on economists' radar screens. Models which show financial markets to be efficient – as most of them did – will not give you the collapse of 2008. The spate of papers offering explanations of the crash came *after* the crash. We now learn that, with a bit of uncertainty, 'multiple equilibria' can be 'endogenously' generated. But there was no 'uncertainty' before the crash, only insurable risk. So, this book aims to discover why the most influential discipline for making public policy is so often cut off from reality.

Economists usually scorn the study of methodology. 'Those who can, do science', said Paul Samuelson (1915–2009), 'Those who can't, prattle on about methodology.'[2] Frank Hahn (1925–2013) similarly claimed, 'I want to advise the young to avoid spending too much time and thought on methodology. As for them learning philosophy, what next?'[3] In other words, these eminent economists didn't see the need for students of economics to think about what they were doing. Their message was not how to think, but what to think.

If economics were a natural science, this would be good advice. Natural scientists don't spend their time agonising about their methodology. They believe, with good reason, that the methods they have evolved for understanding physical matter are adequate for discovering the truth. (In fact, reflections on method have always intertwined with developments in physics from Descartes to Einstein. But for all practical purposes, the methodology of the natural sciences is fixed.) Most economists take the same line. Their world is peopled with human robots and they aim to establish 'laws' about the behaviour of these machine-like creatures. A complete set of laws is not yet to hand: but they will catch up with the natural scientists in the end, perhaps after the neuroscientists have completed their work on the brain. They are loathe to admit that the material they study and try to understand does not behave with the law-like regularity of natural phenomena. Humans are, uniquely, inventive animals. They are aware of who they are, reflect on their experiences, set themselves goals, relate to each other and their environments in complicated ways, puzzle about the morality of their actions, adapt creatively to new situations. By the exercise of their minds and imaginations, they modify the future – their own, and the world's. Their games cannot be 'sussed out'. The most secure laws of economics are tendencies at best.

Open and closed systems

John Maynard Keynes (1883–1946), one of the greatest economists of all time, pointed to the inescapable fact of uncertainty:

> It is as though the fall of the apple to the ground depended on the apple's motives, on whether it is worthwhile falling to the ground, and whether the ground wanted the apple to fall, and on mistaken calculations on the part of the apple as to how far it was from the centre of the earth.[4]

The implications of this statement are profound. Keynes is saying that humans are not 'programmed' to behave like apples. Humans are parts of complex systems, whose motions cannot be explained by the causal laws on which natural science is built.

The difference between natural and human material can be expressed by saying that a *closed* system is one in which 'if X, then Y'-type statements apply, whereas an *open* system is one in which they don't.[5]

True enough, there is a lot of variety in a closed system: in a game of chess, there is a vast number of possible combinations. But the variety is finite, and in time all optimal moves will have been made. (Or so it seems: mathematicians claim that chess is so complicated that potential optimal moves approach the infinite.) The principle of limited variety is true of the physical world. If you roll a fair die, there *is* a ⅙ chance of each outcome. This 'truth' does not depend on how the die views the situation. But if you say that a fall in interest rates by X *will* lead to an increase in investment of Y amount you are converting an open system into a closed system. Only if the rest of the economy is frozen by assumption or decree would a change in X produce a predictable effect on Y.

What economics does is to convert open systems into closed systems by excluding 'moves' which would render the system unstable. Dictators 'freeze the frame' by order: economists do it by 'modelling'. They model the world as a giant computer network in which every possible move has been programmed, and anything 'outside' the frame excluded by assumption. We will have more to say about the freezing technique in Chapters 4 and 5. But even at this point one can assert that their claim to be able to predict behaviour is greatly exaggerated. Apples do not choose whether or not to fall to the ground, any more than a hurricane chooses whether or not to happen every few years. They have no choice; the task of science is to explain why they behave in the way they do, not why they choose to do what they do. Economists are seduced by the thought that, because humans are part of nature, their code can be cracked just like that of physical objects. But even those who hold out this hope admit that humans are uniquely complicated. This makes social systems for all practical purposes almost infinitely complex.

The method of freezing the frame, and including in it only measurable moves, works well enough in the analysis of individual markets or firms in isolation. But it breaks down when applied to a whole economy. This reminds us that economics has its roots in microeconomics – the study of the logic of choice in a single market without money. Money, the errant or wandering cause, which causes whole economies to misfire, was added as a separate field of study. In the standard textbook it is introduced in later chapters as a 'complicating' factor. Keynesian macroeconomics tried to take this complicating factor into account in explaining economy-wide malfunction. More recently, economics has reverted back to microeconomics, with macroeconomics squeezed out by assuming that money can be got to behave in a non-disturbing way. Microeconomic theory can then be 'scaled up' to explain the behaviour of the whole economy. However, the big questions of the macroeconomy – what causes prosperity or depression, inflation or deflation, growth or stagnation – cannot be satisfactorily answered with the tools of microeconomics.

The method of economics

The study of the methodology of economics is the study of the methods which economists use to gain knowledge, rather than a study of the knowledge they claim to have acquired. That is to say, it is not primarily a study of economic doctrines. Rather, the proliferation of economic doctrines testifies to the failure of the established methods to generate knowledge, if by knowledge we mean *true belief*. The methods which produce 'laws' in physics produce doctrines in economics. The hypotheses of economists are largely untestable. In this they resemble religious beliefs. The question is not whether economics can be made more like a natural science, but whether different methods might enable it to improve its understanding of human behaviour. The charge is not one of false reasoning, but of reasoning from over-simple premises.

In today's classroom, students are fed models: the better the university, the more complete their drilling in the conventional models. The basic model is that of a perfectly competitive economy, in which prices adjust the preferences of perfectly informed buyers and sellers to each other. Students must be taught to learn such models, not question them. The collapse of the financial system in 2008 took nearly all economists by surprise, because such collapses were 'outside' their models.

Economic models are supposed to be closely related to the real world: once mastered, the model offers reliable knowledge of 'what is going on'. But this relationship is not obvious. Economic models are not like model aeroplanes, which are scaled-down versions of a real aeroplane. It's easy to see if you have a bad model aeroplane – it looks nothing like the real thing. But economic models are not miniaturised replicas of real things. They typically consist of logical deductions from axioms (truths treated as self-evident). How do you know that your economic model has any relation to reality? That the premises of the argument have not excluded parts of reality important to understanding what might happen? A reply might be that the model is a caricature which nevertheless contains the essential features of the real thing. But a caricature is only identified as such because we have an actual face or body to compare it with. Economists, like natural scientists, are committed to bringing their caricatures 'to the data', and rejecting those which are disconfirmed by the data. But I shall argue that no secure tests exist for many models which claim authority. Economics' inability to validate its most important hypotheses empirically means that it has a strong tendency to slide into ideology. The pretence to science makes invisible the rhetorical character of much of its thinking.

Economists suffer from 'physics envy' because they believe that their material – human beings – being rooted in nature, are only more complicated versions of natural objects. Like the technologists, they believe that with enough data and computing power they can 'crack the code' of human behaviour. This quest – and the envy which inspires it – is misplaced. It drives economists further away from the 'real' world of humans whose behaviour they are trying to understand. They can get closer to the real world by making use of the insights of painting, music, and literature, and, in the narrower sphere of social science, by collaborating with other disciplines like psychology, sociology, politics, and history. Such cooperation will broaden economics' view of what is important and true about human life, without losing the sharpness of its particular angle of vision. These studies ought to be part of the education of an economist because they suggest valid ways of seeing the world which lie outside the frame of mainstream economics. The demand for pluralism is not a demand for a new theory, but a demand for a wider vision, from which new theories (plural) may emerge, applicable to different parts of social life. The historian Eric Hobsbawm looked forward to a terrain of enquiry on which history, economics, and sociology could meet. Add psychology and politics and you have the agenda of this book.

The value of pluralism can be illustrated by the ancient Indian parable of six blind men trying to identify an elephant. One grabs the trunk and thinks it is a snake. Another thinks its flank is a wall, another the tail a rope, another feels an ear is a fan, another still thinks the legs are tree trunks, and the last reckons the tusk to be a spear. The point is that, blind, none can see the whole picture; to do so they must collaborate, share what they have found from their own vantage points, and piece together the elephant from their combined insights. Economists must learn to listen: to those in other disciplines, and to their own dissenters.

The other disciplines do not, of course, speak with single voices, and it is greatly over-simplifying to talk of a 'psychological' or

1. *Blind Monks Examining an Elephant* by Itcho Hanabusa, 1888.

'sociological' or 'historical' point of view. But they each shed a distinctive light on the topic of human behaviour, which is my justification for giving them separate chapters.

So what does the study of economic method involve? Most obviously, it involves philosophy – thinking about the conditions needed for making true statements, and how far these conditions apply to economic propositions. Almost entirely lacking from economics is any explicit argument pertaining to its epistemological status – its status as knowledge. Only a total disregard for philosophy enables economics to claim that it is a positive science, immune from judgments of value.

A key issue is whether logical deduction from tight assumptions is the best way of 'getting at the truth' of the world or whether it is better to pay more diligent attention to the facts even though this might mean using a looser logic. As failure to foresee the crash of 2008 testifies, precision can be purchased at the expense of usefulness. For the purposes of policy, it is important to ask how far, and in what areas, the propositions generated by current methods of doing economics are sufficient pointers to good policy, and where they need to be complemented by understandings gleaned from other ways of studying human behaviour.

Mainstream economics believes social phenomena are best understood as the summed-up behaviour of individuals, an approach known as *methodological individualism*. This method has two characteristics: the only *actors* or *agents* recognised on the economists' social map are persons (this 'realistically' includes households and small firms, but not organisations or classes), and individual choices and decisions are *independent*, that is, specific to those making them. This twofold claim enables economists to use a simple additive formula to demonstrate that aggregate outcomes 'are the result of an enormous number of discretionary decisions by individual actors'.[6] With the further assumption that individual plans are, on average, fulfilled – that is, there is no uncertainty – one can derive an aggregate number simply by adding up the individual plans.

There are two huge flaws in the approach which represents individual choices as parallel straight lines. The first is that explanations in terms of individuals alone omit the relations between them, and thus the social structure in which choices are made. Individuals are part of 'networks' of choice. So aggregate outcomes of any kind are the sum of individual choices plus the social structure. The second flaw is summed up in the phrase 'the fallacy of composition'. Even if made independently, individual choices affect each other. We each decide how much of our income to save. But an increase of $1 in my saving does not increase total saving by $1, because it reduces your income by $1, so if everyone else saves the same proportion of income as before, the total of saving goes down not up. In the words of songwriter Leonard Cohen, 'You can add up the parts, you won't have the sum'. (For further discussion, see Chapter 7.)

For mainstream economists it is not enough simply to specify individual persons as the sole choosing units. Their units choose 'rationally'. They have coherent plans; act purposively to achieve them; and calculate the most efficient means to get what they want. Mainstream economics presents to us one human type – Economic Man or *homo economicus*, the human calculating machine, continually calculating how to get the most ('maximum') gain he can for the least cost. This calculation is done in prices, everyone and everything has a price.

These two methodological rules – the concentration on individuals, and their depiction as calculating machines pure and simple – are the clue to what goes wrong in mainstream economics. Economists reduce social structures to economic transactions and erect one aspect of human behaviour, calculation of costs ('how much will it cost me to do X rather than Y?'), into a universal law of all human behaviour. They are in a quandary when you point to motives for action like love, devotion, pity, courage, honour, loyalty, ambition, public service, which on any reasonable interpretation are not motivated by subjective calculation of gain or outcome. The codes governing such behaviour may be 'beyond price', because it would be felt shameful to break them. Economists have to say that such motives appear to be irrational, but may be rational in situations of limited information. They are forced by the requirements of their own reasoning to squeeze their explanations of human behaviour into absurdly narrow channels.

This raises a hugely important question which will run through this book. Is the unlovely creature *homo economicus* intended to be a realistic description of a human, an ideal type, or simply a requirement of deductive theory? My own view is that, from the start, physics envy drove economists to think of the social world as a potentially perfect machine. This induced them to model human behaviour to fit the requirements of such a conception. Once economics became formalised in the twentieth century, the requirements of 'ideal' modelling started to dominate theory. Theories needed to be couched in terms of isolated (deterministic) atoms to facilitate modelling. So, the possibility that under conditions X the outcome could be any of a range of outcomes could no longer be allowed. It could be prevented by specifying that in any conditions X there is a unique optimum Y, and that human beings (under the compulsion of 'rationality') everywhere seek and find it. However, in the early phase of the discipline matters were not quite so clear; and the lack of clarity as to whether economists' depictions of human nature were intended to be descriptive or prescriptive has bedevilled the discipline to this day.

The crudeness of its own psychology cuts the economist's picture of the individual off from any serious study of psychology. Until quite recently, economists dismissed the findings of psychology as of no use to them. 'Economics', wrote Lionel Robbins (1898–1984), 'is as little dependent on the truth of fashionable psychoanalysis as the multiplication table'; he waved away its main rival, behavioural psychology, as 'this queer cult'.[7]

Following the financial crisis, widely attributed to 'irrational exuberance', economists have started to modify their views: behavioural economics is the new vogue. As Andrew Lo says,

> the crisis hardened a split among professional economists. On one side of the divide were the free market economists, who believe that we are all economically rational adults, governed by the law of supply and demand. On the other side were the behavioral economists, who believe that we are all irrational animals, driven by fear and greed like so many other species of mammals.[8]

What is wrong with behavioural economics is that it dubs irrational any behaviour which does not meet the neoclassical specification of rationality. It then tries to formalise that behaviour as rational in the circumstances; for example, it is rational, when faced with partial information, to 'follow the crowd'. These concessions to reality produce incoherence, not progress.

Treating the economy as the sum of individual choices leads to one of economics' greatest defects – its failure to understand the nature of the social world. Economists typically see rational individuals choosing in isolation; as a result they have paid scant attention to the 'sociology of knowledge' – the part played by society in structuring the knowledge on which individuals act. They typically treat social relations as irritating complications to the study of individual choice, rather than as essential components of the choosing process. Interactive behaviour can only be brought into the maximising framework by modelling it as a strategic game, as in the Prisoner's Dilemma, in which actors calculate the value of the payoffs from cheating or cooperating.

Sociology is partly responsible for economists' neglect of it. The demand for sociology as a science of society may have weakened, but there is also a problem with the supply. Contemporary sociologists have, by and large, left the economy to the economists, even though the economists' image of a world in which the 'invisible hand' of the market guarantees social stability is profoundly opposed to the sociological standpoint. Sociology, writes Wolfgang Streeck, must rediscover political economy.[9]

The choice between the individual and the social is not straightforward. One strong defence can be offered for methodological individualism: it guards against treating individuals simply as members of groups, deprived of agency. Its weakness is that it ignores the architecture of choice. Our choices are affected by the social positions we occupy, our place in society's power structure, our reflections on what is good and bad behaviour ('morals'), and our state of knowledge, and these choices in turn help restructure the social world.

In mainstream economics, individual actions typically take place through voluntary exchange in competitive markets, in which, by definition, no transactor has power. This means that its models are blind to the role of power in shaping economic relations: the mythical power of numbers replaces the actual power of elites. The power imbalances between workers and bosses, the influence of money on politics, the role of big business in shaping beliefs and market behaviour – these are all 'outside the model'. The rational agents that economists assume we are would never allow themselves to be bamboozled by advertising. Political science, the science which deals with relations based on power, should be part of the education of every economist, since power structures shape the structure of choice. Karl Marx understood this better than anyone, but his writings are outside the standard curriculum.

History offers students of economics another powerful tool to understand the nature of economic life. All the disciplines have their histories – the histories of how they were done in the past, how they came to be what they are today. Like natural scientists, economists like to claim that the science they do today – the economics of the latest textbooks – is better than the science of a hundred years ago, or even ten years ago. Time, they say, has purged economics of its mistakes.

However, students will discover that economic theory, far from progressing like a giant tapeworm towards better knowledge, is rife with interminable arguments. In the course of this history, no single school has achieved unchallenged dominance. Classical and neo-classical economics may be regarded as the main line of advance, but there are many other schools of thought, including the German Historical School, Marxism, Institutional Economics, Keynesian economics, Behavioural Economics, Ecological Economics, and many others. This pluralism is typical of the social sciences; but it is rare in the natural sciences. It points to the extreme difficulty of *falsifying* any theory in economics. After centuries of debate, there is still no agreed theory of money. A study of the history of economics is an invitation to join in conversation with some of the greatest dissenters in the field like Karl Marx and John Maynard Keynes. Whatever doubts students may have about the way economics is now done, they will not find themselves alone.

Just as striking as the violent attacks that have been made on mainstream economics is the fact that its methodology has, by and large, remained intact. This is because of economics' undying aspiration to be a hard science. There is an accepted, 'professional', way of doing the subject which exerts a gravitational pull on the way it is done.

Two eminent philosophers of science, Thomas Kuhn (1922–1996) and Imre Lakatos (1922–1974), help explain the roots of methodological persistence. They show that all established sciences erect virtually impregnable methodological defences to safeguard themselves from assault. (For further discussion, see Chapter 10.) These defences include a considerable power of absorbing contradictory thoughts. Economics soaks up heresies, which it turns, where possible, into maths. Occasionally the defences crumble altogether, not so much under the weight of disconfirming facts, as from a changed view of the world. The two candidates for 'paradigm shifts' in economics are the marginalist revolution of the 1870s and the Keynesian revolution of the 1930s. Of these, the marginalist revolution has proved the most *methodologically* durable; its methodological persistence, in fact, doomed the Keynesian attempt to erect an alternative doctrine on neoclassical foundations.

The study of history proper is valuable, because it shows that economic *doctrines*, far from being the universal truths they claim to be, are connected to particular historical conditions and episodes. The conditions of time and place explain not just why they arose when and where they did, but why some doctrines swam while others sank. Influential social theories satisfy 'needs' which arise from outside their own system of thought. Thus the protectionist doctrines of the nineteenth-century German Historical School answered the desire of late-comers to the capitalist feast to 'catch up' successful pioneers like Britain; Marxism tried to explain the miserable conditions of factory workers in the early Industrial Revolution; the Keynesian revolution offered a theoretical explanation of the persisting unemployment of the interwar years; twentieth-century development economics took up the argument that free trade keeps poor countries permanently poor. Today we have behavioural economics, feminist economics, and other branches. In all cases, doctrines are partly intended to do political work. It is important for students to get a sense of which period and place they are living through, and the power relations of their societies without swallowing the view that economic doctrines are 'merely' reflections of the historical conditions and power structures of the day. If economics fails to give history its due weight as evidence, historians are also guilty of self-absorption: with notable exceptions like Niall Ferguson and Harold James, they have simply failed to engage with economic theory, leaving the field to the econometricians.

Because economics is not a natural science, the 'right' or 'wrong' answer to an economic problem is as much ethical as positive. Economics is the study of people who make ethical judgments: it cannot simply be treated as a matter of good or bad logic or arithmetic. Economists will tell you that moral questions are above their pay grade – 'a matter for politics' – but this is only because they have defined their subject in a way that deliberately excludes them. Yet economists' values determine what they pay attention to, what models they use, and what policies they prefer. Ethics can be used to criticise method.

Except for philosophy (whose job is to sort out everyone else's mistakes) all the disciplines have their biases. Psychologists tend to think of human behaviour as irrational; sociologists, to think of humans as creatures of groups. Historians tend to see only relations of power, and students of politics have traditionally followed their lead. Economics offers a useful corrective to such slanted views. But it also has much to learn from them. A well-known study showed that broadly educated people had better judgment about future economic possibilities than narrow experts.[10] Curiosity may have killed the cat but it leads to better forecasts.

John Maynard Keynes grasped the truth of this when he wrote that:

> The master-economist must possess a rare combination of gifts ... He must be mathematician, historian, statesman, philosopher – in some degree. He must understand symbols and speak in words. He must contemplate the particular in the light of the general, and touch abstract and concrete in the same flight of thought. He must study the present in the light of the past for the purposes of the future. No part of man's nature or institutions must lie entirely outside his regard.[11]

An ideal, no doubt; nonetheless, worthy to be put before the mind of students of economics.

2
THE BASICS: WANTS AND MEANS

I ain't ever satisfied.

Nat King Cole

Philosophy talks about ends and means. Economics talks about wants and means. The difference is important. Ends to philosophers are about what is good; to economists 'ends' are simply what people want. What they mainly seem to want is money, or at least what money can buy. By collapsing ends into wants, economics cuts itself off from ethics – the study of what is good. It also cuts itself off from an important part of reality – the fact that humans have always struggled with moral choices. It also makes the problem of scarcity insoluble, as we shall see.

Economics was not always as ethically colour-blind as it is now. Historically, there are two main definitions of the subject. The first makes it the study of wealth; the second the study of choice. The first dates from Adam Smith (1723–1790) who called his famous 1776 book *An Inquiry into the Nature and Causes of the Wealth of Nations*. In discussing the nature of wealth, Smith set out to controvert the 'erroneous opinion' that wealth consists of money (gold and silver). Rather, he defined it as the 'annual produce of the land and labour of society'.[1] Wealth arises from the production and exchange of 'useful' things like provisions, houses, clothes, and furniture. Wealth is a means to comfort.

Alfred Marshall (1842–1924), writing after a hundred years of economic growth, opened up a broader vista when he wrote in his *Principles of Economics* that economics was the science which studies the 'material requisites of well-being'. Money, he said bluntly, was a means to an end.[2] But he did not define 'well-being'; and his notion of requisites is fuzzy. Well-being lends itself to the interpretation of 'feeling well', which collapses all too readily into 'feeling happy' – a sad constriction of philosophical usage. And how much of 'requisites' are required for being or feeling well? Traditionally requisites had to do with the physical upkeep or 'provisioning' of the species. People needed money to buy food and 'comforts'. But is the internet part of the provisioning? There is nothing very material about it. Any gross national product (GNP) measure of 'enoughness' runs into this problem.

Nevertheless, the older definition in terms of wealth had three advantages. It isolated for the purpose of study an extremely important, if not at all times overriding, motive for action. Secondly, it could measure the inputs and outputs of this activity by quantity, and thus develop into a causal science. A third attraction was moral: there was a presumption that the pursuit of wealth was more benign than other forms of striving, because, unlike the quest for power, it was inherently cooperative. It could thus be conceived as the benign, or peaceful, form of social competition. The combination of these advantages go far to explain why economics eventually established a policy primacy over the other social sciences. Its propositions could be made more exact; and it was more optimistic.

The view of economics as the study of the causes of wealth and poverty was superseded by Lionel Robbins in 1932. In his book *The Nature and Significance of Economic Science,* Robbins defined economics as the science which 'studies human behaviour as a relationship between ends and scarce means which have alternative uses'. It was 'the form [of behaviour] imposed by the influence of scarcity'.[3] Robbins made scarcity the central, and indeed only, topic of economics, when he pointed out that it was not the materiality but the scarcity of goods which made them 'economic'. Every decision involving choice of means has an economic aspect. People's ends are various but 'life is short, nature is niggardly'.[4] Maximising outputs was essentially a matter of economising inputs. There is no presumption that people will or should prefer material to non-material goods; the task of economics is to point out the difference between efficient and inefficient ways of getting whatever it is that people want. Economics, that is, is indifferent about ends, but far from indifferent about means.

The Robbins definition was the culmination of the shift from 'political economy' to 'economics' – from the idea of economics as part of the wider study of society to that of a self-sufficient technical discipline. This went together with a shift from the view of an economy 'embedded' in social institutions to that of a self-regulating market of calculating individuals. In presenting economics as the general science of rational choice, applicable to all objects of human striving, Robbins staked the claim of economics to be the 'master social science', able to penetrate the dark, hitherto un-theorised, corners of human behaviour with its language of mathematics. This claim helped to sharpen economic thought, but there was a twofold price to pay. The first lay in the assumption that all choices are commensurate, that is, that they can be weighed on a common scale, the scale being money. There are no 'tragic choices', only trade-offs. The second was the elimination of history. The Robbins method focuses attention on the efficient allocation of *given* resources at a point in time. It ignores the question of most concern to the classical economists, which was how to explain the *growth* and *stagnation* of resources over time. Since the 1960s, Robbins's has been accepted as the working definition of economics. Economics is about the logic of choice. This logic is hard-wired into individuals because of scarcity.

Of course, in saying that all choices have an economic aspect, Robbins was not claiming that it was the only aspect. Many aspects of human life lay outside economic calculation. However, there was a 'money-mindedness' bias in the Robbins conception of rationality, since money was the only standard against which the efficiency of action might be judged. Almost by default the view developed that only measurable choices were rational. Robbins's efficiency criterion thus opened the way to the economic analysis of non-market institutions like law and marriage. A string of Nobel prizes rewarded the working out of this insight. The Chicago economist Gary Becker (1930–2014) received this honour for his analysis of the economics of marriage and crime and punishment. The equation of rational choice with efficiency, measured in money, is a classic *pars pro toto* (a part taken for the whole) error – treating a specific aspect of human behaviour as a proxy for human behaviour in general.

The contrast between the earlier and later definitions of economics can be overdrawn. Robbins's scarcity perspective was implicit in classical discussions of economic growth. Wealth does not fall like ripe fruit from a tree; it has to be worked for. Classical economics was known, not unfairly, as the 'dismal science'. This was based on its two most famous 'laws': Malthus's law that population would inevitably outstrip food supply; and Ricardo's law of diminishing returns. Both ignored the cumulative impact of technological innovation. Classical economics also taught efficiency in the use of time: not cashing all the fruits of one's efforts today but spacing their enjoyment over a lifetime. Marshall called it 'waiting', economists today know it as 'saving'.

Economists, it might be said, come to the feast of life like spoil-sports to a party. They continually remind people of the need for calculation and efficiency, for working hard and postponing satisfaction. Even people plentifully supplied with 'upkeep' still have to *price their time*. Since scarcity of time can never be overcome, the day when efficiency will no longer be needed will never arrive. To give the devil her due, economic reasoning is a useful antidote to politicians who promise today what they know cannot be paid for tomorrow.

Economists have typically believed that the most efficient mechanism for achieving coordination of production and consumption decisions is the 'invisible hand' of the market. To this day, this insight remains the single most important contribution of economics to the economy. Although economic choices are hard, economic life need not be a *zero-sum* – winner take all – *game*. This is because economics assumes that no voluntary trade will occur unless both sides see an advantage in doing so.

Wants

The Robbins definition of economics pivots on the tension between wants and means. Wants may exceed given means; alternatively, means may fall short of given wants. Both are potential sources of scarcity, to which 'economising' is the right answer.

The word 'wants' draws on an earlier association with 'needs', as in the idea of a person 'wanting' or 'lacking' the means of livelihood. But the idea of 'wanting something' has long shed its objective grounding in 'needing something' and has acquired the purely psychological meaning of wishing for something one hasn't got. Contemporary economics, following Robbins, takes wants in this sense as 'given' – that is, not subject to further explanation. He didn't say that wants were insatiable, merely that at any point in time an individual's wants normally exceed his budget. There is, nevertheless, a strong implication that wants are insatiable. For example, in their standard textbook *Economics*, McConnell, Brue and Flynn write that 'For better or worse, most people have virtually unlimited wants'.[5] Robbins even conceived it possible that 'living creatures might exist, whose "ends" are so limited that all goods for them were "free" goods'.[6] The American anthropologist Marshall Sahlins (b.1930) considered that such was the happy condition in the first hunter-gatherer communities. He called these the 'original' affluent societies, able to get what they wanted at very low cost of effort and time.[7] But our own experience – at least ever since we were expelled from Paradise – has been the reverse of this. We want – or are induced to want – more than we need, or can easily get. We suffer from a kind of divine restlessness. We are always seeking to improve our lot. Economics takes this striving for improvement as a fact, or datum. It just assumes it is human nature never to have enough.

This is not enough to make it rational. *Rationality* is not about what we want, but how we set about getting it. The main requirement of rationality is that one should act consistently towards one's goals, whatever they might be. You judge which satisfactions are more or less important to you, and rank your choices accordingly.

If you prefer A to B and B to C, it is irrational to prefer C to A. Inconsistent preferences are taken to be signs of delusion, neurosis, madness. From the assumption of consistent preferences most of microeconomics follows: the idea of the substitutability of different goods, of the demand for one good in terms of another, of an equilibrium distribution of goods, of the equilibrium of exchange, the formation of prices, and so on.

The logic of the argument is plausible enough. Economists argue that the relentless pressure of wants on scarce resources *forces* people to 'economise'. But we still need to ask whether economists believe that is how people do behave, or whether they think this is how they should behave, or whether the postulate of such behaviour is the only way to make 'tight' predictive models. This is an excellent question for a student to ask her teacher. With mathematical models the suspicion is that the last is the most important reason. As Robbins noted, the means-ends problem would still exist if people acted inconsistently; it would just be that no determinate result could be obtained.[8]

Earlier economists distinguished between needs and wants. The usual argument was that first we aim to satisfy our physiologically unmet 'needs', then the needs of the imagination take over, in a progression up the ladder of wants. But economists have rarely stopped to consider the social origin of 'wants' or the economic implications of the shift from needs to wants.

For Adam Smith, 'desire of food is limited in every man by the narrow capacity of the human stomach; but the desire of the conveniences and ornaments of building, dress, equipage, and household furniture, seems to have no limit or certain boundary'.[9] The Austrian economist Carl Menger (1840–1921) recognised that the different needs of men are not equally important in satisfying wants, 'being graduated from the importance of their lives down to the importance they attribute to a small passing enjoyment'.[10]

To illustrate his analysis, Menger assigned numerical values to the different intensities, starting at 10 (highest) through to 0 (no need), arranged as in the table below. If the need for food is 10 and for tobacco 6, the consumer will not buy tobacco until his need

I	II	III	IV	V	VI	VII	VIII	IX
10	9	8	7	6	5	4	3	2
9	8	7	6	5	4	3	2	1
8	7	6	5	4	3	2	1	0
7	6	5	4	3	2	1	0	
6	5	4	3	2	1	0		
5	4	3	2	1	0			
4	3	2	1	0				
3	2	1	0					
2	1	0						
1	0							
0								

2. Menger's Hierarchy of Wants.

for food has been satisfied sufficiently. Each increment of satisfaction is subject to diminishing marginal utility, so the baton is passed, so to speak, to the next less urgent need. Thus psychological, not physiological, needs drive the growth of wealth. Menger's table illustrates the principle of how needs of different intensity are brought into equilibrium. Good I (food, say) is consumed until it reaches need 9, at which point both goods I and II (shelter, say) are consumed until they reach need 8 and so on.[11]

Implicit in both Smith and Menger is the idea of a hierarchy of wants, starting with the primacy of physical need. For most people, for most of history, *absolute* wants – the 'needs of the stomach' – have in fact been by far the most important of their wants, so economists understandably paid much less attention to the existence of *relative* wants – those generated by the existence of other humans.

The American Thorstein Veblen (1857–1929) was the first economist to attend seriously to the primacy of relative wants in consumption patterns. No one understood better than Veblen that the insatiable wants which most economists attributed to human nature were socially constructed. He originated phrases which have become household words, such as 'status symbols' and 'conspicuous consumption'. We desire a good or service not because of the value we get from its use, but because of the opportunity its possession brings to display our superiority to those who cannot command it.[12]

His work is an exploration of the exploding culture of consumption in nineteenth-century America. Its background was the rise of a new class of *nouveaux riches* – 'robber barons' – who were building their gaudy palaces and lifestyles out of the profits of railways, steel, and oil. Extravagant display was the hallmark of the new class; a display designed to impress rivals and awe inferiors with its wealth and power.

Consider an auction of vintage Burgundy wines. The winning bid may be $50,000 or even $100,000 a magnum or bottle. Does the winner love Burgundy wine? Not necessarily. Can he or she tell the difference between a $20,000 glass of it and a $5 glass? Not necessarily. The winner is telling the other bidders that his pocket is deeper than theirs. His purchase is an act of conspicuous consumption.

Veblen's ironic pen could be turned onto any of society's cultural institutions; on gender, he writes that 'the dress of women goes even farther than that of men in the way of demonstrating the wearer's abstinence from productive employment', which in turn is useful to signify the status of her husband. The long skirt is especially valued because 'it is expensive and hampers the wearer at every turn and incapacitates her for all useful exertion'.

Veblen argued that 'the struggle of each to possess more than his neighbor is inseparable from the institution of private property'. It is capitalism which focuses the emulation complex so completely on material goods. In doing so it reproduces itself, as people demand more and more, but also bars them from ever fully succeeding, since dissatisfaction with the present state of being is the system's driving force. Veblen saw this 'emulation complex' as wasteful, because it results in expenditure ever ready to absorb any margin of income that remains after physical wants and comforts have been provided for. Indeed, 'a general amelioration cannot quiet the unrest whose source is the craving of everybody to compare favourably with his neighbour'.

Veblen alerts us to the role of advertising in shaping our wants. For mainstream economists, advertising is primarily an information system that tells consumers about products, old and new. For Veblen and his intellectual descendants, its role is to stimulate wants which can never be satisfied.[13]

Inspired by Veblen's work, the economist Fred Hirsch (1931–1978) developed the notion of 'positional goods', goods whose chief function is to position their owner socially or politically. A good is positional as long as not everyone can have it. As soon as it is generally available, it loses its value. Some goods like Old Masters are naturally scarce; others like dwellings with fine views, or degrees from top universities, can be kept artificially scarce by restriction on entry. Power is an archetypal positional good. Ownership of such goods is necessarily a zero-sum game: not everyone can have power at the same time.[14]

We are rather a long way from economists' laudable desire to ensure enough provisioning for people to lead good lives. Relative wants build insatiability into human striving and ensure that the poor are always with us: someone will always be poor relative to someone else. There is no 'end' beyond more and more consumption.

Means

What about the other side of Robbins: 'scarce means which have alternative uses'? It is true that we cannot easily conceive of a general situation in which there are no costs to an activity. But is it true that scarcity is as general or acute as economics makes it out to be?

First, one should notice that Robbins closes the circle of scarcity by including time in his scarcity of means. Life is simply not long enough to accomplish all that one wants: it is in this deeper sense, he says, that 'your economist is a tragedian'. Students are taught that every activity involves an 'opportunity cost', which is a cost not just of money at a single moment of time, but of time itself: 'time is money'. If someone can earn $10 an hour by working, and prefers to be idle in that time, he has actually 'spent' $10. Common sense suggests that the greater your budget of money (wealth), the more time you will have to pursue other interests like going to concerts.

So, with the growth of wealth, the psychological pressure of scarcity might be expected to recede. In fact, this is not necessarily so: one now has a choice between different kinds of music; one cannot listen to them at the same time. Today, information overload helps keep time scarce. We are constantly being bombarded with choices we might make which promise more satisfaction than choices we used to make. Thus the dream of abundance is a delusion: we are stuck with scarcity of time unless our deaths can be indefinitely postponed.

Secondly, mainstream economists, following Robbins, take means, like wants, as *data*. 'We assume an initial distribution of property', writes Robbins.[15] In taking means as given, economists take the distribution of resources available to satisfy wants off their agenda. But the problem of scarce resources is caused not just by the 'niggardliness' of nature, which affects everyone, but the niggardliness of some people's incomes. If incomes are highly unequal it will be the wants of the rich which make the first call on 'scarce' means. Poverty in today's world is not due to scarcity but to inequality. There is enough food to feed an even higher global population than today. An economics which made the reduction of poverty and disease a priority would attend to the efficiency of distribution as well as to the efficiency of production and exchange.

Examples of artificially created scarcity – the scarcity arising out of particular social and political structures and policies rather than from natural causes – are legion. War and war preparations are conspicuous examples of the continuous creation of scarcity. There is an economic cost to buying a new aircraft carrier as opposed to paying for a new hospital or school. The more wealth devoted to military consumption, the less will be available to satisfy civilian needs. Enforced scarcity of this kind was a decisive feature of communist systems, in which the military sector consumed up to 30 per cent of national income. This enforced scarcity was made possible by state ownership of land and capital, and its ability to allocate labour for its own purposes. Nobel Laureate Amartya Sen (b.1933) has pointed out that famines in poor countries are as much the consequence of a politically determined distribution of food as of natural shortage.[16] Eradicable diseases like malaria and leprosy fail to be eradicated not because nature is niggardly but because some rulers prefer to spend the money buying arms and enriching themselves and their families.

Economists may reasonably point out that such artificial scarcity is produced by bad politics, not by bad economics; and indeed they have been persistent critics of 'rent-seeking' by governments. However, they have been relatively blind to the ability of big private corporations to extract rent. Today the biggest rent-extractor is the cartel of big banks, which controls the means of financing production. The method of mainstream economists has blunted criticism of actual market distributions by setting out to 'prove' that in fully competitive markets consumers are sovereign and all the factors of production are paid what they produce. These proofs minimise the extent to which unregulated market distribution is bound to be skewed in favour of the rich and powerful. By insisting that scarcity is given by nature, not by institutions, mainstream economics blunts the edge of efforts to regulate markets and redistribute income.

It is commonly said that there is a 'trade-off' between efficiency and equity. Economists can tell you what an efficient distribution of income is; it is up to politics to secure a just distribution. Neoclassical economists of left-wing persuasion used to busy themselves with working out schemes for an 'optimal' distribution of income which satisfied the requirements of both efficiency and justice. But the propaganda for productive efficiency has latterly become so powerful that interest in moral efficiency has waned. The growth of inequality, in turn, has produced growing popular disenchantment with supposedly 'efficient' market outcomes. (For a further discussion, see Chapter 13.)

Finally, the assumption of mainstream economists that economies have a spontaneous tendency to full employment leads them to ignore the ever-present possibility of crashes and weak recoveries. The heavy unemployment, poor growth, and depressed wages in most of Europe since 2008 is an example of scarcity created by bad economic policy.

✗

We are now in a position to criticise the way the Robbins definition sets up the economic problem. We can consider the issue from the point of both demand and supply. As far as demand is concerned, three points can be made.

First, and most obviously, the Robbins view expels morality. By making efficiency God, it fails to ask: what is efficiency for? Robbins writes: 'Why the human animal attaches particular values . . . to particular things is a question we do not discuss.'[17] By collapsing ends, needs, and wants into the single category 'preferences', and taking these as 'given' – not subject to further investigation – mainstream economics precludes itself from questioning the value of wants, of asking whether what is desired is desirable.

How much 'wealth' is needed for 'well-being'? Economists who stuck to the older view of their subject were not so shy about considering this question. John Stuart Mill (1806–1873) believed that once poverty has been overcome, the need for efficiency would decline. The economist Marshall, writing in 1890, gave a precise number for sufficiency. He thought that with $150 a year (about $10,000 in today's money), a family 'has . . . the material conditions of a complete life.'[18] Average global per capita income today is $17,300. If we accept Marshall's standard, there is no need for further economic growth, only redistribution. But, as we have seen, the notion of 'materiality', no longer anchored in food supply, has lost its clarity; and in a world of 'relative wants', there is never enough.

Second, by taking preferences as given, mainstream economics is debarred from exploring the instruments of persuasion used to make people want more of one thing rather than another. It takes consumer sovereignty for granted. It is only interested in the logic of, and the consequences for, behaviour of people having the wants they have. It is not interested, that is, in the history and sociology of wants. Yet, though the acquisitive tendency has always existed, it became a driving force in economic life only with capitalism. In the pre-modern world wealth was simply regarded as the means to the good life; moralists condemned money-making and custom restricted its scope. 'Scientific' economics took the desire for money to be the main psychological drive of human nature, and emphasised its utility for begetting wealth. Ethics was reshaped to accommodate the spread of commerce. Greed became the power which wills evil, but does good.

Mass consumption, the modern form of insatiability, entered history at a definite time and place, with mass production in the United States at the start of the last century. Before that the possibility of *mass* consumption did not exist. Today it is promoted by economists, advertisers, and politicians as the democratic form of happiness. In the words of Andy Warhol, '... the President drinks Coke, Liz Taylor drinks Coke, and just think, you can drink Coke, too. A Coke is a Coke and no amount of money can get you a better Coke'.

But is giving everyone a Coca-Cola enough? If insatiability is taken as given, there is clearly no end to scarcity, for there is no obvious top rung in the ladder of wants. This means that the economic problem will always be with us. Paradise never arrives. The realisation, though, that wants are shaped by culture opens the door to thinking how they are created – particularly by relentless marketing – and how they might be limited to reduce the constraint of scarcity. But talk of culture makes the economist, like Goering, reach for his revolver.

Finally, failing to distinguish between needs and wants allows mainstream economics to ignore the problem of fluctuations in demand. In the Robbins view, economies are always supply-constrained, never demand-constrained. As J.B. Say (1767–1832) said: 'supply creates its own demand', that is, people would not produce things unless they needed them. This of course makes sense if one is considering just the needs of the stomach: there is never enough caviar to go round. But insofar as wants and not needs direct the larger part of economic activity today, the stability of economies depends on what goes on in the mind, not the stomach. Neoclassical economics took over the older mechanistic psychology of need without grasping that the shift from needs to wants undermined the stability of behaviour.

On the other, supply, side, we have never really shed our anxiety about sufficiency of means, and with reason. The sanction economics has given to unlimited wants has brought back the Malthusian problem, as consumption presses on the planet's natural resources. Low entropy energy and materials are dissipated in use and return as high entropy waste. Our industrial and farming systems release masses of carbon dioxide, methane, and other gases into the atmosphere, which destabilise the world's climate, while destroying the absorptive and recuperative capacities of nature. Put bluntly, there are too many people, wanting too many things. As Nicholas Georgescu-Roegen (1906–1994) pointed out, humanity is destined to physical extinction if a growing population continues to consume at the same rate as it now does. Economics is about minimising inputs. But because it sets no limit on outputs, the efficiency requirement alone cannot guarantee a sufficiency of natural resources to satisfy wants.

The neoclassical economist will tell you that the price system guards against this result. Scarcity is only relative, he says. Price movements will shift demand for goods which are relatively costly to produce to those which are relatively cheaper. But this presumes two things: that there will always be sufficient inputs (energy from the wind or sun, for example) to satisfy the present scale of production and consumption; and that an unimpeded market system will generate the 'correct' prices before disaster strikes. No one not thoroughly trained in the neoclassical method is likely to believe either proposition.

To sum up: scarcity is by no means as 'natural' a long-run condition as post-Robbins economics makes out. A great deal of it is artificial, arising not just from the continuous need to stimulate demand, but from the artificial restriction of supply. Capitalism creates the demand it requires through advertising; while in many parts of the world, political control of allocation keeps supply artificially scarce. By failing to question the sources of demand or the political obstacles to supply, mainstream economics neuters the most urgent parts of today's economic problem.

It would be absurd to claim that the faulty methods of mainstream economics are responsible for global warming. But by failing to distinguish between needs and wants, and by taking wants as 'given', economics has powerfully reinforced the ethical blindness which threatens the human species with extinction. Insatiability in face of climate change is not rationality, but madness.

3

ECONOMIC GROWTH

If theories, like girls, could win beauty contests,
comparative advantage would certainly rate high.

Paul Samuelson, *Economics*

The only defensible purpose of economics is to help abolish poverty, opening up a more spacious life for humanity. Beyond that it has no obvious purpose, and should leave the stage to others. Abolition of poverty was the improvement in the human condition offered by the first economists. Over the centuries, though, the means has become the end, so we no longer dare to ask what economic growth is for, especially in rich countries who already have more than enough to meet their basic needs.

What has economics contributed to the growth of wealth? It is the spectacular growth of prosperity, reduction of poverty, and decline of violence since Adam Smith's day that is economics' main claim to have added value to economic life. By demonstrating that the striving for wealth, unlike the quest for power, need not be a zero-sum game, economists set public policy an altogether more benevolent prospectus.

However, their contribution cannot be considered in isolation. It came on top of the prior emergence of scientific and market institutions, legal rules, the 'spirit of capitalism', and technological applications favourable to economic growth.[1] This was the platform on which Adam Smith built his 'science'. The unique contribution of 'scientific' economics was to *empower* these dynamic forces with an improved understanding of their place in the scheme of improvement, and thus prevent any relapse into bad old habits. It gave commercial society intellectual and psychological legitimacy.

The question asked by the early economists was: what is the path to prosperity? The challenge the classical economists Adam Smith, Ricardo (1772–1823) and Malthus (1776–1834) set themselves was to understand how it is that some countries become rich and others stay poor. The answer they gave – in Smith's case based on extensive historical enquiry – was that it depends on their laws, morals, and institutions. Ruling groups could either retard or promote invention, stifle or encourage enterprise, restrict or free up trade. Britain, surging to opulence, and China, stuck in stagnation, were at the opposite corners of Smith's map. However, the first economists, imbued with the spirit of the Enlightenment, failed to understand how institutions, not especially suitable for wealth-creation, might nevertheless serve other human purposes not less essential, like maintaining social contentment – a blind spot which has persisted to this day.

The main policy prescription to emerge from the writings of the 'English' economists Smith and Ricardo was free trade. Free trade increased wealth; restrictions on trade retarded it. The German economist Friedrich List (1789–1846) asked a narrower question: how could continental Europe 'catch up' with Britain? The answer he gave was protectionism. Free trade was fine for the already industrialised; but the industrialising countries needed to protect their 'infant industries' against premature extinction.[2] This idea was taken up by development economics in the 1940s.

The intellectual clash between free trade and protection has dominated thinking about economic growth. It particularly involves the part institutions play or should play in the growth story. Adam Smith and his followers identified the state as an economic monopoly, and tended to see producer groups as conspiracies to restrict trade. Mainstream economics has faithfully reflected this bias ever since: state economic activity hinders economic growth by blocking the mutually beneficial working of markets. For the followers of List, on the other hand, the state was, or could become, an entrepreneur; and they understood that producer groups could be growth engines. The role of the state in the growth story is an unsettled question in economics. There is the question of historical fact: what role did states play in the growth of wealth? This leads to a further question. What kind of state is good for growth – democracy or dictatorship? Are states bound to be corrupt and/or incompetent?

The eighteenth-century classical economists correctly surmised that the growth of material wealth depends on control of population, the 'accumulation of stock' (investment), and the 'widening of the market' (trade). They understood that if they were to prosper, societies needed to control their fertility, to put aside part of what they currently produced to invest in future production, and to trade freely. These were profound insights, on which economics still largely lives. Where they fell short was in understanding how societies develop institutions favourable to such activity. To this day, many, perhaps most, economists take private property rights as given, and explain the greater wealth of some societies in terms of their more efficient distribution of property, without showing much curiosity about why inefficient property distributions persisted for so long, or what functions they played in the life of their societies.

This chapter traces 'growth' economics from the insights of the classical economists to the emergence of development economics as a distinct subfield of economics in the second half of the twentieth century, and the gradual dissolution of the developmental perspective into the neoclassical Washington Consensus.

Population

If the economist is a tragedian, the Revd Thomas Malthus has a claim to be considered its tragedian in chief. Before Malthus there was the allure of a more prosperous future; after him gloom. For the first fifty years of the nineteenth century, economics was known as the 'dismal science'. In *An Essay on the Principle of Population* (1798) Malthus set out to refute the utopianism of writers like Condorcet, Godwin, and Thomas Paine. Excited by the growth of wealth, the advance of science, and the softening of manners, these eighteenth-century thinkers argued that there were no natural limits to economic progress, and with it, human perfectibility. Malthus pulled them up short with his famous ratios. Human life, he proclaimed, is forever poised between 'population' and starvation. Population, driven by sexual passion, increases in geometrical ratio (1, 2, 4, 8) while food supply increases only arithmetically (1, 2, 3, 4), that is, by a constant amount each year.

If every couple has four children, the population is bound to double each generation. Eventually, population will outstrip the agricultural production that can support it. The population of Britain in 1800 was 7 million. So, Malthus reasoned, it would double every 25 years, to 14 million in 1825, 28 million in 1850, 56 million in 1875, 112 million in 1900 and so on up to nearly 1.8 billion in the year 2000. Meanwhile, if food supply was enough to feed all 7 million in 1800, it would feed 14 million in 1825, 21 million in 1850, 28 million in 1875 and 35 million in 1900. So, in 100 years, two-thirds of the population would be starving: a tragic perspective to be sure. Malthus's prediction was based on a type of reasoning which has become standard in economics – logical deduction from tight priors. His was a 'model' with a warning attached.

In the second edition of the *Essay* (1803), expanded to two volumes, Malthus ransacked history to find empirical support for his hypothesis. He did, in fact, discern cycles of rapid population growth followed by large-scale population collapses – the Black Death of the fourteenth century being the most famous instance – and offered a causal explanation: any improvement in productivity led to more population not more wealth, as wage earners took advantage of their prosperity to have more children. Population presses on food supply: wages fall, and population growth is reversed, with a fraction of the population, young and old, carried off by disease, plague, pestilence, and starvation. In this way Nature maintains a rough long-term equilibrium between wants and means. But this mechanism prevents wages ever rising above subsistence. Marx would call this the 'iron law of wages'. So much for the optimists.

However, Malthus offered a crucial check to the destructive power of sexual passion: 'moral restraint'. People should delay their age of marriage and remain celibate outside marriage. Malthus rejected contraception, inside or outside marriage, as a way of checking population growth. His attitude mixed up theological and economic arguments in a way which now seems strange. On the theological side, God, he thought, had planted the sexual passion in humans not just for purposes of reproduction but to spur them to moral effort, first to earn enough to marry and then later to provide for the resultant family. Consequently, reasoning in line with the tenets of the new economic science, Malthus argued that contraception (and other 'vicious' sexual practices) would reduce the incentive to work and self-improvement, by blunting the urge to provide for one's children.

Thus Malthus emphasised moral efficiency as a requirement of economic growth. Societies which 'selected' an efficient moral code prospered; societies which wallowed in 'vice' stagnated or declined. In fact, already by the end of Malthus's third population cycle in the late seventeenth century, diminishing returns to agriculture were being offset by productivity gains. In the nineteenth century a combination of sustained productivity growth and colonisation swept Malthus's numbers into the dustbin of failed predictions – at least as far as the developed world goes. In Europe today the native birth-rate falls short of the replacement rate. Vice, in the form of contraception, has rescued it from the Malthusian trap.

However, the Malthusian bogeyman has cast a long shadow. The best-selling report, *Limits to Growth* (1972), with strong echoes of Malthus, predicted that the world's population would hit 7 billion by 2000, leading to shortages of grain, oil, gas, aluminium, and gold.[3] Global population is now almost 8 billion, and is expected to peak at 11 billion, or, in some estimates, 15 billion. Mainstream economics has largely learned, wrongly, not to think about absolute resource pressures, but Malthus's method left a permanent legacy on economics in other respects. The first was the *a priori* (literally 'from the earlier', and meaning 'independent of experience') character of his economics. His theory was a classic example of deductive reasoning, the premise of which came to him long before he tried to verify it empirically, and which was replete with *ceteris paribus* defences against disconfirming facts. Second is his use of mathematical formulae to give his predictions a precision which they certainly never merited. Third was his propensity to draw large inferences directly from 'the facts of nature'. Finally, he oscillated between the positive and the normative. Like Adam Smith he was in the growth business; and growth required moral efficiency. He was a preacher, using science to reinforce his sermons.

Investment

For Adam Smith, the accumulation of 'stock' (capital goods) was the first key driver of growth. The question was how to get the required investment in capital goods. Ricardo believed that any enquiry into the process of accumulation had to start with the institutions governing the division of the product between the three classes of landlords, businessmen, and workers. If the surplus of production over consumption was the only source of accumulation, the rate of growth of prosperity depended on who got the surplus, and this depended on how much of it went to each of the classes. Landlords lived off the surplus of producers, which they took as 'rents'. These rents were spent unproductively – in building and maintaining grand houses and lifestyles. Since workers consumed what they earned, businessmen were the only possible accumulating class, the only class with the wherewithal and incentive to invest their profits in improving and expanding their business. Thus economic growth depended on depriving landlords of their rents, restricting the 'wages fund' to the minimum necessary to sustain the workforce, and keeping taxes low.[4] 'I shall greatly regret', Ricardo wrote, 'that considerations for any particular class, are allowed to check the progress of the wealth and population of the country.'

Ricardo was a divided soul, torn between an equilibrium theory which proved that exceptional profits would be competed away, and his recognition that economic growth was a dynamic process which required continuous accumulation. He set economics on a course of class analysis which was eagerly exploited by Karl Marx, but proved highly embarrassing to his own neoclassical successors. In effect, Ricardo identified the state with the interests of the landlord class, and argued that control of the state should pass to the business class. Karl Marx claimed that this is exactly what had happened: in the new industrial society, the state was the agent of the capitalist class, a class which used its monopoly control over capital to exploit the worker, in the same way as the landlord class had previously used its monopoly of land ownership to 'exploit' the other classes. The difference was that the businessman's exploitation of the worker was the source of capital accumulation, and therefore economic growth, whereas the landlord's monopoly rent was waste. So the new exploiting class was also the progressive class.

Marx's structural method of analysing economic life was identical to Ricardo's. As we have already noticed, the neoclassical economists who followed Ricardo rejected this institutional view of economic structure: the only actors in their models were individuals. By this means class power was rendered invisible. The shift from a structural to an individualist analysis of economic behaviour marks a decisive break in economic method, a genuine 'paradigm shift'.

Trade

For Adam Smith the division of labour was the second key engine of growth. Advocacy of the division of labour leads directly to advocacy of free trade. It carries to a logical conclusion the message of the pin factory. Smith explained how the production of pins can be greatly increased if each pin maker acquires a specialised aptitude for the production of a part of the pin only. Instead of one pin maker making ten pins a day, five pin makers might make, say, 100 pins a day, thus halving the cost per pin in labour time. This principle of the division of labour into specialised tasks can be extended to countries and regions. Wealth is increased if countries, like individuals, specialise in those trades in which they have an advantage.

Behind the science which Smith and Ricardo brought to the free trade cause was a crucial political objective: to break the landlord stranglehold on the price of food. Free import of food would reduce its price, simultaneously lowering the costs of production, augmenting profits and investment, and raising the real wages of the working class. The connection between trade, capital accumulation, and economic growth was established at the birth of scientific economics. It remains the intellectual foundation of globalisation.

However, the free trade doctrine came in two versions.

Adam Smith believed that God had placed people in different places so they could trade with each other. Trade arises from natural advantage: you get better quality wine if you import it from the Mediterranean than if you try to make it in Scotland. The crucial point to emphasise is that trade based on natural advantage is less disruptive than trade based on competition for the same product. Countries produce different things, they don't compete to produce the same things. Complementary trade – buying from abroad needed or desired goods which cannot be produced at home, or which can only be produced at home at prohibitive cost – minimises the threat of wage and job competition.

However, to base trade on natural advantage alone is to limit the division of labour it makes possible. This limitation was overcome by Ricardo. Ricardo explained that welfare-maximising trade should not be bound by natural advantage. Rational agents understand that their gains will be greatest if they specialise in those activities not in which they have a natural advantage, but in which they are least disadvantaged.

Thus the professor who can both think and type better than anyone else in town, but who can think better than he can type, will hire a secretary to do the typing, leaving himself more time for thinking. Portugal, said Ricardo, should concentrate on producing wine, leaving cloth production to England, because though it can produce both wine and cloth cheaper than the English, it can produce wine at lower cost than cloth. In this way, the gains of both partners will be maximised.[5] The theory of comparative advantage has been the most influential doctrine in the whole of economics. It has turned even the most hard-nosed of economists dewy-eyed; Paul Samuelson described it as 'beautiful'.

As with the Malthusian population theory, Ricardo's comparative advantage theory is a classic example of deductive reasoning: formalising an intuition, and then deducing its consequences.

Committed to the long view, Ricardo ignored any disruptive effects on Portugal in surrendering the production of cloth to England. Unlike Malthus, Ricardo also disdained any empirical attempt to show that trade had in practice developed along the lines suggested by the theory. And to this day, there is no conclusive evidence that inter-country trade flows have followed the 'law of comparative advantage'. It comes into that category of economic theorems which are largely prescriptive.

It is not necessarily good prescription either. Ricardo's was a doctrine of static equilibrium: it called on countries to specialise in what they could do best in the present. This might have made sense when advantages were in natural endowments, but not in manufacture. As soon as 'catch-up' became the name of the game, countries looked to exploit dynamic, not static, gains from trade. This meant developing higher-value industries shielded from premature competition. Friedrich List claimed that free trade can be an instrument to entrench existing trade advantages, and, via these, existing power advantages. Mainstream economists nod to his 'infant industry' argument for Protection but accord it scant respect. Any transitory benefits protectionism might bring, they say, are trumped by the corruption and inefficiency attendant on state interference in trade flows.

The role of the state

Left out of both classical and neoclassical growth stories is the role the state has played in economic development. As a matter of historical fact, much economic growth has been state-led, not market-led, in the sense that a great deal of capital accumulation was done by the state itself. This was true of all European states in the nineteenth century; and has been true of Japan, South Korea, and China more recently. Trade, too, was an instrument of state policy. As many historians have pointed out, most countries industrialised under tariff protection, not free trade.[6]

Why did early economists choose the competitive market and not the state as galvaniser and coordinator of economic activity? The most important reason is that they saw the pre-modern state as a private monopoly, personified in the monarch who pursued his own family or dynastic interests at the expense of the public good. Adam Smith's anti-state diatribes were directed against pre-modern forms of rule. The ruler was the 'Prince' who had neither the knowledge nor integrity to direct the economic affairs of society. The conclusion seemed to follow that the state's role in the economy should be kept as small as possible, by restricting its sources of revenue and patronage. This anti-statist bias in economic thought, briefly disturbed by the Keynesian revolution, has persisted to this day.

Even in the eighteenth century, the economists were wrong. The monarchy was already in the course of becoming part of a wider entity, the state, with a better quality of bureaucracy. In Adam Smith's day despots, like Joseph II of Austria, could be 'enlightened'. It was the 'absolute' monarchies of central and eastern Europe which spearheaded the drive to modernise their backward societies, against the strong opposition of nobles, wedded to their traditional rights and privileges. And by the end of the nineteenth century, the state was increasingly accountable to voters.

The negative view of the ruler was matched by a positive view of the market. This was part of the deep-seated eighteenth-century liberal belief that, in the absence of power, private interests did ultimately harmonise. A competitive market system made possible voluntary cooperation in pursuit of prosperity, with only a minimum of regulation.

The view that states do best which govern least persisted, at least in the Anglo-American mainstream. Even when governments did start to accumulate capital for economic purposes in the nineteenth and twentieth centuries, mainstream theorists were quick to argue that public investment was bound to be less efficient than private investment. This was because the state could not direct capital in line with any choices other than its own. Today's neoclassical economists love telling stories of how governments invariably 'pick losers', constructing roads which lead nowhere, towns which no one wants to live in, and steel mills which use lots of capital and very little labour, and whose products cannot be sold for hard currencies.

The sweeping denunciation of government failure pays no attention to the character of governance, or the distribution of power. It assumes that all states are inherently incompetent, if not also corrupt and predatory. But performance of the pre-modern state is no guide to what a modern state might achieve. The neo-classical parody ignores the fact that governments, dedicated to full employment or growth, have often picked winners. Consider Toyota, the Japanese automobile manufacturer. Starting as a tiny textile manufacturer it was propelled to world rank by acts of government: tariffs, exclusion of competitors, and subsidy. In Ha-Joon Chang's words: '. . . had the Japanese government followed the free-trade economists back in the early 1960s, there would have been no Lexus. Toyota today would, at best, be a junior partner to some western car manufacturer, or worse, have been wiped out. The same would have been true of the entire Japanese economy.'[7]

The real story behind Silicon Valley and other dynamic centres of innovation is not explained by the state getting out of the way, so that risk-taking venture capitalists and garage investors could do their thing. From the internet to nanotechnology, most of the fundamental technological advances of the last half century – on both basic research and downstream commercialisation – were funded by government agencies, with private businesses moving into the game only once the returns were in clear sight. Even military spending which is, almost by definition wasteful, can have growth-creating spinoffs.[8]

This profound disagreement about the role of the state in economic development has run through economics from the start. In every epoch you find a debate between those (the majority of economists) who believe laissez-faire desirable, with 'every departure from it, unless required by a great good, a certain evil' and those who believe that economic development needs the active support, and often the leadership, of the state.[9]

Development economics

'Development economics' marries two distinct concepts. The first is economic growth. Economic growth is simply the growth of gross national product (GNP), calculated as the total value of all market transactions in a given period. GNP is a purely quantitative measure. Provided it grows faster than population, it leads to what is termed an increase in 'living standards'. Economic development is a broader idea, in which economic growth contributes to the 'well-being' or human enrichment of the population.

There is no harm in using the words 'growth' and 'development' interchangeably, provided one recognises that their requirements might – and should – diverge after a certain level of 'provisioning' has been achieved.

Once economic growth started to be a conscious aim of policy after the Second World War, growth policy has been through two different phases of theoretical fashion. First in the field were the 'big push' theories of the 1940s and 1950s, designed to turn poor countries into rich ones in double-quick time. These were based on a structuralist analysis of the economy, ancestrally derived from the doctrines of Friedrich List. The alleged failure of the big push growth policies led, in the 1970s and 1980s, to a swing back to neoclassical economics, which came to be embodied in the Washington Consensus.

Structuralism

Development theories can be called structural because they take as their unit of analysis the structure of the world capitalist system. They viewed this not as an integrated market peopled by competitive firms but as a binary system with an advanced centre and a lagging periphery. The dual structure of the economy required a dual system of economics and economic policy – one suited for rich countries would not suit poor ones.

Like Adam Smith, development economists saw capital accumulation as a motor of growth, but, unlike Smith, they did not believe it would come about naturally. The reason was that poor countries lacked a business class. Therefore it was the state which needed to mobilise savings (foreign or domestic) and invest them in manufacturing industries, drawing on 'unlimited supplies of labour' in agriculture.[10] The key assumption was the existence of increasing returns to scale in manufacturing. The larger the manufacturing sector, the larger the domestic market would be, thus producing a self-sustaining 'virtuous circle' of growth.

Advocates of the big push theory attacked free trade as locking rich and poor into their pre-existing positions in this global structure. The Argentinian economist, Raúl Prebisch (1901–1986) argued in 1959 that the gains from trade are systematically biased against the poor countries in the periphery. This is because the prices of primary products, in which poor countries specialised, were set in competitive markets, whereas the manufactured goods of developed countries were priced in monopolistic markets. Poor countries are subject to declining terms of trade, equivalent to transfers of income from the poor to the rich world. In addition, manufacturing industries have a permanent cost advantage, because technical change benefits them more than primary producers.[11]

So Prebisch and his followers demanded that the state institute policies of import substitution to improve developing countries' terms of trade. Under cover of protection, the state would shift resources out of agriculture, subject to diminishing returns, and low-productivity services where 'disguised unemployment' was rampant, to higher-productivity manufacturing industries, which enjoyed 'economies of scale'. This would enable developing countries to create their own 'infant industries', which in time might become export giants, and so 'catch up' with the developed countries. As Harry Johnson (1923–1977) put it: 'The notion that there exist masses of "disguised unemployed" people leads easily to the idea that "development" involves merely the mobilisation and transfer of these presumably costless productive resources into economic activities.'[12] In the 1950s and 1960s most of Latin America, as well as India, pursued policies based on this kind of analysis.

By the 1970s there was growing doubt that government push was working. The data for developing countries showed rapid population growth, widening income inequality, and small growth in industrial employment. Import substitution was also producing inflation and balance of payments problems. Borrowing abroad for infant industries led to the pile-up of debt, which peaked with the debt crises of the 1970s and 1980s. There was also evidence that forced growth policies were producing deleterious side effects ranging from civil wars to the establishment of murderous authoritarian regimes. Increasing attention was paid to lack of 'social capability'. Governments, it turned out, were perfectly capable of enriching themselves and their families, but not at developing their countries' economies. 'As in the myths which demonstrate the danger of wresting secrets from the gods, the policy-makers abused their newly discovered knowledge and applied to excess the magic formulae that had paid such early dividends.'[13]

To this disappointment with the big push policies, there were two reactions. The first was *dependencia* ('dependency') theory, the Marxist theory of exploitation applied to international economics. Low-income countries aren't just up against bad odds, they said, the game itself is rigged against them. 'Unequal exchange' is not a contingent outcome that can be remedied by state policy within the world capitalist system, because it is the necessary condition of capitalist profitability. The prosperity of the core depends on the poverty of the periphery, with the periphery being required to provide cheap raw materials, and unskilled labour to keep up the profits of the core. The villains of the story were the multinational corporations whose control over global capital enabled them to extract rents from poor countries.[14]

A crucial point made by *dependencia* theorists is that capitalism at the centre developed on the basis of the home market, whereas capitalism on the periphery was imposed from outside. Thus the capitalist economies on the periphery lacked any internal dynamic of their own. Capitalism in such conditions leads to an 'enclave' economy, which not only has no beneficial spillover effects, but kills off the remaining economy, by diverting resources to 'artificial' export activities, substituting luxury imports for home-produced products, shrinking the tertiary sectors of traditional economies, and encouraging wasteful modern production techniques.

Dependency theory brings us back to the picture of the economist as tragedian. Because development of the periphery within the capitalist system is cut off, a socialist revolution is the only path to the conquest of poverty. This will at the same time destroy capitalism at the centre, by undercutting its sole remaining source of profit.

Washington Consensus

A more durable reaction to the alleged failure of import-substitution policies was a drift back to neoclassical economics. It started to be argued that what was needed was not expensive steel mills and motor car industries which could not sell their products for hard currencies, but labour-intensive production based on exploiting the existing comparative advantage poor countries enjoyed in cheap, docile labour. Rural labour reserves could be switched into low-cost manufacturing for exports. The spectacular success of a handful of East Asian 'tigers', like Japan, Taiwan, and South Korea, in break-ing into world markets gave some evidential backing to the new approach.

In the 1980s, the Latin American debt crisis and low commod-ity prices swung the policy discussion to the kind of 'structural adjustment' needed to secure export-led growth. This shift coin-cided with the global ideological shift to freer markets associated with Reagan and Thatcher. In the 1990s the growth agenda was taken over by the so-called Washington Consensus. Significantly, developing economies became 'emerging market economies'.

Economists of the International Monetary Fund and World Bank induced poor countries, as a condition for loans, to 'liber-alise' their financial markets, reduce trade barriers, privatise pub-lic enterprises, cut down on state spending, and allow production decisions to be taken in the global marketplace. A related realisa-tion was that most Third World governments were too incompe-tent and corrupt to be entrusted with ambitious 'catch-up' plans.[15] Instead, in line with the New Institutional Economics (see Chapter 8), increasing emphasis was placed on creating enforceable private property rights, so as to equalise private and social rates of return.

Exploiting comparative advantages became the accepted name of the game in east and south-east Asia. The new growth engine was market integration. Instead of trying to accumulate physical capital, developing countries should concentrate on exporting what they could get most for and importing what they had to pay least for, and using the profits of trade to build up 'human capital'. Growth through globalisation is the accepted position today.

So we have three stories of development.[16] The free trade theory shows us different cars on the same road with some ahead, others behind, but assures us that those in the rear will catch up with those in front by following the free market recipe. The structuralist theory shows some cars stuck in the slow lane, but argues they can move over to the fast lane by following statist import-substitution policies. The exploitation theory argues that capitalism has consigned most peripheral countries permanently to the slow lane from which they can only escape by a revolution against their exploiters.

Structuralist theories still have considerable purchase in Latin America. What makes them a theoretically dissident strand of modern economics is that, in contrast to orthodox or neoclassical economics, they model the world economy as a binary system, borrowing from Marxian class analysis and replacing 'capitalist' and 'worker' with 'centre' and 'periphery'. The two contrasting methods of modelling economic life reflect different views of reality.

Both can be criticised for ignoring important aspects of that reality. Structuralists were alert to the distribution of power in the world economy, but blind to the absence of a competent state to deliver the results promised by their 'big push' policies. Globalisers put their faith in the 'invisible hand' of the market, but paid far too little attention to the fact that successful marketisation requires entrepreneurs. Both approaches thus neglected two vital institutional requisites for economic growth: a strong, relatively uncorrupt state and a commercial middle class. Most of East Asia had these; most of Latin America and Africa did not; hence the different results.

Who is right?

A flavour of the difference between the structuralist and orthodox views of development is given by the following exchanges in

2002 between Professor Robert Wade of the London School of Economics and Martin Wolf, chief economic commentator of the *Financial Times*.[17] This took place in the heyday of the Washington Consensus, before the collapse of 2008.

They start with a dispute about the facts. Wade denied that globalisation had lifted hundreds of millions of people out of primary poverty. World Bank figures showed that the numbers of people in absolute poverty (with incomes of less than $1 a day) remained roughly constant in 1987 and 1998 at around 1.2 billion. Since population had increased, the *share* of the world's population in absolute poverty fell sharply from 28 per cent to 24 per cent; but the absolute numbers may even have grown. Inequality had been widening if one compared the average incomes for each country and treated each one as an equal unit (China=Uganda); it had been decreasing if each country was weighted by its population. But the latter result was entirely due to the fast growth of China and India. While data on income distribution among all the world's households was lacking, the falling wage share from 1982 suggested a growth in inequality. Thus globalisation had been nothing like the poverty and inequality reducing engine the orthodox view supposed.

To this, Wolf responded that World Bank data showed a decline of 200 million living in absolute poverty since 1980. This made nonsense of the claim that poverty reduction had been blighted by globalisation. Further, a big decline in world-wide inequality had occurred since it peaked in 1970. So the previous two decades had seen a decline not just in absolute poverty but also in world-wide inequality between households. The explanation of both was the fast growth of China and, to a lesser extent, India.

The debate shifted to the causes of growth. For Wade the main cause is the diffusion of technical capacity; for Wolf it is multi-causal, with globalisation as an important ingredient. He pointed out that the experience of South Korea and Taiwan in the 1950s showed that countries experience faster growth as they move from autarchy to trade. But economic success, Wade replied, is not evidence of the benefits of globalisation. China and India had started growing before they opened themselves up to trade and foreign capital.

Wade rejected the prescription that all countries should liberalise to speed up growth. History showed that countries didn't liberalise to become rich; they liberalised once they had grown richer. By forcing premature liberalisation on poor countries, the Washington Consensus was impeding the growth of their technical capacity. World Trade Organization (WTO) rules prevented poor countries from doing things which had previously helped rich countries nurture their technological learning, like subsidising their labour-intensive industries, or limiting foreign investment.

Wolf replied that one can't separate technological innovation from the context in which it is applied. Among other preconditions, economic growth requires a stable state, security of person and property, widespread literacy and numeracy, basic health, adequate infrastructure, ability to develop businesses without suffocation by red tape or corruption, broad acceptance of market forces, macro stability, and a financial system able to transfer savings to effective use. In successful countries these emerge in mutually reinforcing ways. In Africa few such preconditions exist. Liberalisation of goods and capital markets won't fix this, but they are handmaidens of growth.

Wolf conceded that infant-industry promotion, buttressed by trade restrictions, may 'occasionally' accelerate economic growth. But the record of their use in poor countries is 'dreadful'. He failed to see why restraints on policy discretion should be good for rich countries and bad for poor ones. Poor countries need more not less protection from bad governments.

A final set of comments related to the reliability of World Bank data. Wolf wrote: 'All data on incomes and distribution are questionable, above all those generated in developing countries. But contrary to what you [Wade] say, World Bank researchers have calculated the numbers ... on a consistent basis.' Wade persisted that the World Bank had 'an official view about how to do development and is subject to arm-twisting by its major share-holders.' It was under pressure to fudge its GDP data base, most glaringly in the case of China, whose growth, he suspected, was far less stellar than World Bank numbers showed.

Wolf had the last word:

> Economic growth is, almost inevitably, uneven. Some countries, regions and people do better than others. The result is growing inequality. To regret that is to regret the growth itself. It is to hold, in effect, that it is better for everyone ... to remain equally poor. [This] seems to me ... morally indefensible and practically untenable ...

✕

This debate illustrates very well why economics is not a hard science. At issue is correlation versus causation (if two or more events run in parallel, which, if either, causes the other?), reliability of the data (how much trust can you put in official statistics?), the ideological complexion of economic models (is the world economy best understood as a unitary or binary system?), universal versus contingent truths (do different economic structures have the same laws of development?), the role of power (are market transactions spontaneous or induced?), the type of policy prescription (free trade or protection?), and last but not least, whether the already affluent West provides the right model of development for poor countries to follow. The next two chapters will address the central question facing the claim of economics to be scientific. Are the stories we have told just stories? Or can they be subject to scientific sifting?

4

EQUILIBRIUM

As in the physical sciences, equilibrium is a
central concept in economics.

Edward Lazear, 'Economic Imperialism'

Equilibrium

Equilibrium is economics' principle of order. The fact that it is supposed to be the spontaneous outcome of market transactions means that alternative systems of maintaining order – those based on power – can be minimised. Markets will do most of the work needed to ensure social cooperation. The state can be restricted to a few political duties – 'law and order'. Thus the equilibrium of the market is the traditional answer of economics to the political claim that societies have to be 'kept in order' by the exercise of power.

In technical terms, equilibrium is the concept of a system at rest. No one has any incentive to change what they are doing. Economics shares the concept of equilibrium with physics. The idea is that there exist forces in nature which automatically balance each other. Any disturbance to the balance will set up an opposing force to restore it: you swing the pendulum one way, and gravity pushes it back.

Joseph Schumpeter (1883–1950) described equilibrium as the 'magna charta' of exact economics.[1] But it poses a severe problem. How do economists reconcile, even notionally, the idea of a state of rest with the undoubted dynamism and instability of economic life? The answer lies in the notion of 'shocks'. The normal state of

economic life is one of predictable activity, based on stable expectations. But the even tenor of economic life is constantly being upset
by shocks: they could be natural, technological, or monetary. In
the prologue of Goethe's eighteenth-century poetical drama, *Faust*,
God sends humanity the devil (Mephistopheles) to rouse it from
its somnolence:[2]

> Man's active nature flagging, seeks too soon the level;
> Unqualified repose he learns to crave;
> Whence, willingly, the comrade him I gave,
> Who works, excites, and must create, as Devil.

In the development of physics, Galileo (1564–1642) glimpsed
the operation of equilibrium in the curved line drawn by the
moon as it circled the earth. Kepler (1571–1630) was then able to
describe accurately the path it took, from which Newton (1643–
1727) explained the curve by the concept of gravity: a field of
force which pulls matter together. No one has ever seen gravity: it
was a hypothesis to explain Kepler's observation and many others
since. As it was once believed that the planets were held in place by
angels, gravity is a scientific improvement on the angelic host. It is
also a proven hypothesis. With trivial exceptions, gravity holds for
all physical bodies.

Mainstream economists want to make economics as much like
physics as possible. Mechanics came before economics and the first
economists marvelled at the precision and certainty of the laws of
mechanics. So the economic world must be shown to exhibit something like the laws of physics. Economic equilibrium is secured by
the opposing forces of supply and demand. The elementary supply
and demand diagram shows the quantity of a good which will be
demanded and the quantity supplied at different prices. The price
of something goes up, the quantity sold goes down; its price goes
down, and the quantity sold goes up. If a blight makes tomatoes
scarcer, their price will go up, consumers will buy fewer tomatoes.
If farmers grow too many tomatoes, prices will fall, leading some
farmers to stop growing tomatoes, and some to grow something

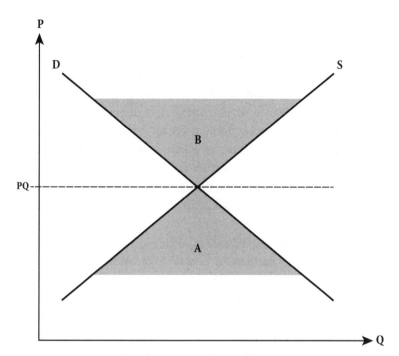

3. Competitive Equilibrium. Note: The first diagram students of economics
encounter: **P** = price, **Q** = quantity, **S** = supply curve, **D** = demand curve,
PQ = equilibrium price. **A**: excess demand forces P back up to equilibrium level,
B: excess supply forces P down to equilibrium level.

else. Either way the market for tomatoes will find its equilibrium
level, a price level at which no producer willing to accept the going
rate will be left with unsold stock, and no buyer willing to accept
the going rate will have empty shelves.

In Paul Samuelson's summary: 'There may have to be an initial period of trial and error, of oscillation around the right level,
before price finally settles down in balance.' Thus competitive supply and demand schedules represent the best response by sellers
and buyers to any disturbance to a pre-existing equilibrium.

The French economist Léon Walras (1834–1910) extended the
notion of equilibrium in a local market to the idea of the general
equilibrium (GE) of a system of markets. He reasoned that if the
whole economy consisted of perfectly competitive markets, supply

and demand would be *simultaneously* balanced in all markets, a balance which can be expressed in a set of simultaneous equations.

In Walrasian GE each market establishes its equilibrium or market-clearing price through a process Walras called *tatonnement* or 'groping'. At the point of trade all prices in the economy have been perfectly adjusted to the supply and demand conditions in each market. It is important to note that all markets in the Walrasian system are *auction* markets, in which contracts to buy and sell are made simultaneously – prices are known to both buyers and sellers. If prices are uncertain, the existence of equilibrium cannot be proved, either in one market, or in the market economy as a whole.[3]

One little noticed paradox of Walrasian GE is that it abolishes the need for markets! A central planner, with a sufficiently extensive computer-generated data set on consumer preferences and producer costs, could just find and implement the equilibrium solution. This unfortunate consequence was pointed out by the Austrian economist Friedrich Hayek (1899–1992). Hayek guarded against this possibility by famously arguing – in the so-called 'socialist calculation debate' of the 1930s – that information was diffused through the system of decentralised markets; it was impossible for even a well-resourced planner to concentrate all the information arising from market processes at his computer's finger tips. It was market transactions which 'discovered' the very information that Walras assumed all agents had in order to solve his system of equations.[4] Hayek's argument seems less convincing in the age of big data and real-time computation.

Although proving the possibility of a general equilibrium may seem to be nothing more than a playful mathematical exercise, it seems quite likely that most economists do believe that something like GE prevails in real life. What Backhouse calls 'Walrasian formalism' is the bedrock of methodological orthodoxy.[5]

Self-interest as economics' gravity equivalent

What is supposed to be the equivalent in economic life of the force of gravity which keeps the natural world in equilibrium? What is the 'energy' that 'pushes down' the price of a good in excess supply, or 'pushes up' the price of a good in excess demand? The economists found the answer in self-interest. An equilibrium is the result of what purposive, self-interested individuals interacting in markets achieve through a process of 'haggling and higgling'.

You will find the germs of this story in Adam Smith. It has, of course, been refined in the telling. Self-interest remains at the core. But today self-interest is identified with acting in such a way as to 'maximise expected utility'. (Some fancy maths will demonstrate that the requirements for rational behaviour are the same as the conditions of Walrasian general equilibrium.)

Maximisation (getting the most for least) as a principle of behaviour seems so obvious to us today that we find it hard to envisage a market in which buyers did not try to buy at the lowest price and sellers did not try to sell at the highest price. Yet this seems to have been the case in many pre-modern markets, in which the prices of goods and services were fixed not by the expectation of 'gaining on the exchange', but by custom; and markets were places where people exchanged goods thought to be of equivalent value, because they could not produce them themselves. People in such markets instinctively recognised that they were simultaneously consumers *and* producers, buyers *and* sellers, so that if they spent less, others would have less to buy what they produced. Thus the economist's idea of intersecting supply and demand curves was alien to the pre-capitalist mind. That mind conceived of only one curve, representing the 'just' price, and any deviation from it as a sign of moral disturbance. This, too, was a principle of equilibrium, or order, with 'natural prices' playing the role later assigned to market-determined prices. But it was entirely static.

Today, the equilibrium achieved by 'haggling and higgling' is an approximation to what happens in auction and fresh food markets and in Arabian *souks*. However, as a general principle of market pricing, and particularly in those markets most important for the working and stability of the modern economy – labour, commodity, financial markets, and markets for information and innovation – it is false, because the stationary conditions needed for equilibrium are lacking. These markets exhibit momentum and bandwagon behaviour which cumulatively push prices upwards or downwards. That is why we get prolonged booms and busts. The human apple may have a tendency to fall to the ground, but this tendency is far too weak to be called a law.

Frictions

To explain the sluggish operations of the see-saw, economists have found it useful to apply the idea of 'frictions', another word borrowed from mechanics, which signifies a resistance to the efficient 'sliding together' of the parts of the market system. The concept of frictions does sterling work in protecting the core theory of equilibrium from attack, by allowing for deviations. When students of physics first start to calculate the effects of gravity, they do so by assuming the object falls in a vacuum. Frictions such as air resistance can be incorporated into the calculation. So long as the shapes of the objects remain simple, the frictions do too, and thus the law of gravitation exhibits high predictability.

But nothing like these conditions exists in economic life. Ideally Walrasian equilibrium is achieved in a time-free world: it makes no difference whether you take midday or midnight to be the zero of time in your calculations. As soon as time is introduced, which allows processes to work themselves through at different speeds, the economist is forced to abandon pure Walrasian GE, and resort to *ad hoc* explanations for the failure of equilibrium to establish itself. (We will consider other protective devices in Chapter 10).

The fundamental impediment to most markets working like auction or fresh food markets is uncertainty about the future. The prices of goods in the auction house or grocery store are 'spot' prices: prices of goods bought 'on the spot' for immediate delivery. But Walrasian equilibrium requires contracts for future delivery of goods and services at prices which can only be guessed at. A great deal of trading in actual markets therefore takes place at the 'wrong', or disequilibrium, prices. This means that equilibrium cannot be proved to be the result of a myriad of voluntary transactions in markets. Frictions in the social world are much more severe than those in physics, because they are caused by the human beings whose behaviour we are trying to explain.

Thus the existence of frictions such as 'sticky wages' might explain persisting unemployment. To the fervent globalist, nations are frictions to the more perfect integration of markets. When humans are shown not to possess the properties needed for perfect efficiency, they too tend to be regarded as frictions. Humans are an endless disappointment to economists. They mess up their equations.

Economic laws, as we have seen, come with health warnings known as *ceteris paribus*: the law holds if other things do not change. In natural science the *ceteris paribus* limitation is not onerous: it is a reasonable assumption that other things do not change. In economics this is not true. Where 'recurring little decisions' are all that are involved, economists can estimate demand and supply functions reasonably accurately.[6] But where decisions are unique and non-recurring the standard models of rational choice, equilibrium and so on, break down. Therefore the scope of any economic law is very much less than the scope of a law in natural science. The main purpose of this book is to show *how much less*.

Questions about equilibrium

At this point in the conversation the student should be thinking of some good questions to put to the economist (or teacher of economics). First, do economists see equilibrium as a necessary property of a market system, a benchmark, a logical requirement for quantitative prediction, or a mathematical ideal: beautiful to behold but of little practical relevance?

Most mainstream economists would see it as a mixture of the positive and the normative. They believe in the spontaneous tendency of markets to equilibrium. But they also believe that 'artificial' impediments to this self-adjusting mechanism – like labour union-controlled wages, over-generous welfare benefits, and erratic government policies – exist, and should be minimised. However, some economists have undoubtedly surrendered to the logical and aesthetic beauties of the concept of equilibrium. They love it for its own sake.

Here is a second question. If the pendulum is set in motion by an impulse ('shock'), how long does it swing before it stops swinging? In other words, how long are periods of *disequilibrium* supposed to last? Equilibrium will be restored 'in the long run'. How long is the long run? Just long enough for equilibrium to be restored! The assumption in financial markets is that it is almost instantaneous. As the trader tells it, 'the long run is what we are going to have for lunch'. Contrast Keynes's reminder that, 'In the long-run we are all dead'.

Thirdly, does the notion of pendulum swings have any power to explain the actual movement of prices and output through time? In other words, is the 'normal' condition of the economy one of equilibrium or disequilibrium? Joan Robinson (1903–1983) stressed the contradiction between equilibrium and history, between the swinging of an economy between points of equilibrium, and the forward movement which time imposes. Time, she argued, is irreversible: innovation builds on innovation. Certainly it seems hard to reconcile the neoclassical equilibrium model, which assumes 'normal' returns to scale, from which economies occasionally deviate, with the classical growth perspective, in which the economy is continually accumulating capital and technology.

※

So what is the status of equilibrium theory today? Duncan Foley believes in the 'immense scientific value' of equilibrium concepts.[7] I would argue rather that it has a baleful influence, by encouraging economists to think that the market system is automatically self-correcting and therefore not requiring policy intervention.

Formally, equilibrium represents a state of affairs in which resources are so allocated that market-clearing prices prevail all round, and no one has any incentive to change their position. This is an 'optimum' equilibrium, in the sense that the economy is at its production possibility frontier (PPF) and all are satisfied with 'what they've got'. However, within this equilibrium framework, economists toy with several different concepts of equilibrium, depending on what they want to explain. Static equilibrium is of the Walrasian kind, relating supply, demand, and price at a single moment of time. Dynamic equilibrium takes past and expected future values of the variables into account in explaining the adjustment process. The stationary state is a kind of equilibrium in which the economy simply reproduces itself. This translates into the idea of balanced growth, with population and capital increasing at roughly the same rate and preferences staying constant.[8] Partial equilibrium traces the adjustment of supply to demand in a particular market in isolation from the rest of the economy.

Joseph Schumpeter contrasted static and dynamic models. Statics refers to an economy of given, known, and constant external conditions, such as tastes and technology. This has no resemblance to modern market economies. In dynamic analysis, external conditions not only change but such change is fundamental to a capitalist economy. Entrepreneurs try out innovations which in a process of creative destruction replace tried methods: 'increasing destruction of age-old relationships for the sake of profit'.[9] Schumpeter, like Marx, understood that technological progress is endogenous: it is impelled by the logic of competitive, profit-maximising capitalism.

Cyclical theories are a long-run type of equilibrium theory. The capitalist economy experiences waves of innovation, each one of which eventually exhausts itself like a receding tide. Karl Marx was an equilibrium theorist in this sense, with the profit rate waxing and waning with the size of the 'reserve army of the unemployed'.[10]

Keynes challenged the idea that an economy is always at, or tending towards, an optimum equilibrium of the Walrasian kind. His equilibria need not be optimal, but they are equilibria none the less. Keynes pointed out that the economy does not correct itself through relative price adjustments as mainstream equilibrium theory claims. Rather there are uni-directional, economy-wide, movements of output and employment, so that it is 'quantities not prices' which adjust, pushing economies to inferior equilibria, in which all income earned is spent, but some factors of production are left without any income at all. Uncertainty is key to generating such equilibria, with a fall in investment prospects producing a flight to liquidity rather than a fall in interest rates. There has always been a debate about whether a Keynesian equilibrium is anything more than a short-period phenomenon.

Economists in the Keynesian tradition, including Nicholas Kaldor (1908–1986), Gunnar Myrdal (1899–1987), George Shackle (1903–1992), Giovanni Dosi (b.1953), as well as many in the Austrian school, such as Ludwig Lachmann (1906–1990), have tried to break out of the straitjacket of equilibrium. Innovation is a fertile field for dynamic analysis. One can't know in advance about the effects of innovation because it hasn't yet happened. New knowledge builds on prior knowledge so you get an accumulation of positive feedbacks which push the economy ever further from equilibrium. Innovation builds 'first starter advantage' analysis into explanations of economic growth.

To sum up: without making unrealistic assumptions about human behaviour, and without assuming stationary conditions, the existence of an equilibrium of supply and demand, either in single markets, or in the system as a whole, cannot be demonstrated. There is nothing in the 'market' akin to the law of gravity. There is no coercive force behind the policeman's authority. In a famous exercise, Nobel Laureates Kenneth Arrow (1921–2017) and Gerard Debreu (1921–2004) specified with great mathematical rigour the conditions under which a market economy could achieve perfect allocation of resources. These included perfect information, no frictions, no public goods, consistent preferences, as well as complete competitive markets which include all contingent and future contracts.[11]

Theirs was a formidable intellectual feat. There are some conditions under which GE is true. But the conditions are too severe for it to have any general application. The two economists' health warnings against GE's practical usefulness are so muted that it would surely have been better to have said straight out that GE was a mental fantasy, despite the great pleasure they derived from the challenge it presented to their mathematical and logical skills.

How then to explain the continued hold of equilibrium modelling? The most important reason, as we have suggested, is physics envy. But the certainty of physics can be achieved only by making heroic assumptions about human behaviour.

There is also a strong ideological motive. If markets are naturally self-balancing, they don't need governments to balance them. Governments, rather, appear in this account as one of the frictions preventing markets from working optimally. (Unless, that is, one assumes an omniscient government, which most economists have been understandably reluctant to do.) Thus the notion of equilibrium reinforces the anti-statist thrust of economics.

But there is something deeper than that, which is not unique to economists. This is the conviction that underneath the messiness of appearances there exists an underlying order that can be captured by logic and mathematics: a conviction that goes all the way back to Plato (c.428–348 BC), and in modern philosophy to René Descartes (1596–1650). Equilibrium is thus a mental construct to explain a feature of social life whose explanation is not evident at first sight, viz. its apparently spontaneous orderliness.

It is undoubtedly true that markets are not violently disorderly. Even their oscillations exhibit certain patterns and regularities. Where do these (weak) principles of order come from? For Adam Smith the world was a providentially ordered cosmos. We no longer believe the order comes from God, so we invoke reason. We then find that individual rationality is not enough to guarantee equilibrium in the face of uncertainty. But there may be an alternative explanation for the orderliness of markets, to be found not in the rational behaviour of 'maximising' agents, but in mutually reinforcing social conventions or politically coordinated action. The gravitational forces, so to speak, are external and not internal to the market.

Thinking about equilibria and disequilibria prompts one to reflect that if balance exists in economic life it is part of the wider balance of social life evolved to prevent society itself from exploding. It expresses itself in the tendency of an excess in one direction to produce a reaction to its opposite. It is in this, but only in this sense, that the tendency to equilibrium can be thought of as natural. But this tendency is far too complex to have the precision required for a prediction of specific events.

5

MODELS AND LAWS

> When faced with incomprehensible phenomena the human
> mind gives forth hypotheses, the most plausible, convenient
> or expedient of which are dressed up into a theory after
> which tranquillity may be restored . . . this chaos of jarring
> and discordant appearances brought to order, this tumult
> of the imagination allayed.
>
> Adam Smith, *Essay on Astronomy*[1]

According to Paul Samuelson it is economics' ability to make
quantitative predictions that makes it 'the queen of the social sciences':[2] its theories are engines for generating predictions, which
can therefore become the basis of successful policies. The challenge
for economics has always been to 'model' economic life in such a
way as to generate reliable predictions. The standard technique is
to isolate a single motive for action, and deduce its consequences
by excluding the influence of other possible motives. This is no
different from the technique of other social sciences: for example,
political science takes love of power to be overriding. What makes
economics 'queen' is that its subject matter is what Marshall called
'measurable motives' – motives whose strength can be measured
and compared on the single scale of money. No other social science has found a way of bringing disparate quantities of stuff into
such precise relationships with each other. As Lionel Robbins put
it: 'Scientific generalisations, if they pretend to the status of laws,
must be capable of being stated exactly.'[3] Furthermore, predictions stated in terms of quantities of money can be properly tested.

Hence, economic generalisations are said to be open to improvement in a way that generalisations in other social sciences are not. Economic generalisation can be falsified; generalisations made by other social scientists remain matters of opinion.

How do economists seek to establish their so-called laws? There are two main theories of knowledge in economics (as in all sciences, natural and social): the inductive and the deductive. The empirical theory sees economics as reliant on induction, testing, and refutation. The logical theory portrays economics as a system of logical deduction from axioms – premises 'known to be true'. Provided the axioms are correct, the results will follow. The actual practice of economics is a compromise between these two views. Logical reasoning is at its heart. But its premises are not entirely plucked from the air, and it tries to test the validity of its conclusions against real-world outcomes. There is a third view, to which few economists subscribe, which treats economics as a branch of rhetoric, engaged not in the science of discovering truth, but the art of persuading people of the truth of its own utterances, and by persuasion causing them to behave in a desired way.

Modelling

The answer to the question of how economists seek to establish their laws is through modelling. Modelling is the act of creating a simplified theoretical structure to represent real-world events. In economics, this structure is now overwhelmingly mathematical, with three parts: input variables, a logical process that links them, and an output variable.

Economists claim that building a model is like drawing a map: the object is to leave out cluttering matter, while leaving in place crucial information. A model that is just as complicated as the world is of no use at all, just like a 1:1 map. Economic reality – whatever that is – is too complicated to be directly interrogated; so it must be simplified to the point of caricature. Critics argue that this is simply a rhetorical ploy. The open world is 'modelled' as closed, not to simplify reality, but for mathematical convenience.

The issue is what to include in the map and what to leave out. What one includes in the map depends on what one wants to do. If it is to get from one place to another as quickly as possible the map will highlight coastlines, motorways, express railway connections, and airports. A more leisurely itinerary will require a map with scenic routes. If the modeller wants to map a social terrain, he might populate the map with individuals, and leave out firms and classes, or he might include these. All of this, of course, leaves the modeller, like the map maker, considerable latitude to choose which features of 'reality' to emphasise. There is ample room for ideology. Neoclassical economics claimed it rediscovered the individual buried under the institutional lumber of Marxist theorising.

Models start with hypotheses, which then have to be tested by experiment, or by some other means if experiment is impossible. This is as true of natural science as of economics. Physics has, in nature, its own ready-made laboratory, where events regularly repeat themselves. The social world lacks such stationary features. The standard economic model is typically a theoretical representation of a closed system. But to model an open system as though it were a closed system 'introduces a damaging rift between ontology and epistemology – i.e. between the way the social world actually is, and the way it is represented in economic models. Once in place, the rift cannot be healed.'[4]

Economists use many techniques to 'close' open systems, of which the following are the most important. First is *ceteris paribus* – working out the consequences of a particular change by 'freezing' the other variables specified in the model. David Ricardo's *Essay on Profits* (1815) is an early explicit example of its use: 'We will ... suppose that no improvements take place in agriculture, and that capital and population advance in the proper proportion ... that we may know what peculiar effects are to be ascribed to ... the extension of agriculture to the more remote and less fertile land.' This technique gives you a single starting point leading to a single destination. A second stratagem is to remove potential disturbances from the model entirely by calling them 'shocks' – random events 'exogenous' to the model. A favourite is a technology 'shock'. This preserves the predictive power of the model itself, while allowing for failure of a change in the input variable to produce the predicted change in the output: 'non-linearity' in maths-speak. A third stratagem, which we have already noticed, is the concept of 'frictions'. This allows for any lags in the adjustment of the different parts of the model to a change in the input variable. It is closely related to the idea of 'transitions' and the short-run/long-run distinction.

Thus the introduction of machinery may make workers redundant in the short run. But it sets in motion forces which will preserve employment in the long run. Given that economists want to achieve a high level of model predictability, these are perfectly legitimate stratagems. But the predictability is too often achieved at the expense of realism – the models are, in effect, rendered immune to criticism. With the increasing use of formal mathematical modelling, the zones of exclusion become ever larger. The subject matter of the enquiry comes to be defined by the requirement of model tractability.

There are three main views of how to construct economic models. The first says you must start with 'realistic' assumptions or your models will be merely fanciful. Second, in his influential paper, *The Methodology of Positive Economics*, Milton Friedman (1912–2006) claimed that the important question is not whether the assumptions of a model are realistic, but whether the model yields good predictions. Any premise will do. If it happens to hit the nail on the head, one can test for whether this was a coincidence or a causal law. The third stresses the deduction of conclusions from self-evident axioms. (Malthus's population theory as described in Chapter 3 is an example.)

The following questions arise. Are models to be thought of as descriptive or prescriptive? Do models aim to show how people behave or get them to behave as the modeller thinks they ought to behave? The normative or prescriptive purpose of modelling is hardly ever acknowledged, because economics is supposed to be 'scientific' and 'value-free'.

The economist Jevons put one view of the task of economics simply: 'The investigator begins with the facts and ends with them.' In his conception, there are three stages in model-building: the inductive hypothesis, the deduction of a conclusion, the testing of the conclusion against reality.[5]

The process may be illustrated as follows. An observation suggests a 'conjecture' or 'hypothesis' as to why something may be the case. You then develop a theory which involves establishing a causal link between your conjecture and other factors called variables. The deductive stage involves working out the logical consequences of your hypothesis. You then test the conclusion against reality. Jevons realised that a deductive argument can do no more than link a set of premises to a set of conclusions. If the assumptions are unrealistic, the conclusions (predictions of the model) will not hold in the real world. So in his view the assumptions need to be realistic.

A standard workhouse model in modern macroeconomics is the Phillips Curve. The statistician A.W. Phillips (1914–1975)

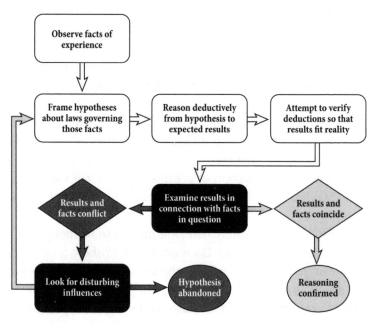

4. The Method of Modelling.

noted (1958) an empirical relationship ('correlation') stretching from 1861 to 1957 between inflation and unemployment.[6] This suggested that governments could 'trade off' a bit more inflation for a bit less unemployment, and vice versa.

The problem with the original Phillips Curve was the disappearance of the postulated trade-off between inflation and unemployment in the later 1960s. To explain this 'change in the facts' a hypothesis was suggested: rational agents 'learn from experience'. They come to realise that the current inflation rate is the rate they can expect and adjust their wage-bargaining behaviour accordingly. This resulted in the 'expectations augmented' Phillips Curve, which predicts that over time, government attempts to reduce unemployment by allowing a bit more inflation lead only to accelerating inflation. Notice that in this model there is no attempt to investigate changes in institutional facts (in trade union organisation, historic levels of unemployment, among others) which might explain the breakdown of the original Phillips Curve: the single postulate of 'utility maximising behaviour' does all the work needed.

A close inspection of this procedure points to some of the difficulties inherent in model construction.

1. What is the status of the 'facts of experience'? Are they based on casual observation, observed regularities, interpretations of the facts, or known *a priori?* In other words, are they already 'contaminated' by prior conceptualisations? – for example, that human behaviour is rationally calculated?

2. What lies behind the inclusion of some, and the exclusion of other, possible causal variables? What, in other words, guides the modeller's judgments of relevance?

3. What constitutes verification? Results are rarely black and white, so how dark a grey can we accept? How large a pile of 'disturbing influences' is it possible to accumulate before the theory is more exception than rule, and should be abandoned? What if the results and facts appear to coincide, but do so only by chance?

The facts of the matter

In practice, economists almost never start with the facts; there are too many. Nor do they normally start with 'vigilant observation': numbers arranged as statistical series from which they try to discern patterns and suggestive anomalies. They start with a hypothesis and then try to prove it. The hypothesis is not 'plucked from the air'. Nor is it based on systematic observation, even though economists often appeal to the 'indisputable facts of experience'. Rather, it is based on the claim to 'direct acquaintance' or 'intuitive' knowledge of how humans think. Ronald Coase (1910–2013) recalled the English economist Ely Devons (1913–1967) saying to him, 'If economists wished to study the horse, they wouldn't go and look at horses. They'd sit in their studies and say to themselves, "What would I do if I were a horse?" And they would soon discover that they would maximise their utilities'.[7] This joke gives a profound insight into the economic method. Economists see themselves as forming their theories by looking into the minds of their subjects and seeing how they think. This is what enables them to make sharp predictions about their behaviour. 'Vicarious problem solving,' writes Nobel Laureate Thomas Schelling (1921–2016), 'underlies most microeconomics'.[8]

So economists' models may be interpreted as starting with intuitions about what goes on in the horse's mind.[9] They claim they are merely formalising 'models' which are already 'there'. But this may not give you a good way of understanding behaviour. The chances are they have put into the mind of the human horse what they want to find there. So a key question concerns the relationship between the economists' hypotheses of human behaviour and how humans actually behave. Are economists' models intended as replications or simplifications of actual behaviour, or are they intended to create behaviour consistent with the economists' models – to create self-fulfilling prophecies, so to speak? It seems pretty obvious that economic models are intended to be both descriptive and prescriptive, wobbling between claims that this is how humans behave in fact, and this is how they should behave, both converging on a predictive claim.

Paul Krugman (b.1953) has described the model-building process as follows: 'You make a set of clearly untrue simplifications to get the system down to something you can handle; those simplifications are dictated partly by guesses about what is important, partly by the modelling techniques available. And the end result, if the model is a good one, is an improved insight into why the vastly more complex real system behaves the way it does.'[10] The argument here is that economists need the untrue simplifications to get the generalising machinery going. But it can be argued that heroic (untrue) assumptions should have no place in a discipline intended to be useful. To start off one's reasoning with a basic premise (axiom) that is immune to challenge cannot justify certain knowledge of a conclusion, unless one (irrationally) accepts the premise as true.[11]

Macroeconomic models have tried to get beyond 'untrue simplification'. The economist Nicholas Kaldor wrote,

> The theorist, in my view, should be free to start with a 'stylized' view of the facts – i.e. concentrate on broad tendencies, ignoring individual detail, and proceed on the 'as if' method, i.e. construct a hypothesis that could account for these 'stylized' facts, without necessarily committing himself on the historical accuracy, or sufficiency, of the facts or tendencies thus summarized.[12]

A good hypothesis accounts for the stylised facts. Kaldor's was a notable attempt to ground macroeconomic models in 'vigilant observation' rather than 'inner understanding' of human nature. However, an over-enthusiastic reliance on stylised facts may lead the modeller seriously astray when the facts change.

All economic models have a tight logic, amounting to mathematical proof of the conclusion. The name of the game today, as depicted by Nobel Laureate Robert Lucas (b.1937), is to 'get logically consistent mathematical conjectures of various degrees of complexity'. But economics cannot live by logic alone. To be useful a logical argument has to be based on true beliefs about something. Logic can tell you nothing about the real world; it can only tell you about itself. Students should be aware of the pitfalls of reasoning *a priori*: the argument 'If all swans are white, and X is a swan; therefore X is white' is valid in logic, but not in fact since not all swans are white. If the starting point was that 'most swans are white', then one will know more about what colour swans actually are but won't be able to make a definite prediction about the colour of the next one encountered.[13]

The most important name in the philosophy of testing is the Austrian philosopher Karl Popper (1902–1994). Popper believed that what demarcated science from non-science was not whether theories could be proved but whether they could be falsified. Popper's point was not that verification is less powerful than falsification, but that it is impossible. Scientific laws claim to hold true universally, and to verify a universal statement is impossible for finite minds.

However, falsification is also rarely possible. Even in the natural sciences there can be no conclusive disproof of a theory in the strict logical sense that Popper wants because it is difficult to know which of several hypotheses you are falsifying.[14] It is always possible to say that the experimental results are not reliable, or that the discrepancy between observation and fact will disappear with the advance of understanding, rather like Cesare Cremoni's doubts about whether Galileo's telescope had been tampered with.[15] Although a lot of scientists still swear by Popper, among philosophers of science his view has long been rejected. The problem, as Lakatos pointed out, is that scientists don't reject theories the moment they encounter problems; they construct 'auxiliary hypotheses' to account for the disconfirming instance.

Popper believed that his verification principle applied equally to the natural and social sciences: in fact, he failed to distinguish between the two. But falsification in economics encounters even worse problems than in any natural science, because the ubiquity of the 'other things staying equal' condition serves to immunise an economic theory against the disturbing influence of untoward events. One can get robust predictions only by waving away the disturbing causes.

Testing hypotheses in economics encounters the general problem of testing faced by all social sciences. First, although one can, with some difficulty, do experimental work on a small scale, it is impossible to experiment with whole economies; the second is the weakness of econometrics, the substitute for experiment.

Economists are mostly debarred from using the experimental method, typical of applied natural sciences like medicine, to test their hypotheses. Suppose you invented a new drug which you expect to lower cholesterol. How would you test for it? In a laboratory test you could secure the equivalent of the 'vacuum' situation by ensuring that the two sets of lab rats are subjected to identical conditions, except that only one group is given the drug. If the outcome between the two groups is identical this would amount to a refutation of the hypothesis, calling for a new one. A difference of outcome would corroborate the hypothesis that the drug lowers cholesterol. But it would not confirm that it does so in all, or even most, conditions, because these have been equalised by design. So no irrefutable 'law' has been established, but perhaps a useful indication, which can be further refined.

The technique of randomised control trials, borrowed from medicine, suggests a way round the difficulty of conducting controlled experiments with rats. In the lab experiment you have taken steps to ensure identical initial conditions. But you might achieve the same result by administering tests to individuals selected at random – that is, those whom you have no reason for thinking are different in any relevant respect. The trial then proceeds in the same way. Divide your test subjects into two groups, at random, then administer a 'treatment' to only one of the groups, and compare the results.

This method was used to evaluate the famous PROGRESA scheme in Mexico, which involved providing cash transfers to households for sending children to school. The finding was that more education resulted in higher wages. It is unlikely that a trial of this kind would satisfy a convinced Popperian, but it is fit enough for purpose.

The randomised evaluation of public policy interventions works well in fields like public health economics, where one can plausibly assume equal susceptibility to disease and interventions. It has been used to develop effective vaccines for treating pneumonia and meningitis in developing countries.[16] But it is useless for testing the effect of interventions in 'open' systems, where the constancy of the underlying structures cannot be plausibly assumed. Each country has its own particularities of geography, climate, culture and institutions, so would make poor experimental controls. Even if this were not the case, the sample size would be too small to draw the types of robust conclusion required.

Econometrics

By far the most prominent testing technique in economics is econometrics. The economist Guy Routh described it as 'mock empiricism, with statistics subjected to econometric torture until they admit to effects of which they are innocent'.[17] Econometrics is a kind of statistics, but one in which empirical evidence enters not as a foundation for the argument, but as a health-check on the conclusion. It is used not to display the facts of the world in statistical form but to test the statistical significance of the relationships hypothesised by the model. We run a regression to estimate the quantitative influence of the independent variables on the dependent variable, according to a model specification set out by the researcher. Typically, this amounts to assuming a linear (straight line) relationship between the independent variables and the dependent variable (or some transformation of it).

Two problems are commonly raised with econometrics. Firstly, it is almost impossible to isolate the hypothesis which needs to be tested from the many other hypotheses which have had to be assumed in order to make the test possible. This includes the possibility that there might be a circular relationship, where the variable you have assumed is purely dependent exerts influence on the independent one, or that important aspects of the relationship are omitted from the model. This objection highlights the fact that a correlation (the association in time of two events) tells you nothing about the causal relationship between them. A celebrated example of an econometric 'proof' which has failed to escape from the trap of circularity is the claim by Alberto Alesina (b.1957) that cutting government spending in a slump causes economic recovery.[18]

Secondly, time-series cannot establish the laws which economists seek. If the time-series is too short, there is not enough data. If it is long enough, the conditions are not stationary. So something true at one time may not be true at another. The heterodox economists are right. All so-called economic laws are dependent on time and place.

There can also be too few observations. Studies by Harvard University's George J. Borjas and others suggest that net immigration lowers the wages of competing domestic labour. Borjas's most famous study shows the depressive impact of 'Marielitos' – Cubans who emigrated *en masse* to Miami in 1980 – on domestic working-class wages. In reply, others pointed out that there were sampling issues: the census bureau had recently made an effort to sample more black males, who tended to have low incomes, and the sample was too small not to be swayed by this. Borjas in turn accused his critics of bad faith.[19] Far from clarifying the matter, econometrics had spun everyone around in circles. There are too many examples of studies whose econometrics were subsequently discredited, either by spreadsheet mistakes, or cognitive bias.

These problems point to the fundamental weakness of econometric testing: that the conditions needed for its success arise only in controlled experimental situations. Most econometricians recognise that these conditions fail to hold strictly but proceed as if this wasn't important. They fail to understand that the very act of writing papers in learned journals using these techniques gives authority to faulty procedure. Students are told: if everyone does it this way, it must be right. Economists' health warnings are like the small print in a statement of business accounts which no one reads.

Modelling complexity

Following the crash of 2007–2008, there has been a surge of interest in how best to model 'complex' systems. This stemmed from the realisation that the simpler models like the 'efficient market hypothesis' completely failed either to foresee or understand the crash. 'Complexity refers to the density of structural linkages and interactions between the parts of an interdependent system'.[20] In other words, because there are so many relationships and potential feedback loops between variables, even small changes have the potential to produce large knock-on effects. This not only makes it difficult to understand the system intuitively, but also excludes traditional modelling techniques which generally require sparse structural linkages. The chief approaches to understanding complexity are agent-based modelling, network analysis, and system dynamics.

Agent-based modelling tries to avoid fallacies of composition that would occur by using the 'representative agent' hypothesis, which assumes that the entire economy can be represented by a single individual who thinks like everyone else. Instead, it simulates the actions and interactions of a multitude of agents who may have different characteristics and display adaptive behaviour. The modeller sets up relationships between the agents and defines the conditions of their world. The fictional agents are then left to interact, possibly under a shock or change in conditions of some kind. The simulated outcomes churned out thus constitute the results of the model. These outcomes can serve as indicators of what will happen in the real world without the need for further interrogation.

Network analysis studies economic networks, which are 'webs' whose nodes represent economic agents (individuals, firms, consumers, organisations, industries, countries, etc.) and whose links depict market interactions. This is useful for studying the rise of networks in the global supply chain. The most important networks today are programmed computer networks.

System dynamics, derived from Forrester's (1971) attempts to model the world ecosystem, take a similar approach but focus on links between aggregate variables rather than agents. These can be economic variables such as GNP or capital stock, but could also refer to physical quantities such as forested areas or oil stocks, which has made this technique particularly popular in ecological economics.

Although an improvement on mainstream methods, these techniques presuppose the same atomistic ontology in order to generate their predictions. They must in turn make assumptions about behaviour and relationships. These may be based upon observation, intuition, or simply plucked from the air, but must necessarily be simplified or idealised descriptions of the real world. They will be internally and logically consistent, but the results largely follow from the premises: they are not really 'new knowledge', and in any case the 'art' of calibrating the model is often what really generates the results. The chaos of the interacting agents and conditions can throw up vastly different results even from the same initial conditions, so the best a simulation can do is act as a useful guide to the range of possible outcomes, and shed light on the dynamics of the system.

It might be tempting to apply the well-known aphorism 'garbage in, garbage out' to economic modelling. Certainly there are cases where this is true, but it does not apply universally. The purpose of the modelling exercise is key: if precise predictions of real-world outcomes are desired, models are likely to disappoint, except in special situations. If they are intended as tools to investigate the consequences of certain assumptions, clarify thinking, and make general claims about how events might respond to certain actions, they are useful.

Platonic modelling

Economists may construct models as ideals, just as a model in ordinary language can mean not a simplification (as in a model aeroplane) but an ideal of goodness or beauty: perfect 'forms', of which objects in the everyday world are imperfect copies. Platonic models are pictures of what reality might be like if it attained to an ideal state. One can think of them as 'benchmarks'. To the economist this means a state of perfect efficiency: the efficiency of a perfectly frictionless machine. They have a powerful ally in computer technology, able to assemble and process masses of data in 'real time'. This promises to realise, at no distant date, the economist's vision of the human as a perfect calculating machine.

The writings both of neoclassical economists and technological utopians reveal the prescriptive nature of their callings. They are allies in their ambition to 'make the crooked timber of humanity straight'. So economists' theories are meant to inspire greater efficiency. There is some evidence that the prescription works. In a marvellous book, *I Spend Therefore I Am*, Philip Roscoe (2014) reports studies which show that students of economics were markedly more calculating than those of other subjects, though whether it was their calculating nature which drew them to economics, or economics which made them more calculating, is not clear. 'Rational expectations' models are examples of such ideal modelling. They assume that economic agents are perfectly rational and perfect processors of their information. The assumption hides the hope that in time people will come to behave in the way the ideal model says they should.

Science versus rhetoric

Deirdre McCloskey is the best-known exponent of the view of economics as rhetoric. Coming from a mainstream economics background, she denies that economics can prove its arguments, because there is no possibility of falsification. There are no true or false arguments, only persuasive and unpersuasive ones. Maths is neoclassical economics' most emphatic metaphor: the economic researcher has only to produce a correlation, and the statistically unsophisticated are persuaded he has discovered a cause. Nevertheless, McCloskey believes that the rhetorical character of neoclassical economics is socially useful, because it strengthens the case for free markets.[21]

To say that economics is purely rhetorical is to deny that there is a reality outside the language of persuasion itself. How does rhetoric work? It normally starts with an appeal to some thought or prejudice already in the mind of the audience, like 'we all know that . . .' The rhetorical articulation of this 'common sense' makes it *consciously* common. This, as we have seen, is precisely the way all economic arguments start, with the 'facts of experience' being the 'premises' of the deductive logic. The rhetorical character of this procedure is disguised by the claim that what 'we all know' is true.

Economics has to assert the truth of its premises to generate its prized 'quantitative predictions'. But this is a rhetorical device. The 'facts of experience' cannot provide the universal premises necessary to demonstrate the truth of the conclusion. There are too many contrary facts. This does not make the conclusion utterly false. It makes the argument incomplete. Rhetoric is the art of incomplete argument, a 'heuristic' device, or story, to point the mind in the right direction. In this sense all the social sciences are rhetorical. This simply means that the conditions required to make them universally true do not hold, or only hold under special conditions. They are only partially true.

The claim that economics is rhetoric has been heavily influenced by post-modernism, the movement which has dominated cultural studies since the 1980s, which claims that all arguments in the humanities are of the persuasive rather than demonstrative kind. As Jacques Derrida (1930–2004) put it, 'there is no outside text': there is no reality outside the circle of language. Post-modernist literary criticism 'deconstructs' the 'text' by shifting attention from the truth of what is being asserted to the means by which people are persuaded of its truth. From this perspective, economic modelling is a persuasive undertaking: it does not aim to discover truth, it tries to persuade people of the truth of its own 'text'. All reality is 'socially constructed'.

Philip Mirowski carries the argument further by saying that natural sciences, too, are built on persuasive utterance. There is a fundamental gap between our thought and reality which can only be bridged by metaphor, simile, analogy. Logical proofs are part of the persuasive machinery.[22]

There are three valuable implications of this approach. First, it emphasises that stories or narratives are the ways in which people try to make sense of complex situations. They assume, that is, that much social landscape is mysterious, or uncertain. Their ways of making sense of it should not, therefore, be considered irrational, but rather reasonable in the circumstances. Second, it points out that belief in the story rests on confidence in the story-teller. This is undoubtedly true: knowing that our own predictions are worthless, we rely on the testimony of those supposedly better informed. Third, while the stories are not the engines of prediction envisaged by Samuelson, they illuminate problems which escape formal modelling. The question, then, is whether economic modelling can improve significantly on story-telling or whether it is part of the story-telling.

McCloskey is almost unique among methodological critics of mainstream economics in viewing the overall programme of the mainstream as a success. Economics may be rhetoric dressed up as science, but its effects are positive. Quite simply, it tells the right story. Unlike most of those who think of economics as rhetoric, McCloskey believes that the market system has ensured progress and prosperity. The scientific pretensions thus take on a life of their own; they are not methodological mistakes, but choices of communication strategy which allow economics to be seen to be consistent with the dominant scientific-rational mode of engagement with the world.

However, the claim that economics is just rhetoric is itself rhetorical, because it fails to distinguish between what makes some arguments persuasive and others unpersuasive. Economists may tell stories, but these are stories about something. They may be reflections of folk stories, but where do these stories come from? The stories we tell each other may not be the complete truth, but an incomplete argument is not the same as one that is just made up. It has to have some basis in experience and evidence. Without it, it would not be persuasive. The point to remember is that economics is not the only 'text' in the social sciences. There are many 'truths' out there about the human condition, of which economics is just one.

So is economics a science?

Economics is not like a natural science in that it does not, and cannot, use experimental methods to generate laws. A scientific theory cannot require the facts to conform to its assumptions, but this is what economics tries to do. The failures of mainstream economic theory are not, on the whole, due to the internal inconsistencies of its models, but the failure of the models to account for observed facts. Except in special cases, economics has not advanced beyond what Rosenberg calls 'generic', that is, qualitative, predictions: predictions of broad tendencies, not of specific events.[23]

Macroeconomic models have fared particularly badly. The big Keynesian macro forecasting models broke down in the 1970s, because the assumed stable relationships between aggregates, like the consumption function or the relationship between unemployment and inflation, broke down. Models which start with large 'stylised facts' have fallen victim to breaks in trend. For example, Kaldor's 'law' of a constant wage share in national income fell foul of globalisation. Verdoorn's 'law' of increasing returns to scale in manufacturing industry became much less relevant when manufacturing ceased to be a major part of production in advanced economies. The Kuznets Curve, which predicted decreasing inequality after a period of growth, has broken down, partly because the state became indifferent to questions of income distribution. Such breaks in trend – partly at least – reflect changes in behaviour caused by the discovery of the trend, and the attempt to exploit it for policy purposes.

It is tempting then to abandon the attempt to map the movement of macroeconomic variables directly, and concentrate on mapping the supposedly unvarying (maximising) motives of individual agents. This, indeed, was the response of the mainstream to the failure of the Keynesian macroeconomic forecasting models. Micro-models, it was claimed, would be better forecasters than macro-models. But this hinged on economists getting human behaviour right. The failure of the neoclassical financial models to predict not just the crash of 2008, but even its possibility, suggests that their account of human psychology was deeply flawed. It was not just that they got the 'facts' of human behaviour wrong; but that, from the rhetorical point of view, they put much too much faith in the persuasive power of economic theory to make behaviour conform to the assumptions of the model.

The conclusion to which we are drawn is that there are no 'laws of economics' valid at all times and places. At best, theories can lead to approximately reliable predictions over such time periods as other things stay the same. This is true of short periods in particular markets and in specialised areas such as in health economics. Macroeconomic forecasts are reliable over very short periods but not when the parameters are shifting.

One important implication of this is that mathematics plays an oversized role in modern economics. The role of maths in any social science is to formalise its logic, and to make specific the relationships between different variables. But the wholesale formalisation of economics rests entirely on the premise that the variables of interest can readily be expressed as mathematical quantities. Many behavioural facts such as friendship or love of power do not lend themselves to such treatment. The tight logical relations, therefore, simply exhibit the theoreticians' prowess in tight logical reasoning.

As Robert Solow (b.1924) has pointed out, 'there is enough for us to do without pretending to a degree of completeness and precision which we cannot deliver'. The functions of analytic economics are 'to organise incomplete knowledge, see connections that the untrained eye might miss, tell plausible causal stories with the help of a few basic principles, make rough quantitative judgments about consequences of economic policy and other events. These are worth doing, science or not.'[24]

It's because economics is not a science that it needs other fields of study, notably, psychology, sociology, politics, ethics, history to supply the gaps in its method of understanding reality. We should not be afraid to say to the economist, 'There are more things in heaven and earth, Horatio, than are dreamt of in your philosophy'. The task is no less than to reclaim economics for the humanities.

6

ECONOMIC PSYCHOLOGY

Rational people are people who systematically and
purposefully do the best they can to achieve their
objectives.

Gregory Mankiw, *Principles of Economics*[1]

Homo economicus[2]

To many encountering economics for the first time, the crudeness
of its psychology is disconcerting. The lecturer can barely get past
'let's start out by assuming everyone is rational' before someone
points out that this is quite obviously false. Nor do students take
readily to the idea that they are motivated solely by self-interest,
even if it is said to be enlightened. In this chapter we explore the
economic interpretation of human action, show how far it is from
the truth, and consider why it is so difficult for economists to shake
it off.

Psychology, the study of the human mind, is used by economics
to construct explanations of why market participants behave in the
way they do. Why do these reasons need constructing, when it might
be possible to find out reasons for actions from surveys? The main
reason is that these usually turn out to be too complicated. People
will inevitably end up contradicting each other, and even themselves. The standard solution to this dilemma has been to eschew
evidence altogether – to start with assumptions about behaviour
based on the 'facts of experience', deduce the logical conclusions
of these assumptions, and present the results as incontrovertible.

A psychological construct such as utility maximisation 'allows an analyst to make predictions in new situations'. Other social sciences, trapped by the non-numerical nature of their subject matter, can't do this.[3]

The fruit of this procedure has been *homo economicus*, the human robot or calculating machine. The human robot 'has the cognitive capacities of a superhero': his 'ability to churn unlimited information and unflinching self-knowledge into instant and accurate decisions is infallible'.[4] Relations with other human robots are purely instrumental; *homo economicus* interacts with others, but is unbound by social ties. His axiomatic character is designed to ensure the autonomy of economics from history or culture.

If this seems like an unfair characterisation, we need only take economists at their word. Nobel Laureate Robert Lucas said: 'My aim is to construct a mechanical, artificial world, populated by ... interacting robots ... that is capable of exhibiting behaviour the gross features of which resemble those of the actual world.'[5] The catch is in the claim to capture 'the gross features' of the actual world.

Once again we must ask: is this a claim about how humans actually behave? Is it a prescription of how they should behave? Or is it a statement of the form 'if they do behave this way, I can get my model to work'. In *The Economist as Preacher*, fellow Nobel Laureate George Stigler (1911–1991) set out a view of *homo economicus* that was clearly normative: 'Efficiency in the sense of the fuller achievement of uncontroversial goals has been the main prescription of normative economics', because 'one sets up a perfect standard to define an imperfect performance'.[6]

One should always remember that for economists, as for some other social scientists, humanity has always been 'work in progress'. They have seen their task not as describing but improving; as engineers of the soul not dispassionate students of the mind; their task being to liberate rationality from the fetters of superstition. *Homo economicus*, the rational calculator, would emerge from the cave of history. So, much of economics must be seen to be about fabricating the human nature it purports to describe. Nevertheless, since the stories economists tell of humans are part of the stories humans tell about themselves, to some extent humans start behaving in the way economists say they should behave. This is called progress.

The behaviour of *homo economicus*

How is *homo economicus* supposed to behave? Nobel Laureate Thomas Sargent (b.1943) defines a person as a 'constrained, intertemporal, stochastic optimising problem'.[7] The constraint is one of resources; the optimising takes place over time; and is subject to random shocks. This leads to the central claim of the rational expectations school that economists' models are the formalisation of models already 'in the minds' of persons. Everyone has an incentive to forecast the future. Beliefs about the future (which include what others are expected to do in the future) affect what people do today. All agents behave in this forward-looking way. One therefore has only to specify the information set possessed by the agent, and the forecasting 'problem' is 'solved'.

The key to understanding the rational expectations revolution is that mainstream economists believe they have cracked the uncertainty problem. Expectations about the future are simply probability distributions over a sequence of events. Uncertainty is reduced to probability, and can thus be labelled a special case of certainty. Economists like Nobel Laureates George Akerlof (b.1940) and Joseph Stiglitz (b.1943) have pointed to the existence of 'asymmetric information' – situations in which one party to a transaction has more information than another: a problem rife in insurance and second-hand car markets.[8] But unless such inequalities of information are regarded as inherent, they will be overcome by computer-generated big data. Provided this is freely available, all persons will have near-perfect forecasting ability about any decision they need to make. They will be on an information highway linked directly to God.

Homo economicus in action

Here is how the rational basis of criminal activity was revealed to the economist Gary Becker. One day he was rushed for time. He had to weigh the cost and benefits of legally parking in an inconvenient garage versus in an illegal but convenient spot. After roughly calculating the probability of getting caught and potential punishment, Becker rationally opted for the crime. Becker surmised that other criminals make such rational decisions. 'However, such a premise went against conventional thought that crime was a result of mental illness and social oppression.'[9]

This insight into the criminal mind hardly had to wait on Becker's parking problems. It has deep roots in Jeremy Bentham and the Utilitarians, the thought being that if you raise the cost of crime and improve policing there will be less of it.[10] However, this insight into the 'mind of the horse' cannot be proved statistically. If we tried to test it we might well find that the crime rate varied with the number of young males in a population. What they were thinking is neither here nor there.

Here are three further examples of *homo economicus* in action. The first comes from Becker's 'A Theory of Marriage' (1974). Becker argued that people marry for the same reason that nations trade: comparative advantage. Selection of a partner takes place in a competitive market, and marriages occur only when both partners expect to gain. It's a very sophisticated theory, constructing a model of the complementary nature of male and female work, but ends up treating marriage as little more than a cost-reducing mechanism. Each partner is assumed to know all the expected payoffs from the union over an indefinite future. This is equivalent to asserting that the marriage market is always in equilibrium, and thus succumbs to the critique of equilibrium theory in Chapter 4. To act on the precepts of *homo economicus* is to renounce love for the gold one can never be sure of getting.

A second example comes from the work of Jon Steinsson and Emi Nakamura. Paying someone else to fold your socks, they say, is a way to maximise your own earnings and those of the sock folder. Even as penniless graduate students, the two economists borrowed money to pay people to do their household chores, calculating that 'spending an extra hour working on a paper was better for their lifetime expected earnings than spending that same hour vacuuming.'[11]

Finally, the economists Betsey Stevenson and Justin Wolfers, pioneers of "lovenomics", conducted a cost/benefit analysis before having a child. As Wolfers explains,

> The principle of comparative advantage tells us that gains from trade are largest when your trading partner has skills and endowments that are quite different from yours. I'm an impractical bookish Harvard-trained empirical labor economist, while Betsey is an impractical and bookish Harvard-trained empirical labor economist. When your skills are so similar, the gains from trade aren't so large. Except when it comes to bringing up our baby. There, Betsey has a pair of, um, endowments that mean that she's better at inputs. And that means that I'm left to deal with outputs.

As Stevenson helpfully clarifies, 'it turns out that fathers can be pretty good at dealing with diapers'.[12]

Within the rational expectations framework, these arguments make a good deal of sense. Assuming, as neoclassical economists typically do, that what we aim to maximise is our life-time earnings, we must admit that it is irrational to spend time dealing with matters which cut into our earning power, if we can avoid it. Time spent on changing nappies is time stolen from inventing, say, new software (unless nappy changing helps the invention).

Is it rational?

Take our two economists who outsource their house-cleaning. Is their behaviour really rational? What they are doing is calculating in terms of money the lifelong consequences of doing one thing rather than another: writing academic papers to doing housework. But they can have only the vaguest idea of what these consequences are. The suspicion must be that the two economists are simply rationalising their dislike of housework.

Let us take a more winning example than folding socks. Say the greatest pleasure our economist gets is going to the cinema. But he calculates that time spent at the movies will reduce the available time needed to maximise his earnings as an economist. So he cuts out, or minimises, going to the movies, that is, he gives up a certain present benefit to himself for the sake of a doubtful one in the future. This is not rational because there is no basis for calculating how much filmgoing he will need to give up to maximise his income. The prices he attaches to future goods are conventional, and easily upset by a 'change in the facts'. It is no use being a consequentialist if you can't calculate the consequences of your actions.

Economists should spend less time working out the consequences of rational behaviour under conditions of certainty, and more trying to understand what is reasonable to do in conditions of uncertainty. This would bring out the rationality and indeed moral worth of forms of behaviour they are now bound to condemn as irrational. They should also take more care to distinguish situations of imperfect information in which information is contingently incomplete, from situations of uncertainty, in which no complete information is obtainable under any circumstances.

However, the fundamental objection to *homo economicus* is ethical, not epistemic. If, *per impossibile*, all outcomes could be assigned probabilities, would there be any objection to thinking of choice as utility maximisation? The answer is surely yes, because values cannot be neatly traded off against each other, and therefore there is no escape from moral choices. We understand the need for compromise and fine adjustments, but we admire people who make of their lives 'songs for singing'.

So, as humans, we should be ready to follow the precepts of *homo economicus* when they apply and ignore them when they don't. We should certainly not consider this unlovely creature a general model for behaviour. In many cases it is far better to do what you want to do, or what you are good at, or what you think is good, and not waste time on the calculation. We ought more often to be in the state of mind of not counting the cost at all.

Behavioural economics

Behavioural economics is an attempt by economists to replace the caricature *homo economicus*, the human robot, with a more realistic actor. As such, it attempts to make use of the insights of psychology and neuroscience, hitherto a closed book to the economist. Behavioural economics does not challenge the idea that behaving like *homo economicus* is the best way for individuals to secure their own well-being. The disagreement comes over the extent to which this behaviour actually occurs.[13] For neoclassical economists, deviations from rationality are assumed to be non-systemic. People might make errors in estimation, but they overestimate as much as they underestimate, so it cancels out without altering the overall trajectory of the system. Behavioural economics claims to have uncovered empirically systemic, and therefore predictable, deviations from rationality: situations where individuals consistently over- or underestimate benefits or costs. They behave like robots with restricted information.

Behavioural economics came of age in 2002 when the psychologist Daniel Kahneman (b.1934) got a Nobel prize for the work he had done with Amos Tversky (1937–1996). It flourishes as a subset of economics only because the standard behavioural assumptions of economists have been so thoroughly unrealistic.

Thinking fast and slow

Kahneman and Tversky claimed that we make choices according to two mental systems, the first intuitive, the second calculating, which they label fast and slow thinking. Slow thinking is logical; fast thinking is intuitive, and frequently irrational. They have found impressive evidence of 'irrational' choices – for example, investors' preference for high-cost actively managed funds which underperform zero-cost index funds. Behavioural economists identify the following 'systemic' errors that people make.

1. Survivorship bias
We tend to look only at what was successful. Think of a newspaper article that claims it can help you imitate Mark Zuckerberg's morning routine. The obvious implication is that you too could become a billionaire if you just wore grey t-shirts and ate the right breakfast, but this ignores the multitudes of non-billionaires doing just that.

2. Loss aversion

It is fairly well established that people hate losing something more than they love gaining it. Dropping a $10 note is more bitter than finding one is sweet. We are hard-wired, to some extent, to hold on to what we've got. Students given coffee mugs free from the campus bookstore will not part with them for $6 even though this junk fell out of the sky, and had they desired them they could have got them at the nearby store for the price of $6.

3. Prioritising available information

When making decisions, we are likely to weight striking information more highly. Shocking, sensational information sticks in our memories and so plays an outsized role in decision-making. If you are walking home in the dark, one gruesome news story is far more 'available' than all the times you know of people walking home without trouble.

4. Anchoring

We don't evaluate things independently of context, and so providing context can influence a decision. If a shop puts its most expensive products by the door, everything else seems cheap by comparison. If something says 50 per cent off, it somehow seems more appealing than a normal price half as much. People will drive across town to save $10 on an electronic gadget which costs $50, but not to save $10 on one which costs $500. Why? $10 is $10. Someone who will drink wine from his own collection would never dream of buying the same vintages at current prices of $100 in a market into which he could easily sell. A much noticed discovery is that the way choices are framed has an effect on the decision. This is especially clear in sales pitches. It should be that if something is worth $25 to you, you buy it, if not, you don't. But a good ad 'frames' the choice in such a way as to make it seem that you are getting $50 worth of goods for $25. Quite literally you are being framed! The discovery that decisions can be manipulated by marketing will seem surprising only to those who have buried themselves so deep within their assumptions as to lose sight of reality.

5. Confirmation bias

This is the most famous. Changing your mind is always annoying. Much better to just wait until some evidence that confirms your view comes along! Humans have an amazing ability to rationalise the decisions they have made out of habit or whim. The inverse to this is automation bias: thinking that automated instructions must be correct even when common sense tells you they are wrong. A bunch of Japanese tourists drove their car into the sea because their satnav told them they were on a road. Airplane crashes have happened because pilots trusted their faulty navigation systems rather than the evidence of their eyes.

6. Sunk cost fallacy

This is a combination of anchoring and loss aversion. People will keep on ploughing money into a failed investment, because they can't face the psychological pain of admitting that it had failed, or carry on waging a war that they should have abandoned long ago, because they cannot bring themselves to admit that it was in vain.

7. Hindsight bias

This is central to human thinking and makes the social and economic worlds appear much more predictable and less erratic than they really are. No prominent economist predicted the financial crisis. Yet almost the next day commentators were rushing in to explain why it 'must' have happened when and how it did. It was the same with Brexit and the election of Trump. An analogy in everyday life is when a seemingly happy couple suddenly split up. Everyone then says, 'Oh, I always knew there was something wrong there ...'

These examples upend the central verity of modern economics, that people always have rational expectations. They often make choices which they ought to know will leave them worse off. Advertisers were exploiting this propensity long before economists started to notice it.

In their book, *Phishing for Phools* (2015), Nobel Laureates George Akerlof (b.1940) and Robert Shiller (b.1946) show, with many examples both amusing and appalling, that misperception and deception are rampant in market economies. 'Phishing' is a 'fraud on the internet in order to glean personal information from individuals' to get them to do things in the interest of the 'phisherman' rather than the 'phools'. The two authors divide 'phools' into two classes – those too emotional to make sensible choices, and those victimised by misleading information. Modern economics, say our two economists, should be reoriented to recognise a phishing equilibrium, not a welfare-maximising equilibrium. A defence of markets that rests on the premise that consumers know what they are buying won't work if they don't know what they are buying, or are buying things they don't need. To illustrate his point, Shiller tested different flavours of cat food – turkey, tuna, lamb, and duck – and found that the flavours were not that different. As a reviewer of the book remarked: 'Few of us would want to replicate that study. And its empirical validity is undermined by the fact that Shiller is not a cat.'[14]

Behavioural economists are especially interested in quirks of behaviour which seem to defy rational explanation – like lecture audiences filling up the back seats of the auditorium before the front seats. Mainstream critics say that the quirks detected by the behavioural economists cancel each other out, that average behaviour ends up much as economists would have predicted, before behavioural economics started to complicate matters with unnecessary puzzles. But the real objection to behavioural economics concerns not the frequency or infrequency of 'quirks', but calling irrational any behaviour which doesn't correspond to the neoclassical model of rational choice. Many kinds of human behaviour are rooted in uncertainty. We cling to our sunk costs because we have no certain evidence that they are sunk for good: what is civilisation but a web of sunk costs? We hope for miracles because miracles sometimes happen.

Another finding of behavioural economics is that imperfect information, complexity, uncertainty, and limited calculating capacity force agents to use of rules of thumb, or heuristics, rather than 'pure' optimising behaviour. Widespread use of heuristics – short-cuts – produces systematic behavioural biases. These mean that it might be both possible and desirable for government to 'nudge' (aka incentivise) people to act more rationally. Nobel Laureate Richard Thaler (b.1945) and Cass Sunstein (b.1954) argue people might be 'nudged' to eat more healthily by taxing sugar or to save more by making wage increases conditional on savings commitments.[15] How successful this last 'nudge' would be is open to question. Saving for the future implies a belief that money will hold its value, and that government will honour its commitment to keep savings for retire-ment tax-free or tax-deferred. In light of well-known facts to the contrary, consuming more and saving less may be highly 'efficient'.

A deeper objection to the fashionable 'nudge' approach is that creating incentives for more rational individual behaviour may decrease the amount of morally efficient behaviour. All organisa-tions rely on moral commitments, which cannot be specified in contracts, to achieve efficient results. Companies which introduce monetary incentives like bonuses to promote efficient effort, often experience worse 'bottom lines' than those that allow greater scope for natural sociability. Thus the 'nudge' cure may easily turn out to be worse than the disease.[16]

We may also point to the artificial nature of the experimental situations economists set up to establish their claims for irratio-nal behaviour. The experimenters place the subjects of the experi-ment in atypical situations, assess their answers to trick questions according to the neoclassical benchmark of rationality, and dis-cover large amounts of hitherto unsuspected 'irrationality'. They ask their subjects to make hypothetical choices like 'would you rather toss a coin for a half chance of $1,000 or get a certain $450?' To settle for $450, the majority choice, is not 'rational' in the sense of maximising expected earnings, but as Lars Pålsson Syll remarks, 'The important activities of most economic agents do not usually include throwing dice or spinning roulette-wheels.'[17] The effect of this testing procedure is to draw attention to the irrational ways people behave rather than to the faulty ways economists model their behaviour. Instead of concluding that the subjects are giving reasonable answers to the tests they have been set, they conclude that their thinking is delusional.

The most important possibility opened up by behavioural economics is that the neoclassical model of rational behaviour based on fixed preferences, complete contracts, and ample relevant information is the wrong one. The way most people behave much of the time should carry no implication of irrationality, but should rather be thought of as reasonable behaviour in the circumstances in which they find themselves. The sin of behavioural economics is to dub such behaviour irrational.

X

As an account of how human beings behave in general, the model of *homo economicus* has been repeatedly disconfirmed by behavioural, cognitive, and other social sciences. We are not always counting the cost in time or money of what we are doing. Nor ought we to be. If we are to condense human behaviour down to a single axiom for the purposes of deduction within a closed system, the neoclassical principle of rationality is probably the best axiom to use. The question then is not about rationality, but about the generality of the axiom.

The neoclassical model of rationality which Kahneman and Tversky set up as their benchmark might make sense in a small, closed world with well-defined limits. The coin-toss experiment is supposed to replicate this – it is either a head or a tail – but it is irrelevant as a test of rationality in open systems admitting of many different outcomes.

Behavioural economics has not come up with a decisive alternative to *homo economicus*. In fact it rather misses the point. It has made some progress in penetrating the working of the mind, and has come up with some systemic quirks, which economists had previously assumed they could treat as statistical noise. What it has signally failed to do is to link the neural networks it posits to social networks. It looks into our minds and finds some unexpected things going on there, but fails to connect what goes on in our heads with what goes on in other people's heads. It leaves methodological individualism intact.

The next chapter will attempt to shed the loneliness of *homo economicus*, to explore how people relate to each other socially, how society shapes our values, how we shape social institutions and the social dimensions of economic cooperation.

7

SOCIOLOGY AND ECONOMICS

It is not 'I' who acts, but the automatic logic of social
systems that work through me as Other. That logic is the
real subject. It is only in the interstices of this logic that
autonomous subjects emerge.

André Gorz, *Ecologica*[1]

Can sociology help economics?

Homo economicus – the human calculating machine – is a fiction.
Humans are born into, nurtured within, and protected by groups.
Groups may be regarded as built-in insurance against misfortune and loneliness, the cost humans pay for the curtailment of
individual freedom. Insurance premia are highest in tribal societies, lowest in the kind of open societies most of us now live in.
Nevertheless, groups always impose some membership costs. If
individuals could calculate exactly the probability of attaining their
desired ends they would not need to live in groups: they would
be exactly as the neoclassical economists describe them. But since
they lack the required information base, *homo economicus* is not
just a simplified basis for theorising, but, outside special situations,
an impossible one. It presupposes a calculable future which does
not exist.

Economists, of course, understand that humans interact with
each other, just as atoms do. Game theory is the study of how rational individuals make choices which depend on the expected choices
of others. But such choices are always autonomous. Sociologists
make a key distinction between *interaction* and *interdependence*.

With interdependence, the parts, whatever they are, *depend* on each other, like the parts of a body. They cannot function on their own. This means that outcomes in many situations cannot be predicted, unless the relationships between the parts can be specified accurately, a much more difficult task.

As soon as 'agency' (the capacity to act) is introduced as an explanatory variable, the problem of where the agency is located becomes crucial. The standard view in economics is that agency is located only in individuals. So-called 'collective agents' like states or football teams are simply the sum of the individual agents who compose them. It therefore seems sensible to start the analysis of how the economy works with the individual, treating the group merely as a tool of individual purpose. Further, it seems sensible to treat social outputs as nothing but the sum of individual inputs. Thus if there is unemployment, we must assume that the unemployed persons prefer leisure to work.

We have already dubbed this approach to social analysis *methodological individualism*. Adam Smith's account of how markets result from the human propensity to 'truck, barter, and exchange' is a good example. You start with some simple axiom of individual behaviour – self-interest, for example – and then deduce the outcome of the whole economy from this premise. Although sociologists also try to understand the economy, they start in a completely different place, with groups rather than individuals. The position of most sociologists can be broadly called *methodological holism*. This asserts that the behaviour of the parts can only be understood in relation to the whole, the 'whole' here standing for the complex of relationships and institutions which 'frame' individual behaviour. The whole is different from the sum of its parts. We can call it the 'system'. Most people understand that they are not independent particles, but part of a system which either helps them or screws them up. 'Wholes', too, have 'agency' – they are actors in their own right.

The attraction of treating individuals as unique actors is easy to understand. They are the *smallest* of the social particles with the capacity for independent action. (Humans, too, are made up of parts. But it would be odd to talk of the leg or arm as exercising 'agency'.) They are also the only actors with *moral* agency. Methodological individualists often confuse agency (the power to act) with moral agency (the power to distinguish between right and wrong). There is also a moral grandeur in individualism, which is lost by treating individuals as puppets of groups. We owe most of our great achievements in art, science, and action to individual defiance of the group mind.

Nevertheless, the individualist perspective misleads as much as it illuminates. If agency is the capacity to act, it is not absurd to talk of collective agency, in the sense that, in many situations, collectives have a power to act which individuals lack. An army regiment, a business firm, a trade union is not just a group of contracting individuals. In an important sense it possesses independent agency: the power to make things happen.

The sociological claim is twofold: first, that it is perfectly legitimate to talk of group action; secondly, that individual action is framed by the individual's social position in the group. If either holds, policies which presuppose that social outcomes are simply the sum of voluntary individual choices can be seriously misleading. In the first case, it ignores the existence of groups except as tools of individual purpose; in the second case, it ignores the power structure within groups. When neoclassical economists talk of the need for macroeconomics to be properly 'microfounded', they mean that it should be possible to explain patterns of behaviour by reference to individual intentions alone, that these patterns are nothing but the sum of such intentions. For example, GNP is merely the weighted average of all the individual transactions in the economy. However, it might make just as much sense to talk of 'macro-founding' microeconomics, that is, showing how individual intentions are shaped by individuals' economic or social positions. David Ricardo and Karl Marx did just that with their theories of class interest.

That one's 'position' in society affects one's choices is obvious to anyone not thoroughly trained in neoclassical economics. An anonymous friend of Donald Trump's told CNN that 'I always thought that once he understood the weight of the office, he would rise to the occasion. Now I don't.' The phrase 'the weight of the office' clearly evokes the idea that the 'office' of US president is an entity separate from its temporary incumbent. There is a two-way causation. The incumbent's performance influences the evolution of the ethics of the office, but the ethics of the office influence the behaviour of the incumbent.

Any economics can be called sociological which rejects methodological individualism as the general rule. Marxist economics, Keynesian economics, and some kinds of Institutional Economics, are all sociological in that they see individuals as inseparable from wholes, which they influence, but which also influence them. For neoclassical economists, on the other hand, the causation runs only one way, from the individual to the institution. Individuals create institutions as tools for making individual action more efficient. Firms are viewed as reducing the costs of transactions. The state is a device to economise on the costs of protection. The church reduces the costs of transacting with God. In this view, society is simply the sum of individual transactions. The logic can be further simplified by treating all individuals as having identical motives. An institution can then be reduced to the behaviour of just one individual – the 'representative agent'.

Sociology offers two routes out of the individualist trap. It offers a way to understand the structure of economic life apart from individuals; and it focuses on the value system or 'culture' of groups which shape the behaviour of its members. It claims that humans are 'cultural animals'.

If in standard economics the key behavioural abstraction is rational calculation, in sociology it is the 'norm'. The first abstracts from society; the second presupposes it. Of course, Robinson Crusoes also exhibit 'normal' behaviour. Normal in this sense is simply an abbreviation of individual calculation. However, in sociology 'the norm' refers to a code of conduct. In other words, it presupposes a social relationship.

The concept of 'norms' in the sociological sense is needed to explain human behaviour because organisations have rules and codes of conduct which shape the motivational structure of their members. For example, do we really believe that the coal miners' strike in the United Kingdom in 1984–5, which resulted in the virtual extinction of the coal industry, can be explained by the rational self-interest of individual miners? Perhaps by a fanciful argument one could explain the behaviour of individual miners in terms of rule-utilitarianism. But surely, one does not have to, nor should one need to, go beyond ideas like 'loyalty' and 'solidarity'. The existence of group actors means that a lot of neoclassical microeconomics – the standard textbook teaching of the subject which takes the utility-maximising individual as the sole independent variable of the microeconomic model – is plain wrong.

As John Harvey puts it 'We live, eat, reproduce, grow and die in packs . . . No individual animal in any . . . species chooses to live with the others. It is hard-wired into them because it evolved as a survival mechanism.' It follows from this that the basic object of study should be not the individual, but the group, and more especially its culture. Very roughly, culture is the value system of a group. It is what we mean when we talk of 'common sense', 'received wisdom', or 'playing by the rules'. It provides formal and informal incentives to good behaviour, and sanctions bad behaviour. Mostly, though, cultural conformity is instinctive. Despite outbreaks of rebelliousness, 'it is in our nature. It is part of what makes us human.'[2]

So why stick to the individual as the unit of analysis? There are two reasons, one instrumental, the other ethical. Individualism offers a more efficient basis for modelling than holism or organicism. It is much easier to posit individuals equipped with a single motive – rational self-interest – than work one's way to a conclusion through the complexity of social relationships. There is also an ethical motive for individualism. Most economists think, like Popper, that holistic models of society are implicitly totalitarian. Freedom of choice is as much an ethical imperative as a scientific assumption.

All that a holistic approach claims is that there is system-level behaviour that cannot be understood at the individual level, and in particular that the dynamics of the system itself are liable to change in unpredictable ways. Economics is the study of 'closed' systems, in which particular outcomes can be reliably attributed to individual actions. Sociology is the study of 'open' systems, in which individuals depend on each other in complex ways. Only in the broadest sense are their choices 'predictable'.

The opposition between individualism and holism is deliberately set out here in a simplified, undialectical way in order to bring into focus the nature of the methodological choices which economists face. Ideally, economics and sociology should complement each other. The rationality assumption offers the path of 'least resistance between ends and means, while sociology is needed to explain the friction of bias and error which usually gets in the way'.[3] Nonetheless, for the most part the two disciplines have made little progress in appreciating each other's methodological strengths. They are self-referential: each views the other through a glass darkly.

The social and the individual

Historically, economics and sociology may be contrasted by their reactions to the Enlightenment and its consequences. In the pre-modern world it was understood that economic activity was an aspect, albeit a very important one, of communal life. In their economic lives individuals were glued to groups by customary norms, expressed through family, village, church, guild, and corporation. The social order was hierarchical: everyone knew their place in the scheme of things. The task of the ruler was to generate 'nourishment' to all appropriate to their rank, including limits to market access, price fixing, and controls on consumption. Work should befit one's rank. 'Temporary wealth' was at best a path to eternal wealth. It was 'irrational' – miserly – to pursue temporary wealth at the expense of eternal bliss.[4] Pre-modern society was not static, but its fluidity was largely circular, with one dynasty replacing another in bloody succession at the top, while the mass of serfs, peasants, townspeople lived their lives in a rhythm interrupted only by natural catastrophe.

With the Enlightenment, the medieval cosmology broke down. This movement to 'light up' the mind had as its object the release of individuals from the social chains that shrouded their lives in darkness. In the memorable words of Immanuel Kant (1724–1804) it was 'man's emergence from his self-imposed nonage'.[5] The convulsions of thought and events freed people from pre-modern relations of power and dependence to assume an expanding variety of roles, or 'identities' as we now call them. The French revolutionaries championed people's political emancipation, the economists their economic emancipation. This was the double revolution of the eighteenth century, welcomed by both political and economic liberals. Progress would bring about a world of elective, not forced, affinities.

Sociology has a different, and much more sombre, way of understanding these events. Its starting point was the 'absolute reality of the institutional order ... bequeathed by history'.[6] To the founders of sociology, what the revolutionaries and economists welcomed as the liberation of the individual from social fetters appeared as a wrenching from the protective ties of community. The material order was decoupled from the moral order. Sociologists have typically depicted the breakdown of society as a process of social atomisation – people losing their functional place in the whole, and therefore their sense of duty to others.

So both disciplines looked at the social question from opposite perspectives. Whereas economists defined the central problem of the age as one of securing the most efficient production and allocation of scarce material goods, the problem which concerned sociologists was about how a sustainable moral order could be created out of the disintegrating fragments of religious and communal life. Economists looked to individual rationality to bring about an age of growing freedom and plenty; sociologists to the nightmare of despotic power exercised over, but in the name of, disoriented and stupefied masses. Sociologists have not been uniformly pessimistic, since institutions can be viewed either as carriers of progress or reaction. Conservatives lamented the passing of the hierarchical order; radicals like Karl Marx accepted the gains of industrialisation, but argued that what Thomas Carlyle (1795–1881) called the 'cash nexus' must be transcended by new 'rational' social bonds. Sociological liberals emphasised the role of free association. Thus sociology is not without its 'improving', or prescriptive, element. Nevertheless, the bias and – it could be argued – the weakness of sociology is its tendency towards conservatism. It could hardly be otherwise, since its map is cluttered up with immovable presences.[7]

No one has summed up the continually restless, contradictory dynamics of the new economic order better than Karl Marx. He was fascinated by Mary Shelley's novel *Frankenstein: The Modern Prometheus* (1823), the story of the hominoid monster which, having been designed to serve its master, Victor Frankenstein, 'went rogue', turned on its inventor, and wreaked havoc wherever he went. Marx saw in this a metaphor for capitalism. The bourgeoisie, he wrote, had created 'more massive and more colossal productive forces than have all preceding generations together'. It had drawn 'even the most barbarous nations into civilization ... created a world after its own image'. But the cost had been horrendous: 'All fixed, fast-frozen relations, with their train of ancient and venerable prejudices and opinions, are swept away, all newly formed ones become antiquated before they can ossify. All that is solid melts into air, all that is holy is profaned ...'[8] Capitalism, the 'creature' Frankenstein created, must be destroyed once it had done its work.

The comment by Alexis de Tocqueville (1805–1859) on Manchester, the hub of the new nineteenth-century industrialism, is similarly double-edged:

> From this foul drain the greatest stream of human industry flows out to fertilise the whole world. From this filthy sewer pure gold flows. Here humanity attains its most complete development and its most brutish, here civilisation works its miracles, and civilised man is turned almost into a savage.[9]

So sociological enquiry has been, on the one hand, the study of the forces leading to social breakdown; on the other hand, an analysis of the new types of association thrown up by the breakdown itself.

The sociological perspective

The minimum sociological doctrine is that humans are inseparably bound to each other by their biology, experience, and culture. Further, all sociologists believe in the reality of the institutional order: institutions exist. The institutional order, though, is not unchanging, nor is it all of a piece. In pre-modern times the economy was 'embedded' in the moral order, in modern times it has become separated from it. A further key idea is that different institutional orders generate different character types. For most of history social organisation reflected military needs, with the warrior as its archetype. *Homo religiosus* was the medieval archetype; *homo economicus* emerged with capitalism. All the social sciences have debated the question of which parts of the institutional order are to be regarded as primordial, reflecting our biology, accumulated experience, and innate moral sense, and which parts should be treated as variable, that is, susceptible to changed beliefs and conditions of existence.

An important ancillary question is: what kind of institution is the state? The state as we know it is the creation of modern society. Before that there was the ruler and his family and court. Is the state to be seen as a private interest? As the executive arm of the capitalist class? Or in some way as representing the general interest? The key question is to whom it is accountable. We will explore this in more detail in Chapter 9.

To put some flesh on these abstractions, let's consider three topics which have historically formed the core of sociology: the nature of community, the spirit of capitalism, and the relationship of the market to society.

Gemeinschaft and *Gesellschaft*

Ferdinand Tönnies (1855–1936) distinguished between a community bound together by affective and customary ties, which he called *Gemeinschaft*, and an association of interest, like a business corporation or a political party, which he called *Gesellschaft*. In *Gemeinschaft* individuals remain united despite separating factors, while in *Gesellschaft* they remain separate despite uniting factors.[10] In similar vein, the great sociologist Max Weber (1864–1920), himself a professor of economics, distinguished between 'communal' and 'associative' types of relationship. A relationship is communal when based on 'the subjective feeling of the parties that they belong to each other, that they are implicated in each other's total existence'. Examples are a military unit, a labour union, a religious brotherhood, marriage, and so forth. The relationship is 'associative' when it rests on a 'rationally motivated adjustment of interest or a similarly motivated agreement'.[11] The associative group is a community of choice; we 'elect' those with whom we want to associate, rather than being stuck with them.

The point to emphasise is that sociologists have regarded *Gemeinschaft* as typical of the pre-modern type of association and *Gesellschaft* as typical of the modern, and have interpreted modernity as a movement from the first to the second. The legal philosopher Henry Maine (1822–1888) called it the movement from status to contract. Status is ascribed; but in a contractual association, the relationship between individuals is based on their choices. The obvious question is: what constitutes the social glue of the associative form of relationship? Is the rational adjustment of interest enough?

According to Jürgen Habermas (b.1929), modern citizens inhabit two separate worlds: the moral-social dimension of domestic, communal, and cultural life and the instrumental relations of the economy. He called the first the domain of 'communicative' rationality, the second of 'strategic' rationality, in other words, calculation. Both apply to different sets of circumstances and activities. The first is indispensable to the moral order; the second to the material order. Habermas's fear, as that of many sociologists, has been the encroachment of strategic rationality on morality.[12] The warrant for this was, as we have seen, given by Lionel Robbins when he argued that all choices have an 'economic aspect' (see above, p. 16). In a world based on contracts, it is no use appealing to morality, because it will no longer be there.

The issue is: is self-interest enough to establish relations of obligation? Mainstream economists have generally supposed this to be the case. Systems of law and regulation have their roots in individual self-interest: it 'pays' to be honest. This picture was powerfully challenged by Émile Durkheim (1858–1917). In his *Professional Ethics and Civic Morals*, Durkheim argued that,

> Contract of any type could not be sustained for a moment . . . unless it was based on conventions, traditions, codes in which the idea of an authority higher than contract was clearly resident. The idea of a contract, its very possibility as a relationship among men . . . comes into existence only in the context of already sovereign mores.[13]

No one, for example, would make a money contract without a belief that money was a trustworthy token of value.

'Anomie' was the word Durkheim used to define the social pathology of a morally uprooted society. He found that the suicide rate of Protestant countries was higher than in Catholic countries because family ties were better maintained in Catholic society.[14] In Durkheim's view, the breakdown of community would lead not to new instrumental relationships but to further disintegration, generating an unlimited expansion of state regulation. We encounter here a recurring motif in the sociological literature: that the spread of marketisation is paralleled by the expansion of bureaucracy, trapping the liberal hope of individual liberty in an 'iron cage of bondage'. A temporary escape only is offered by 'charismatic' leaders, who 'set new goals and open up new paths for societies hampered by political stagnation and bureaucratic routine'.[15]

Since Weber's time, the world of custom has shrunk relative to the world of 'business'. Modern life has become increasingly 'transactional'. The ideology of *homo economicus* together with digital technology suck people out of local communities, and even nations, into a 'global village'. The student of economics needs to balance the economist's enthusiasm for ever-widening markets against the sociological insight that this can be highly disruptive to settled ways of life. Without a sociological imagination, we cannot hope to understand the political revolt of today's 'left-behinds'.

One type of hugely influential institution stands apart from the binary divide between custom and contract: this is the religious community, the community of believers. We are tied to church and religion neither by kinship nor calculation, but rather by a sense of our own human insignificance, which religious belief is uniquely able to convert into confidence in the future. Ideology can be seen as the secular replacement of religious belief. It emerges when custom starts to be contested. The ideological community is the most powerful form of association today. And this carries its own obvious dangers, because it offers completely unwarranted promises of secular utopia.

The spirit of capitalism

Neoclassical economics assumes an unchanging human nature, marked by an unlimited desire for gain. This leaves it unable to explain why this motive for action failed to ignite any significant growth of wealth for most of human history. It is not enough to say that it was prevented from expressing itself by inefficient institutions, because that leaves unexplained the persistence of such institutions. 'What needs to be explained', wrote R.H. Tawney (1880–1962) in his introduction to Max Weber's *The Protestant Ethic and the Spirit of Capitalism*,

> is not the strength of the motive of economic self-interest, which is the commonplace of all ages, and demands no explanation. It is the change of moral standards which converted a natural frailty into an ornament of the spirit, and canonised as the economic virtues habits which in earlier ages had been condemned as vices.

In *The Protestant Ethic and the Spirit of Capitalism*, Max Weber denied that individuals are maximisers by nature. 'In traditional society, a man does not "by nature" wish to make more and more money, but simply to live as he is accustomed to live and to earn as much as is necessary for that purpose'. The 'spirit of capitalism' entered history at a particular time (sixteenth century) and place (north-western Europe), and for a particular reason. It was an unintended consequence of belief in predestination.[16]

God had divided people into the saved and damned, and there was nothing they could do to influence His selection. Believers responded with a redoubling of efforts in order to convince themselves – if not the Almighty – that they were among the saved. Crucially, success in work – accumulation of wealth – was taken as a 'sign' or 'proof' of grace. The worldly asceticism inculcated by Puritanism was the psychological basis of modern capitalism. In embracing the accumulation of wealth as a goal, Puritans were wracked with guilt; personal asceticism or frugality was their way of coping with this.[17]

The value of Weber's brilliant conjecture is twofold: to question economists' belief in an unchanging human nature, and to open our eyes to the link between economics and religion. Economics can be seen as a form of religious belief: in this case, belief in progress. 'If you behave like this, grace will be bestowed on you – at least in the long run.' Economists may be likened to a secular priesthood, fulfilling the ancient priestly function of inducing people to live by the book. God is in the model; outside it lie delusion, madness, evil.

Are markets natural to man?

Following the lead of Adam Smith, mainstream economics has treated markets as part of the natural order, state power a kind of mutilation imposed from outside. In contrast, the social anthropologist Karl Polanyi (1886–1964) distinguished between markets and the market economy. Markets are natural, but the market economy is 'entirely unnatural, in the strictly empirical sense of exceptional'. What was 'natural' were custom and reciprocity. The purpose of exchange was not to make gains but to strengthen relationships through gifts; what was to be maximised was social honour, not money.[18] Thus the economy in pre-industrial times was 'embedded' in a moral order from which capitalism unleashed it. It followed that micro price theory is inappropriate and distorting when applied to non-market relations, as neoclassicals like Gary Becker do.

Polanyi's thesis, in a nutshell, is that in pre-modern societies markets could only exist on the edges of the economy, since the 'factors' of production – labour, land, and capital – were not marketable. Their transformation into 'fictitious commodities', as much subject to buying and selling as food, clothes, and furniture, was the result of state power. It was essential to establish 'national' economies, so that rulers could mobilise their resources for wars. The 'tragedy of the commons' – the private enclosure of previously shared land in seventeenth- and eighteenth-century England – was a notable signpost on the road to creating the first national market.

However, the attempt to create a 'market society' produced a reaction, as society resisted incorporation into the market economy. The market economy brought about increasing regulation by the democratic state to contain its disruptive effects. Thus state intervention today is not a disruption of the natural order of the market. Rather, it is an attempt to prevent markets from destroying the very societies in which they are embedded. Protectionism was the economic response; social democracy and fascism were alternative political responses. All this Polanyi described in his classic, *The Great Transformation* (1944). In a single historical sweep he captures both past economic behaviour and the revolt against laissez-faire in the twentieth century.

Polanyi's critique of market society rests on his belief in the dominance of the social over the economic. He represents a major tradition in sociology which interprets much of modern political and social history as attempts to protect society from the disruptions of the market. Since its earliest appearance, capitalism has evoked spontaneous and deliberate social action designed to maintain our humanity in the face of its inhumanity. The market ideal of specialisation alienates people from society and each other. Through the market, more of our lives are 'commodified', crowding out non-economic values and relations. But human beings are social animals, with a strong need for identity, companionship, security, and a sense of worth, so, while accepting the gains market exchange brings, they devise non-market strategies for protecting their human substance against the encroachment of the market. In political terms, social democracy has been the durable response. But Polanyi offers no obvious solution, simply a dialectic between growing market disruption and growing state regulation.

Reconciliation

There seems to be an unbridgeable gulf fixed between sociological and economic explanations of human behaviour. In methodological individualism, explanations are always in terms of individuals; in methodological holism, always in terms of collectives. This amounts to saying either that 'there is no such thing as society' (as indeed Margaret Thatcher did say) or 'there is no such thing as free choice'. Both statements are clearly false. The cure for treating humans as calculating machines is not to turn them into unthinking automatons; rather, we need to understand better the elusive relationship between the individual and the social.

The philosopher-economist Tony Lawson rejects both the individualist and holist positions, arguing that a proper study of society must focus as much on the organising relations as the individual people and objects that are organised. He uses the term 'emergent' for the social totalities or systems (with independent causal powers) along with their structures that come into being through the chaos of human interaction. (Darwin's theory of natural selection is an influence.) Any system includes both individual elements and an organising structure that includes positions that the individual elements occupy. This organisational structure is fundamental to a system's causal powers, so that the latter are seen always to be irreducible to those of the individual elements involved alone, considered apart from their being relationally organised.

The body is a system of interdependent parts, in the sense that each part is defined by its functional role within the whole. As Aristotle said, a hand is for gripping; thus a hand which cannot grip, because it is severed from the body, is in a sense no longer a hand at all.[19] Similarly, although the organisational structure of society is less well-defined than the body, the parts only function in relation to the structure.

Lawson argues that the organisational structure of a system emerges at the same time as the whole. Pre-existing individual elements become components of the system by slotting into the organising structures. However, those organised individual elements are people with some level of agency. They may accept positional obligations, and thereby have rules, norms, and restrictions imposed upon them, with consequences for transgressions. But this does not mean that the rules are always followed. People may accept the penalties and seek to adapt, evade, rebel against, or ignore the impositions. In this respect, social reality is fundamentally open – powerful, but also changeable.[20]

Given this framework, the question of whether the causation runs from the lower parts to the totality or vice versa, that is, whether it is the collection of lower parts or the totality that is the independent feature, is regarded as posing a false dichotomy. The system as a whole has causal powers, but these powers can be exercised only through the participation of individuals within the system, whether or not these individuals know how their actions fit into the system; so methodological holism is false. At the same time, the individuals involved can exercise the causal force they do only through being relationally organised as system components, even if rules are sometimes broken; so methodological individualism is false.

Consider, by way of illustration, the relationship between language and conversation. To have a conversation, there must first be a language, some agreed system by which meaning is conveyed. But languages are not immutable and nor, for the most part, are they planned. They emerge through the process of uncountable conversations, as tacit rules come to be understood by participants. Sounds take on meanings, becoming words and, as contexts change, the usage of these words can subtly change these meanings or add new ones.

Another example might come from a team sport like football. If a goal is scored, it is the team – Arsenal, say – which would then be winning 1–0, not any individual on the team. But it would be absurd to say that the team is winning without taking account of the participation of the individuals; it's not as though a team has feet, and can kick. But neither is an extreme individualist position appropriate. Eleven individuals running around without reference to each other would play like a village team from the 1850s, just taking the ball and running towards goal until someone tackles them.

Rather, the team is able to score goals because the players are relationally organised into a formation, with each position carrying certain responsibilities. Forwards and defenders have different sets of obligations, and the organisation of the players into a team allows them to carry them out. Knowing that there will be a defender to defend allows the attacker to attack. But at the same time, this structure is not fixed, but interpreted and transformed by managers and players to take advantage of their own strengths and the weaknesses of the opposition, and to exploit the element of surprise. In the 1880s it was virtually unheard of to play more than two defenders, but nowadays any manager attempting to play just two at the back would be regarded as incompetent.

In his book on the history of football tactics, *Inverting the Pyramid*, Jonathan Wilson writes 'football is not about players, or at least not just about players; it is about shape and about space, about the intelligent deployment of players, and their movement within that deployment.' Unlike chess, football is open. Neoclassical economics prefers to treat the economy as a game of chess rather than as a game of football. It reduces complex psychological and social phenomena to simple behavioural axioms or simple linear mathematical models, often without further justification or enquiry.

Football, unlike chess, has a manager, a source of power within the team whose role it is to define the team's strategy. Economics generally assumes that, as in chess, players are totally free to make their moves. It makes more sense to say that they are free to interpret the manager's plan within the game, but liable to face sanction if they deviate too far.

The challenge for the economist then becomes to resist attempting ever more tortured reductionist accounts which either strip humans of their agency (as in a crude Marxist account where an action can be interpreted solely as an expression of class interest) or imbue them with unrealistic powers of choice (as in the neoclassical account which completely denies the possibility of involuntary unemployment by emphasising the freedom to starve).

Rather than presupposing the direction of causality and performing a revisionist exercise to provide a semi-coherent interpretation of apparently disconfirming facts, such as Becker and Murphy's theory of rational addiction, ontological enquiry should be a normal part of economic practice.[21] That is, in attempting to answer any given problem, economists should think seriously about the structures and elements involved, and whether or when reduction to a lower level adds or subtracts from explanatory power.

8

INSTITUTIONAL ECONOMICS

The nature of the firm is not simply a minimizer of
transaction costs, but a kind of protective enclave from the
potentially volatile and sometimes destructive, ravaging
speculation of a competitive market.

Geoffrey Hodgson, *Economics and Institutions*

Anglo-American thinkers of the Enlightenment had an intense
suspicion of institutions, which they saw as impediments to the
flowering of individual liberty. The economists shared this attitude and perpetuated it. They have been wont to explain the fre-
quent lapses from full employment by the existence of institutional
impediments to fully competitive markets. But this begs the question of why institutions exist. Could it not be that many of them
exist to protect society against the market, as Polanyi suggested?
This raises another question. What is the advantage of theorising
as though institutions are absent? The only advantage would seem
be to set up a standard to which institutions should conform. But
to posit, for example, that wages are flexible, when in fact they are
'sticky', and that therefore unemployment is at best a fleeting disturbance, builds a false theoretical prospectus.

Institutionalism is economics' nod to sociology. It took root in
the first decades of the twentieth century when a society which
could have been plausibly understood as one of small firms, individual contracts, and small states had morphed into one dominated by big businesses and trade unions, with a parallel growth
in the size of the state and the scope of regulation. Institutional

economics started out as an attempt to analyse the influence of big organisations on individual behaviour; it has subsided in a vigorous reaffirmation of market logic against institutional logic.

'Old' institutionalism

Institutions are defined as 'organisations founded for religious, educational, professional, or social purposes', or as 'established laws or practices'. Economists had been quite vague about how self-interest played out in different institutional settings. The main interest of the 'older' institutionalism was to understand the ways in which institutions modify the behaviour of their members, just as in the example of the 'weight of the office' modifying the behaviour of the US president. Two prominent examples of this approach were the work of Herbert Simon (1916–2007) and John Kenneth Galbraith (1908–2006).

Simon's acute question was the same as Keynes's: what would be rational behaviour in a world of uncertainty? Humans lack the cognitive ability (computing power) to penetrate the future, so they can exercise only 'bounded rationality' when making decisions in complex, uncertain situations. They will 'satisfice', not maximise: attempt to achieve the best result possible, rather than the best possible result.

This leads to an explanation of why firms exist. They are ways of coordinating the activities of different individuals in a 'satisficing' environment. The firm imposes a shared purpose on the individuals in it through hierarchy and loyalty. Loyalty is described by Simon as 'the process whereby the individual substitutes organizational objectives ... for his own aims as the value-indices which determine his organizational decisions'.[1] Studies have repeatedly shown that employees internalise the *telos* (end or purpose) of the organisation in which they work. By its ability to modify the motives of its employees, the firm is an economic actor in its own right.

John Kenneth Galbraith made a further breach in the neoclassical wall by denying consumer sovereignty. He criticised the conventional sequence which starts with consumers to whom firms respond. His 'revised sequence' starts with large firms which design new production and technology. They do 'market research' to show what's possible to sell. They have advertising and consumer finance divisions to ensure their products can be sold. Big firms internalise many market activities within themselves. All critical interests in firms need to be considered, which means that no one's maximal interest will be achieved. They need size to gain some control over uncertainty: hence the increasing concentration of production in large corporations. Firms do not maximise, they behave in ways to ensure their survival.[2]

In such accounts, the organisation or institution exerts an independent influence on the action of individuals: the causation does not all run one way. In the words of Geoffrey Hodgson, 'Individuals are affected by their institutional and cultural situations'. This does not mean that they are simply 'creatures of institutions'.[3] Institutional economists like Simon and Galbraith study the grammar of society, not its conversation.

The above two analyses of non-market coordination help explain the seeming paradox of organisations which exist to serve the interests of their members imposing codes of behaviour which seemingly fail to maximise their independent utility functions. It helps explain the phenomena of military regiments which sacrifice themselves in a hopeless cause, of firms which fail to maximise shareholder value, of trade unions which fight for higher wages even if it means unemployment. It is true that a map filled with such agents doesn't give you a sparse model. The motives of the organisation lack the hard edge of maximisation, and the outcomes of its behaviour are thereby indeterminate. But we require not better theory, but better understanding.

'Neoclassical' institutionalism

With the 'new' institutional economics of the 1980s, institutionalism collapsed back into neoclassical economics. Its main idea was that individuals form institutions to reduce the 'transaction', especially 'information', costs of trading individually in markets. The neoclassical logic remains intact: individuals create institutions to maximise their utilities. The father of this approach was

Nobel Laureate Ronald Coase (1910–2013), whose seminal article on the firm appeared in 1937, in reaction against the then prevalent theories of oligopolistic competition. It took the overthrow of Keynesianism by the new classical economics in the 1970s and 1980s for his ideas to gain currency. Today they comprise the orthodox microeconomics of institutions.

Why do firms exist? Coase's answer is that they exist to reduce the costs to individuals of doing business separately. His argument is that people organise production in firms when the transaction costs of coordinating production through market exchange are greater than internalising them within the firm. The costs of transacting in markets include discovering relevant prices, negotiating and writing enforceable contracts, and haggling about the division of the surplus.[4]

What gives rise to transaction costs is incomplete information about relevant prices and the costs of monitoring and enforcing good performance. It is because production has a time-element that production transactions are not typically like those which take place in a fruit and vegetable market, where both buyer and seller know the prices of all the products. Within the firm, market transactions are replaced by the authority of the manager who directs the activity of all the productive units. Coase's theory also neatly answers the question of what determines a firm's size. The optimum size of the firm is reached at the point where internalising an additional cost equals the cost of making the transaction on the market. Coase's theorem is a good example of the power of neoclassical economics to absorb apparently incongruous elements of analysis. Individuals lack complete information, but by its control over internal costs, the firm acquires it. So the assumption of profit maximisation can be retained: in setting up firms owners (shareholders) cede technical authority to managers to maximise profits on their behalf. Though somewhat of an intruder on the map of individual maximisation, the firm fulfils the neoclassical criterion of rational choice.

The economic historian Douglass North (1920–2015) received a Nobel prize for using the theory of transaction costs to explain the institutional innovations which led to economic growth in the eighteenth century. The institution 'is an arrangement between economic units which defines and specifies the ways by which they can cooperate and compete'.[5] Economic institutions, like products, are innovated when the gains from the innovation exceed the costs of innovating. North then goes on to explain how the modernisation of property rights in Britain set it on its growth path, by making it profitable for 'improving' landlords to capture the profits of their improvements, thus equalising the private and social rates of return.

While British social historians lament the 'tragedy of the commons' – privatisation through 'enclosure' of common lands on which agricultural workers grazed their sheep and cattle – North commends it as providing for 'easier transfer of property and protection of the peasant'.[6] By contrast, in Spain, the Crown failed to curtail the right of the Mesta (the shepherds' guild) to drive their sheep across the land wherever they wanted. 'A landlord who carefully prepared and grew a crop might expect at any moment to have it eaten or trampled by flocks of migrating sheep.'[7] The result was that England grew and Spain stagnated. What North and Thomas fail to explain was the persistence of inefficient property institutions in Spain (and also France and most of Europe) in face of international competitive pressures, especially those of war. The question can be put more broadly: since technology is a free good, why does its diffusion take so much time?

The American economist Mancur Olson (1932–1998) has argued that even rulers, who originated as 'roving bandits' or mafias, caring only about milking the localities they control and then moving on, rather like slash-and-burn tribes before the age of agriculture, develop an 'encompassing' interest in the economic development of their territories when they become 'stationary' – that is, once they have eliminated their rivals. The self-interest of the stationary bandit is to modernise the economy so as to maximise his long-run revenue.[8] Revolutionary groups in the Middle East can be theorised as revenue-generating mafias in the 'prestationary' phase.

The explanations of Coase, North, and Olson leave *homo economicus* in the driving seat, innovating institutions to maximise his efficiency. The causation is one-way: from the individual to the group. The group has no power to modify individual interest, only to secure its most efficient expression.

But the new institutionalists have identified a flaw that makes all institutions precarious as agents of individual purpose: the principal-agent problem, a form of moral hazard which describes a mismatch between people's incentives and responsibilities. The *principal* wants to maximise something and the *agent* is employed to act on the principal's behalf. The problem arises from the fact that the information possessed by the principal and the agent is unequal, or asymmetric. Often, a principal cannot easily know how an agent is behaving, either because he cannot directly observe the agent's actions, or because the agent (official or manager) has greater expertise: this may very well be why the agent was employed in the task to begin with. This leaves agents free to pursue their own private interests at the expense of the private interests of the principals. This amounts to saying that the principal has theoretic agency, but the manager has actual agency.

The new institutional economics has been used to explain the behavioural characteristics of the state. In the Keynesian age, there was little theorising about the state: it was viewed as a benevolent despot, guided by experts. 'Public choice' theory has reverted to the earlier idea of the predatory state, though now decked out in neoclassical clothes. Far from the 'weight of office' shaping the behaviour of public officials, it is the private interests of public officials which shape the behaviour of the office. 'Public choice' economists like Nobel Laureate James M. Buchanan (1919–2013) use the standard neoclassical methodology to argue that the so-called 'public interest' is 'nothing but' the sum of the private interests of public servants. The 'office' has no influence on their behaviour: they are in the game for private gain.

But what about democracy? Aren't the private interests of public officials constrained by their accountability to voters? Not much, since politicians (the agents) have much greater knowledge, expertise and involvement than the voters (their principals). Political parties are likened to profit-seeking firms, aiming to sell uncosted products (policies) to gullible taxpayers. As Buchanan has written, the main interest of the 'public choice' school is in 'the utility-maximising behaviour of those who might be called on to supply the public goods and services demanded by tax-paying voters.'[9]

In the case of the state, officials are said to maximise their own utilities and attend to the interest of the voters only after they have achieved their own required surplus. In the case of the firm, managers attend to the interests of shareholders only after they have achieved their own private goals. Neoclassical economists have typically seen self-regulating professions as cartels extracting 'rents' from their users.

The principal-agent problem stalks neoclassical economics as a grim health warning, and with it an unequivocal message: do all you can to reduce the costs for individuals of transacting directly *in markets*. It suggested a rationale for the Thatcher-Reagan privatisation policies of the 1980s, and the outsourcing of public functions to private firms. It would be better, so the argument ran, to leave provision of public goods like legal systems, schools, hospitals, homes, and transport systems to regulated 'quasi-markets' rather than to government agencies. Even prisons, that classic emblem of state power, which now incarcerate an increasing proportion of the population, are leased out to competitive tender.

The insight that agents subvert the goals of principals grossly underestimates the natural identification of managers, officials, and employees with the goals of the organisations they serve. The only solution to the principal-agent problem that neoclassical economists can suggest is to improve the incentives for agents not to cheat on their principals. In the aftermath of the financial crash of 2007–2008, which exposed widespread fraud, the talk was of the need to 'align' bankers' incentives with honest dealing. Performance-related pay for teachers is another example. Teachers, it is said, will not do their best for their pupils unless they are given special incentives. This depressing view of behaviour assumes that honesty and duty come at a price.

The neoclassical distaste for institutions has led some economists to argue that business and other organisations are a transitional phase in the process of making markets more complete. If the transaction costs of using markets fall to zero, the cost advantage of firms disappears. What then remains of Coase's theory? What is the function of the firm? What indeed is the function of the state? It can be argued that firms of the old kind are disappearing. Big data and computer technology have lowered information costs so much that billions of individuals can now transact with each other directly 'on line' without the need for institutional intermediaries. Institutions recede before the invasion of social media and on-line shopping. 'All that is solid melts into air', as Marx put it. Radical sociologists, like the Brazilian Roberto Unger, believe that the 'knowledge economy' is bound to generate a decentralised world of small firms wired into global networks.[10]

However, the new individualist perspective is premature. The institutions thrown up by digital technology are less visible than their predecessors, their activities more 'virtual', but this does not mean that they do not exist, or that they are not even larger and more powerful. The highly visible multinational corporations which bestrode the world like colossi in the 1970s, and whose existence and functioning the institutional economists tried to explain, may no longer exist, but this does not mean that the 'democracy of the market' has taken their place. Their place has been usurped by new digital platforms like Google, Amazon, Facebook, and Apple, which establish quasi-monopolies in gathering data on consumer preferences and tastes, which they can exploit commercially. State regulation and monitoring expand to control the exploitation of data for nefarious purposes. Big Brother is (almost) continuously watching you, but most economists, entranced by their vision of an individualist trading utopia, have not spotted him.

Ж

Institutional economics, whether old or new, is a great improvement on the Robinson Crusoe of the pure neoclassical school. It recognises that individuals face situations which lead them to cooperate. These situations can be expressed either in terms of information 'costs' or as an existential problem (uncertainty). Game theory too recognises that games, particularly repeated ones, can lead to cooperative equilibria. The players are conditioned by each other's behaviour.

Nevertheless, new institutionalism remains generically in the instrumentalist camp. It perfectly illustrates the imaginative poverty of neoclassical economics under its carapace of technique. Information is treated as a measurable cost, whereas what causes people to bond together is not the cost of obtaining information but the fear of being alone in an uncertain world.

9

ECONOMICS AND POWER

Mainstream economists have not only found concepts like
exploitation and power to be useless in explaining
economic phenomena, but they worry about introducing
such emotionally charged words into the analysis.

Joseph Stiglitz, *Post Walrasian and*
Post Marxian Economics[1]

Power – how it is acquired, how it is used, its legitimacy – is
the main topic of political science. But it is conspicuous by its
absence from economics. Economics, at least notionally, sets
itself out to study non-coercive relationships: the voluntary bar-
gains of the market. Are the two disciplines, politics and economics, talking about different areas of life – the political realm shaped
by relations of power, and the economic realm shaped by voluntary
contracts?

Political economy is the traditional attempt to bring the two
together. But as an academic subject it has foundered by its association with Marxism; and non-Marxist versions have suffered from
fuzziness about how the power relations and economic relations
are linked together. So the study of political economy has been
marginalised. The two disciplines, politics and economics, pursue
their separate paths, in their familiar silos. In between fall most of
the important questions of public policy.

This chapter is directed at the neglect by economists of the role
power plays in economic relationships. This neglect is deliberate.
By ignoring the extent to which power pervades the economy,

mainstream economists buttress existing structures of power by rendering them invisible.

The first challenge for anyone trying to talk about power is to state exactly what they mean by it. Most simply, it is the ability to secure compliance with one's wishes, by punishment or deterrence. Power is not identical to authority, though the two concepts overlap. Authority is established by accepted superiority of character, brains, experience, or position. This confers a recognised right to be heeded. The doctor has authority, but not power. Nor is all power illegitimate. It may be legitimate, in the sense that the right of some to give orders and the obligation of others to carry them out is generally accepted. However, it is never fully legitimate. It carries an implication of some resistance, actual or potential, to the wishes of the power-holder, which needs to be overcome or prevented. Nor can all authority be divorced from power, though it generally is. We talk of the 'majesty of the law' as something apart from, or above, power. But we cannot avoid the suspicion that there is 'one law for the rich, another for the poor'.

One of the most influential discussions of power, by Steven Lukes (b.1941), argues that it must be understood along three dimensions: blunt power, agenda power, and hegemonic power.

Forms of power

Blunt (or hard) power is the simplest, least controversial, and almost certainly the most important of these dimensions. It is the gun to the head, the hand on the throat: the ability to coerce people into doing what they do not want to do, but what you want them to do. There are different degrees of coercion, but the basic idea is the same. If you don't do what I want, I will make your life either very short, very painful, or very difficult. Blunt power has been by far the most prevalent form of power in history, which indeed has been largely the story of military conflict. Clausewitz defined war as 'an act of violence to compel our opponent to fulfil our will'. War is still important in international relations, though in hybrid forms.

Agenda power, as the name suggests, refers to control over 'the agenda' of politics. It is the ability to keep disturbing ideas out of the decision-making process. If an idea does not suit your interests, you prevent it being discussed. The chair of a meeting sets the agenda and, with a little guile, can make sure that the meeting is over before there's time to discuss an uncomfortable subject. The media and political parties set the language and tone of public discussion. They decide which ideas are 'on the page' and which are 'beyond the pale'.

During the Greek bailout crisis, Christine Lagarde, head of the IMF, famously claimed that there was a need to talk to 'adults in the room', a thinly-veiled allusion to Yanis Varoufakis, then the Greek finance minister. Varoufakis was portrayed as childish; his proposals for debt relief were 'off the page'. The revolver-to-the-head moment came later, when the European Central Bank deliberately crashed the Greek banking system in the run-up to a referendum.[2]

In the same way, if major news outlets decline to cover an issue, and major political parties aren't minded to press it, eventually interest in it fizzles out. People might grumble away on the street or in the pub, but more often than not it comes to nothing. A classic example of this is immigration.

Of course, the attempt to keep issues 'off the page' is not wholly successful. Despite long-term support from the *Daily Mail* and the *Daily Telegraph*, Brexit was not really 'on the page' until David Cameron and George Osborne thought a referendum would finally stop the Conservative Party's perpetual civil war over Europe. Likewise, Donald Trump was not really 'on the page' until he burst onto it during the Republican primary with a cunning grasp of the power of social media, a keen sense of TV news' addiction to drama, and perhaps a little outside assistance. Division of opinion is the biggest limit on the ability to exercise agenda power.

Overlapping with agenda power is hegemonic, or ideological, power. This is not so much about keeping the wrong ideas off the page, but filling the page up with one's own ideas. Ideological power is invisible, so provokes no resistance. Lukes describes it as 'power over thought, desires, beliefs and thus preferences'.[3] French sociologists Pierre Bourdieu (1930–2002) and Michel Foucault (1926–1984) discerned forms of 'cryptic domination' that are so submerged in our subjectivity and our habits that we cannot really become conscious of them.[4] Propaganda supports both agenda and hegemonic power; it sways opinion in the short run, and frames the way people think about things in the long run. Ideological power is the archetypical 'soft' power. You conform from love, not fear. While the definitions above from Lukes, Bourdieu, and Foucault differ subtly, what all point to is the idea that our values and habits of thought can be structured to suit the interests of the power-holders.

'Inducements', in the form of 'carrots and sticks', are elements in the maintenance of all three forms of power. Sticks are obvious with blunt power, which today is virtually confined to state, mafia, or terrorist power. But all organisations have developed systems of inducements (economists call them 'incentives') to tie their members to the organisation's aims. Even hegemonic power (which is largely invisible to those subject to it, acting through their own agency) has its incentive structure.

The hegemonic conception of power draws heavily on the Marxist tradition. For Marx, ideology was 'false consciousness', an idea developed by Antonio Gramsci (1891–1937). In Gramsci's words, hegemony represents 'the intellectual and moral leadership' through which 'a general direction [is] imposed upon social life by the dominant fundamental group'.[5] The idea of religion as 'the opium of the people' is an example of this thinking: through the promise of a blissful afterlife in return for toil in this life, workers are blinded to their true interests on earth. Ideological power can be seen as a replacement for customary authority, including religious authority; the ideological community of nation has been the most potent form of association in the twentieth century.

Gramsci developed the idea of 'hegemonic power' to explain why Marx's predictions of proletarian revolutions in the industrialised countries never happened. The working class had been led to support the conditions of their own oppression. The immediate trigger for his revelation was working-class parties in 1914 putting nation above class in supporting the war. Radical Islamism may be seen as a contemporary example of hegemonic power: young, disaffected men encouraged to throw away their lives for the sake of eternal bliss.

The hegemonic dimension of power is the haziest. How do we know it exists if it is invisible? The answer is that, much like gravity, it is a hypothesis to explain the problem of why people seem to act against their interests. This assertion of myopia, however, assumes that the 'true' or 'objective' interests which are unknown to the person are known to the theorist.

In some cases, involving scientific matters of fact, 'true' interests may be known, and failure to act on them is myopic. In matters of science – say medicine – we talk about the authority of the doctor, not his power. If Marxism is regarded, as it has been by most Marxists, as the 'true' science of society, then the failure of the workers to act as the 'science' required them to needs to be explained. Their behaviour is plainly deluded. This is analogous to the way economists explain as 'irrational' the failure of people to act in the rational way economists expect them to. But in neither case are people being offered a true 'science of society' in the way it is possible to develop a true science of nature: at best, a partial, or incomplete, argument. The charge of irrationality or myopia therefore falls to the ground. It is simply not true to say that the 'working class' had no country in 1914. They felt themselves German, French, British, Russian, Italian. That is why they rallied to their countries' cause in war. This was not delusion: it was reality, a reality which a purely class interpretation of history misses.

The legitimacy of power

Study of the forms of power is heavily influenced by one's view of the character of the institutions through which it is supposed to be exercised. Political science recognises three main structures of power: liberal, Marxist, and Machiavellian.

1. The liberal theory of the state is congruent with, and developed alongside, the economic theory of the state. State power is blunt power, but it is strictly limited by the terms of the social contract which is said to have terminated the 'state of nature'.

This subjects state power to the terms of the contract. The state has rights and obligations; so do its citizens. Provided the state sticks to the contract, its power is legitimate. Crucial to the liberal picture was denial of state power over the market. The state's power was limited to keeping market actors 'honest' – punishing fraud and preventing monopoly. 'Sociological' liberals like Montesquieu (1689–1755) and Tocqueville emphasised the role of a constitutional separation of powers and intermediate institutions as bulwarks against despotic power. Agenda and hegemonic power are not part of the liberal picture, since liberalism denies the state any but coercive power.

2. The Marxist theory of class power reflects its view of history, not just capitalist history. Social organisation has always been shaped by a dominant class for its own purposes, whether the purpose was military glory or booty, with a strong connection between the two, and both involving exploitation of the labouring class according to the prevalent mode of production (slavery, serfdom, 'wage slavery'). Its basis has always been class ownership of the means of production. In capitalist society, class power is wielded by the capitalist class and stems from their ownership of capital. Mostly this is blunt power: either workers accept the capitalist-determined wage or they starve to death. But hegemonic power is not lacking as reinforcement. Control over the means of production includes control over the production of ideas. Marx wrote, 'The ideas of the ruling class are in any epoch the ruling ideas ... The ruling ideas are nothing more than the ideal expression of the dominant material relationships that make the one class the ruling one; therefore the ideas of its dominance'. Class power is per se illegitimate. A revolutionary seizure of power is necessary as a prelude to abolishing it, by abolishing classes.[6]

3. The Machiavellian (or cynical) theory of elite power. For Vilfredo Pareto, economist, sociologist, political scientist, what Marx envisaged as a social struggle for the control of power is simply the struggle for power between incumbent and

opposition elites. 'The sole appreciable result of most revolutions', he wrote, 'has been the replacement of one set of politicians by another set.' Socialism is a form of false consciousness; it leads not to the triumph of humanitarianism, but the imposition of another cage of bondage. 'Play the sheep and you will meet the butcher.'[7] Elite power, like class power, relies on a mixture of blunt power and delusion.

How do economists treat power?

Neoclassical economists typically depict the economy as a power-free zone, with market monopoly as the single recognised exception. This distinguishes them from Marxists, who treat monopoly in the market as no more than an extreme case of the monopoly inherent in all ownership of capital. By modelling markets as competitive, economists help make power invisible.

A monopolist is anyone who buys or sells goods in large enough quantities to affect their price. The ability to raise prices as you wish is a form of power; if you are the only provider, then you can easily say 'it's my way or the highway'. Adam Smith recognised the inherent tendency of markets to monopoly. 'People of the same trade,' he wrote, 'seldom meet together, even for merriment and diversion, but the conversation ends in a conspiracy against the public, or in some contrivance to raise prices.'[8]

Smith understood that as soon as some market participants are monopolists, with power over their own prices, the whole theory of efficient allocation collapses. If someone has a monopoly on water, say, then not only does more money go towards the water supplier than is needed to maintain supply, but that supply will itself be unnecessarily restricted in order to inflate the prices further. In addition, monopoly in the market greatly increases the power of political lobbying. If there are many firms in a sector, then the benefits to any one firm of lobbying for more favourable conditions for the sector go mostly to their competitors, so it doesn't arise. A monopolist, however, captures all the benefits.

Economists have no problem in modelling monopoly, which is simply a market with a single buyer or seller. However, in setting out their stall, they choose to minimise its importance in economic life. Textbooks always start with models of competitive markets, introducing the theory of monopoly later on. This is because ever since Smith's day they have treated monopoly as a blemish or imperfection on an otherwise desirable state of affairs. The prescriptive, or normative, character of economic modelling is here clearly on display.

In line with Smith's attack on monopoly, even governments that were otherwise committed to laissez-faire have often acted decisively against blatant monopolies. The most famous example is the anti-trust Sherman Act in the United States which led to the break-up of Standard Oil in 1911. Recently this hardline anti-monopoly approach has been diluted, particularly in the field of the economics of regulation. Instead of actual competition being required to undercut monopoly power, the mere threat of it can be substituted. If a number of assumptions hold, then, even if there is only one firm in the market, it will be sufficiently worried about new entrants that it behaves as though it is in a competitive market.

The general proposition is that there can be no market power if markets are contestable. This is the most powerful argument for market-led globalisation. Richard Cooper writes: 'Widespread economic capacity, in a globally competitive environment, creates options for all parties; and the presence of alternatives undermines the capacity of any one player to achieve its preferred ends, except through good performance in the eyes of its customers'.[9] This is a highly idealised picture of the actual global system in which large corporations can allocate markets, choose where to invest, and move money from place to place; and, by using transfer pricing – buying at inflated prices from their own subsidiaries – pay tax wherever they want.[10] To these abuses of competition, most economists have one answer: more competition.

A far more common – and complex – form of market power is oligopoly: a market dominated by a few large firms (cars, oil, telecoms, aviation), rather than just one. Each firm knows that any pricing or output decision could provoke a reaction from the others. A few handshakes would be enough to turn this into a cartel. If they cooperate, they are equivalent to a monopoly. It doesn't even have to be overt: firms can reach a kind of tacit truce in pricing strategy for fear of a retaliatory price war. Yet the cartel phenomenon too is immune from the study of economic power. For one thing it is very difficult to model: prices are indeterminate. So economists tend to fall back on saying that sooner or later the cartel will break down due to the economic incentives to cheat, and producers will end up playing a competitive strategic game. But price wars like this don't seem to happen much in practice: oligopolistic pricing displays a remarkable stability in many industries.[11]

Outright monopolies are relatively uncommon in the modern economy. Far more common is the final form of market power students learn about: *monopolistic competition*, first outlined by Edward Chamberlin (1899–1967) in 1933 and later expanded upon by Joan Robinson (1903–1983). The idea of this is that while firms can't hope to hold an absolute monopoly on what they sell, they can establish brand monopolies. Nike don't have a monopoly on all trainers, but they do have a monopoly on Nike trainers. So, as long as enough people feel that the 'swoosh' is worth paying for, Nike have a degree of power, a position to defend.

To establish this type of partial monopoly, firms must differentiate their products slightly from their competitors to find some kind of edge, some 'unique selling point', or USP, as the marketers say. Firms who find a USP can charge a mark-up over the price that a firm in a perfectly competitive market would charge.[12] This actually starts to appear like a more realistic picture of the modern economy, but unfortunately is rarely explored in detail beyond the initial outlining of the theory.

For completeness we should include monopsony power. This is a situation in which the market is dominated by a single buyer. A good example of a monopsony is Britain's National Health Service, in which the state is the buyer of 90 per cent of medical services. The result is a consumers' surplus: the consumers are asked to pay less for their health than they would be prepared to. Similar situations can exist for labour. The state holds a high degree of monopsony power on, for example, police, teachers, and nurses, as would any monopoly provider in an industry with specialised labour.

The hostility to monopoly is a healthy tradition. But in modelling the market system as a self-regulating domain populated by atomistic 'agents', mainstream economics ignores the actual structure of modern markets in which big firms, digital platforms, labour unions (sometimes), advertisers, and governments call most of the shots. Thus most economists minimise the problem of power in the market system.

The contestability of markets is standard economics' answer to Marx's claim that power is inherent in all wage labour. The reply is that it would be true if there were only one job to be had; not if there were a choice of jobs. Even so, quitting has costs. The question is, how high do those costs have to be for the wage contract to count as coercive? The social democratic argument is that it would be coercive in the absence of measures to balance employers' power in the market. This is the justification for labour unions, minimum wage legislation, and welfare entitlements. Yet the neoclassical narrative has been mainly about how trade unions, minimum wage laws, and the welfare state 'price' employees out of work.

The fact that students are nevertheless taught how prices are determined in competitive markets before they are introduced to monopoly or oligopoly pricing strongly suggests that the latter is viewed as contingent and temporary. The student is additionally bombarded by qualifications to the existence of market power, assuring them that competition will usually prevail: the cartel will break down, the threat of an entrant will discipline the incumbent. By contrast, they are largely encouraged not to think too hard about the exceptions and qualifications to the existence of competition. The language of 'market imperfections' supports this. Rhetorically, the default is a perfect market and the rest is just adjusting that template better to reflect reality. Describing a breakdown in a situation where a competitive market cannot exist as a 'market failure' is like describing the collapse of a wooden building as a 'timber failure': in reality, the failures belong to the economists and engineers.

The fault is easy to identify, but hard to eradicate, because it has been with scientific economics from the beginning. The answer is to start at the other end: to accept that markets in general do not, and cannot, satisfy the efficiency conditions required of them, and identify those particular areas where they do and can. In other words, to work out a general theory of markets, with efficient markets as a special case. This, I take it, is what Keynes attempted to do, and he leaves us with an uncompleted task.

Further, by confining itself to studying and worrying about only one particular form of economic power – power in the market – mainstream economics diverts attention from the way in which power is exercised outside the market to influence the economic policy of governments and the tastes, preferences, and values of consumers.

The role of economics in the power system

In the concluding remarks to *The General Theory*, Keynes famously wrote that 'the ideas of economists and political philosophers, both when they are right and when they are wrong, are more powerful than is commonly understood. Indeed the world is ruled by little else ... I am sure that the power of vested interests is vastly exaggerated compared with the gradual encroachment of ideas.'[13] Keynes is not just distinguishing between ideas and vested interests but also asserting the independence of ideas from such interests. Keynes wouldn't have denied that ideas are a source of power. But he would call this *disinterested* power; more precisely, a source of authority. The key argument for the independence of economics from class interests is that economic ideas are the products of the academy, not of business lobbies. Pure research has long been recognised as an independent intellectual pursuit; its hallmark, disinterestedness; its purpose the search for truth. The pecuniary interest of scholars is not directly involved in either the direction of their enquiry or its results.

One can further argue, in Keynes's spirit, that the agenda of economics is set by economists, and not by 'vested interests'. Its leading ideas are not at the mercy of power in any straightforward way. Economic theory, as we have argued, exhibits stability through time, in its concepts, techniques, and language. That is what makes it difficult to apply to it the idea of a paradigm shift.

It is true that economic theory is influenced by the conditions of the times. These produce what John Hicks (1904–1989) called 'concentrations of attention'. The emergence of persisting unemployment in the 1930s produced the Keynesian revolution; the inflation in the 1970s produced monetarism. The theoretical interpretation of these facts cannot be linked up to vested interests in any simple way. But even if we accept (as we must) that ideas are an independent source of power, does this make them independent of vested interests?

'Economics itself (that is the subject as it is taught in universities and evening classes and pronounced upon in leading articles)', wrote Joan Robinson, 'has always been partly a vehicle for the ruling ideology of each period as well as partly a method of scientific investigation.'[14] The question arises why some ideas produced in the academy are considered acceptable, and others marginalised. The world may be ruled by ideas; this does not mean it is ruled by just any ideas. We still need to ask what gives some economic ideas 'legs' and cripples others.

In the natural sciences – physics and chemistry more than biology – the answer is their superior scientific quality. For this reason, quantum physics replaced classical physics.[15] Reality is unchanging, only the theory changes as it improves our understanding of reality. In social sciences this is much less true. The natural world does not interfere with one's observation of it; the social world does. It is the changeability of the object being studied which demarcates social sciences from natural sciences. As a result, propositions in social science do not satisfy the 'universality criterion'. They can rarely be successfully confirmed or falsified, except briefly.

This suggests that in economics, much more than in physics, the profession's own research agenda partly reflects non-scientific interests. It is therefore not irrelevant to ask: who finances the institutions from which economic ideas spring? Who finances the dissemination of ideas in popular form – media, think tanks? What are the incentives facing the producers, disseminators, and popularisers of ideas even in a society in which discussion is 'free'?

The financing of economic research is done mainly by the government and business. We may assume, for the sake of argument, that the government is interested in the public good. It pays for the production of economic knowledge in order to improve the welfare of the community. It does not directly interfere, or has not till recently, with the content of research.

This cannot be said about business. Business is Keynes's classic 'vested interest'. And a lot of economics is paid for by businesses. We may point to the huge influence of 'City economists' – bank analysts, financial journalists, and so on – in propagating a crude version of free-market orthodoxy. And even academic economists have lucrative sidelines in 'consultancy'. Economics is more similar in its funding structure to engineering or pharmacology than to sociology or history.

Economics is the only social science which has a Nobel prize, being bracketed together with the hard sciences. This is seen as the ultimate accolade for a real science. No Nobel prize exists for history, political theory, or sociology. Yet it is funded by the Swedish Central Bank, which is no more a neutral technical institution than any other central bank.[16] So we may ask: what is the interest of business in paying for economic research?

The Marxist charge against bourgeois economics

The Marxists give a clear answer. 'What else,' Marx wrote, 'does the history of ideas prove, than that intellectual production changes in proportion as material production is changed?'[17] Their charge is that the power-holders in a capitalist society, through their control over the media, political, and educational systems, are able to generate a flow of ideas which induce a pattern of working class behaviour which suits them, but is contrary to the objective interests of the working class.

Specifically, these ideas cause workers to accept working arrangements, wages, debt contracts, lifestyles, and forms of consumption which are contrary to their own interests. Economics, say Marxists, serves the interests of the capitalist class by disguising the true nature of things by means of its scientific pretension. This

5. *The Bosses of the Senate* by Joseph Keppler, 1889.

causes people to think of it not as connected to ideology or politics but to something objective like physics or chemistry. It is surely no coincidence that the policy of central bank independence depends largely on the acceptance that economics is a science, and thus the decisions of a central bank are technical, rather than political, in nature. The idea of a technocratic ruling group, above 'class' and ruling in the interests of the whole society, is strongly challenged by those in the Marxist tradition. Capitalism and democracy, writes the German sociologist Wolfgang Streeck, 'are both individually as well as in their respective combinations, the outcome of specific configurations of classes and class interests as evolved in a historical process, driven not by intelligent design, but by the distribution of class political capacities.'[18] The Keynesian revolution itself represented a balance of forces between an increasingly organised working class and a capitalist class on the defensive.[19]

We have already suggested that the claim of economics to be a hard science is largely spurious. Most of its propositions can be neither refuted nor verified. If this is so, economic theory is opinion cloaked in the authority of science. We trust doctors because they have science behind them, though some theorists of power such as Michel Foucault have identified the medical system as, in part, a tool of social control.[20] Economists claim the authority of doctors without the credentials of medicine.

Nevertheless, the Marxist charge is only partly true. The relationship between power and ideas is not a simple base-superstructure one. Not only does economics have its own agenda; practical people – politicians, businessmen, civil servants – are consumers, not producers, of ideas. This gives the producers of ideas considerable latitude vis-à-vis their users. The vested interests are in no position – even were they capable of it – to dictate the precise form of the intellectual defence offered for their preferences. Thus the economist's justification of the free market is likely to be both more general and also more circumscribed than that offered by the business class. For example, economists have almost always opposed protectionism and monopoly, propositions often heavily supported by sections of business.

More damaging to the Marxists is that the base on which the superstructure of ideas is supposed to be erected, is far from being the monolith of the Marxist imagination. In practice, it is usually divided into conflicting interests: in economic life, between exporters and importers, between creditors and debtors, between finance and industry. We get the phenomenon, notable in the United States, of a business class whose ideological hostility to the state is continually subverted by its reliance on state defence and research contracts for its prosperity.

A key matter here is how power is divided. How balanced is the power structure between the state and vested interests, between contending political and social groups, and between capitalists and workers? The more even the balance of forces, the less likely one is to get a single story from economics about the way the economy works. From roughly the 1920s through to the 1970s the balance of forces between capital and labour was such as to enable a policy of social compromise. In the last forty years power has shifted decisively from the old working class to those with superior birth, wealth, and education; and from the old business to the new financial elites.

For these reasons, there is never a 1:1 relationship between an economic argument and a political argument. This gives economics, together with the other social sciences, a relative autonomy from political forces, wherein lies their authority. But the distance, in the Marxist view, is only relative.

Despite its relative autonomy, there are at least three ways in which economics serves the interests of business. First, by investing their interests with the authority of science, economics can make self-interest seem more enlightened. Practical people like nothing better than to have their prejudices dressed up in scientific language. Such language has the power to turn what is really a matter of opinion into a fact of nature.

The second influence is exerted through its agenda power. 'Nothing is so important in the defence of the modern corporation,' writes John Kenneth Galbraith, 'as the argument that power does not exist; that all power is surrendered to the impersonal play of the market. Nothing is more serviceable than the resultant conditioning of the young to that belief.'[21] As he explains,

> The rise of the modern corporations has brought a concentration of economic power which can compete with the modern state . . . The state seeks in some aspects to regulate the corporation, while the corporation, steadily becoming more powerful, makes every effort to avoid such regulation. Where its own interests are concerned, it even attempts to dominate the state.[22]

By modelling economic life in terms of individual optimisation in competitive markets, economics renders any power that is less blatant than outright monopoly completely invisible. For example, an exploitative wage is any wage that falls below the marginal value of labour's product. But under the assumed competitive conditions labour will receive the value of its marginal product, so exploitation is a pathology, not inherent, as Marx claimed.

Similarly with the mainstream treatment of advertising. For mainstream economists, decisions on what to buy are made by rational consumers maximising their utilities in competitive markets. In this model there is no scope for advertising to alter preferences. Advertising as an expression of power is rendered invisible by arguments to the effect that it merely confirms preferences or provides consumers with information. Today the unseen influence of networks of computers known as Cloud storage, owned by virtual companies like Google and Facebook, on the tastes, ideas, and purchases of their mainly young users, is largely ignored by mainstream enthusiasts for the market.

Third, economics supports the dominant power system not just by keeping the role of marketing in shaping consumer choices off its own research agenda, but by giving 'scientific' support to positive political programmes. The chief example in our own day has been the alignment of mainstream economics with the political programme of reducing the role of the state in the economy.

Specific propositions of mainstream economics include the idea that the market system ensures that business leaders are paid no more than they are worth, that globalisation benefits even those who lose their jobs, that government deficits in a slump make things worse than they would have been, and that finance is merely an intermediary in the economic system, not an actor in its own right. All these propositions may be true, or partially true, in special circumstances; it is their generalisation into universal laws that causes the damage.

Milton Friedman has left a charmingly naive account of the relation between science and ideology in his own work:

> During my whole career, I have considered myself somewhat of a schizophrenic ... On the one hand, I was interested in science *qua* science, and I have tried – successfully I hope – not to let my ideological viewpoints contaminate my scientific work. On the other, I felt deeply concerned with the course of events and I wanted to influence them so as to enhance human freedom. Luckily, these two aspects of my interests appeared to me as perfectly compatible.[23]

Friedman peers very briefly over the precipice and then hurriedly withdraws. Yet the whole of his 'scientific' work was directed to demonstrating the futility of government intervention in the economy. Friedman deserves credit for recognising that there might be a problem in reconciling science and values. Most economists simply ignore it.

The link between ideology and economics is complex. It is not that ideology distorts the conclusion of an argument. Rather it invades the way the argument is set up or 'modelled' – the core assumptions (equilibrium, optimisation), the choice of problem to be studied, the choice of relevant variables, the selection of data, the choice of one model rather than another: in short, the research programmes which economists pursue. In this way economics can display a strong ideological slant, while sticking to the accepted canons of scientific enquiry. Its scientific method has served to protect it from the charge of ideological bias or subservience to power.

Economics has not found a way of modelling power. But it is worse than that. Neoclassical economics provides the intellectual backing for the political programme of neoliberalism. Economics is the cement which binds together what Joe Earle, Cahal Moran, and Zach Ward-Perkins (founding members of the Post-Crash Economics Society) call 'the econocracy', a network of technocratic institutions such as central banks, treasuries, large banks, and corporations which have seized control of economies from the nerveless hands of government.[24] It is for these reasons that the reform of economics is more than mere academic self-indulgence.

The weakness of economics in handling power is part and parcel of the absence of institutions from its map of reality. The only actors in its map are maximising individuals. A proper economics would start with institutions – classes, organisations, and social norms – and then try to show how these shape individual choices. The objection is that such an approach is impossible to model mathematically. For mathematical modelling you need tight priors from which you can deduce precise quantitative conclusions. With any other approach you fall into – God forbid! – political economy. To this objection Keynes gave an answer which to me is irrefutable: in matters of public policy it is better to be approximately right than precisely wrong.

10

WHY STUDY THE HISTORY OF ECONOMIC THOUGHT?

Economics is more like art and philosophy than science, in
the use it can make of its own history. The history of
science is a fascinating subject ... but it is not important for
the working scientist in the way the history of economics is
important to the working economist.

John Hicks, 'Revolutions' in Economics[1]

The main reason for studying the history of economic thought
is to question the claim that economic knowledge is cumulative.
Mainstream economics views economics as part of the Ascent of
Man. It believes that all useful economic knowledge from the past
is incorporated in present theories. In fact, economics has been
interminably disputed ever since the start of the 'science'. The reason, I have suggested, is that its theorems, while often contrary to
common sense, are not refutable.

Yet the claim to cumulation has been there from the beginning.
'What useful purpose can be served by the study of absurd opinions and doctrines that have long ago been exploded, and deserved
to be?', asked J.B. Say (of Say's Law fame) in the early 1800s. 'It is
mere useless pedantry to attempt to revive them. The more perfect
a science becomes the shorter becomes its history ... Our duty with
regard to errors is not to revive them, but simply to forget them.'[2]
One wonders whether Say would be flattered or horrified, then, to
learn that his 'law' was still being taught to students 200 years on.

Here is Robbins a hundred years after Say: 'It may safely be
asserted that there is nothing which fits into the old framework

which cannot be more satisfactorily exhibited in the new'. The only difference is that 'at every step we know exactly the limitation and implication of our knowledge'.[3] In our own times, George Stigler has asked: 'Does Economics Have a Useful Past?' and concludes that it doesn't: 'one need not read in the history of economics . . . to master present economics'.[4]

Nobel Laureate Paul Krugman gives a more sympathetic view of the relationship between 'old' and 'new' economics, by means of an analogy with the gradual mapping of Africa. Over time maps of the coastline of Africa got steadily more accurate, but at the cost of leaving out the details of the (sometimes mythical) interiors. The improvement in the art of map-making 'raised the standard for what was considered valid data'. Something similar happened to economics:

> A rise in the standards of rigor and logic led to a much improved level of understanding of some things, but also led for a time to an unwillingness to confront those areas the new technical rigor could not yet reach. Areas of enquiry that had been filled in, however imperfectly, became blanks. Only gradually, over an extended period did these dark regions get re-explored.

In short, 'a temporary interlude of ignorance may be the price of progress'.[5] Despite the interlude (how long?) of ignorance, the history of economics is a story of progress. In the end, the territory is 're-explored' with a better map.

Over the last thirty years, nearly all economics departments have taken Robbins, Stigler, and Krugman at their word by removing the history of economics from their courses, leaving perhaps a lecture at the very start of a course to give a brief overview. In this view, all original formulations have been improved; all 'errors' have been filtered out, leaving nothing but the presently correct statement of the scientific theory. Studying the history of economics is like rummaging in an attic filled with antique gadgets, a pleasant enough pastime, but of no practical use. It also invites the suspicion that the rummager is not competent to do scientific work.

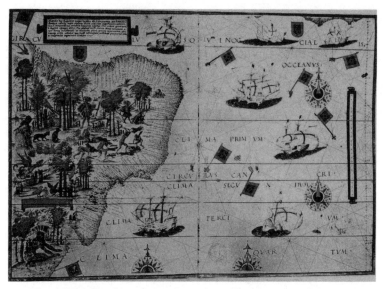

6. The Miller Atlas of Brazil, 1519. Note the stylistic depiction of the interior, compared to the absence of detail in describing the features and settlements along the coastline. It has been suggested that the map served a political purpose: its Portuguese creators sought to discourage Spain's colonial ambitions by showing Brazil fading into the map's outer border, implying that circumnavigation around it was impossible.

The question that such accounts beg is whether 'present economics' is the best economics. The failure of most economists to foresee the possibility of the collapse of 2008 may be thought a refutation of the affirmative thesis. If so, the student cannot, or should not, accept on faith that present economics is best. Some past economics may be better at explaining problems of present interest. One might even argue that the stock of knowledge available to economists has been depreciating. For example, economists in the past knew more than they do today about banking and finance, even though they 'do' the subject more rigorously.

The fact that an idea formerly grasped without maths is now stated in maths is not necessarily an argument for progress, because it ignores the possibility that a great deal of useful knowledge gets permanently lost in translation. Stigler does give one reason for studying the history of economics, which is to understand better how a science evolves, and specifically 'the relationship between the intellectual content of a science and the organization and environment of the scientist'.[6] The study of such relationships might reveal the secret of persistence without progress, survival without evolution.

Methodological debates

The history of economics is marked by a profusion of doctrines but a persistence of method. The one important 'paradigm shift' (see next section for an explanation of 'paradigm') was the marginal revolution – the switch from a cost of production theory of value to subjective utility in the last quarter of the nineteenth century. The commitment to this latter method of analysis either emasculated rival doctrines (institutional economics) or expelled them from economics altogether (Marxism). Persistent sniping from individual dissidents and dissident schools about the mainstream's way of doing economics has been left out of the 'official' story of cumulative progress, and it is this sniping that we shall focus on. The attacks have been mainly directed against unreal behavioural assumptions (*homo economicus*), excessive formalism and abstraction (including the near-mandatory use of mathematics), claims to the universal validity of economic laws, and the demand that macroeconomics be properly 'micro-founded' in individual optimising behaviour.

From the birth of scientific economics, dissidents have argued that too many theories in economics are generalisations made without proper regard to the facts. That is, they lack an inductive basis and are derived solely from 'inner understanding'. Simonde de Sismondi (1773–1842) wrote that 'humanity should be on guard against all generalization of ideas that causes us to lose sight of the facts'. Richard Jones (1790–1850) had as his motto 'Look and see', as opposed to 'See and deduce'. Cliffe Leslie (1827–1882) said that 'instead of investigating actual motives, economists construct a fictional person out of desire for wealth and aversion from labour'. Henry Sidgwick (1838–1900) criticised the approach which undertakes to settle all practical problems 'by simple deduction from one or two general assumptions'. William Beveridge (1879–1963) called economics a 'survival of medieval logic'. Economists were people 'who earn their living by taking in one another's definitions for mangling'.[7]

What is striking about this is not just the similarity but the persistence of the critiques. Economists have not on the whole been too worried about the charge of lack of realism. A typical response has been: the more abstract the theory, the more realistic it will be.

Nobel Laureate Wassily Leontief (1906–1999) attacked the 'nearly mandatory' use of maths in economics. 'Uncritical enthusiasm for mathematical formulations', said Leontief in his 1970 Address to the American Economic Association,

> tends often to conceal the ephemeral substantive content of the argument behind the formidable front of algebraic signs ... In no other field of empirical inquiry has so massive and sophisticated a statistical machinery been used with such indifferent results ... Most of these [models] are ... without practical applications.[8]

In similar vein, and at the same conference, the British economist Frank Hahn said: 'It cannot be denied that there is something scandalous in the spectacle of so many people refining the analysis of economic states which they give no reason to suppose ever will, or have ever come about'.[9] Another speaker, Harry Johnson (1923–1977), noted that 'the testing of hypotheses' on which econometrics rested 'is frequently a mere euphemism for obtaining plausible numbers to provide ceremonial adequacy for a theory chosen and defended on a priori grounds.'[10]

Economists with different politics, from different schools, like Friedman, Coase, Robinson, Krugman, and Stiglitz have complained about excessive maths. It is not just – as some of the more cynical defenders of today's orthodoxy have suggested – that dissident students are unwilling to, or incapable of, getting to grips with the maths. Students who are more than able to cope with the technical demands of mathematical economics have recoiled from the barrier maths puts between them and understanding the real world.

Famous nineteenth-century economists like John Stuart Mill, insisted that economics must be a broad discipline – a branch of social philosophy, he called it – if its conclusions are to have any value, a position echoed by Walter Bagehot (1826–1877), John Kenneth Galbraith, and many others. The claim that economics has discovered 'laws' of universal validity has been repeatedly attacked, without making much impression on the discipline. The nineteenth-century German Historical School introduced the important, but now neglected, idea that the validity of economic doctrines depends on circumstances. A 'law' valid in one time and place may be quite invalid in another. This had an important policy implication: what is good for a nation or society at one time might be bad for it at another.

One variant of this is the theory of 'stages', sometimes called 'stadial': that societies pass through successive stages of development which generate different kinds of economic system, whose precepts are justified by the stage they are in. It all depends where you are in the continuous flow of events. As the ancient Greek philosopher Heraclitus said: 'You never step into the same river twice'. The earliest schools of development economics (see Chapter 3) relied on exactly such a stadial theory, before succumbing to the universalist perspective. Adam Smith was clear that his economics was intended to apply only to the last or 'commercial' stage of economic history. This caveat was forgotten by his followers.

The best economists know that their 'universal laws' are subject to special conditions. But the statement of the law in unqualified form always makes much more impression on the public mind than the statement of the qualifications to it. The demand that macroeconomics be properly 'micro-founded' was part of the reaction against Keynesian economics in the 1970s. Keynes based his economics on the relations between aggregates like saving, investment, output, and money. His micro-foundations of 'animal spirits' and 'conventions' were unorthodox. By contrast, the revived neoclassical tradition claims that macroeconomics should be based on optimisation by firms and individuals. This, as we have seen, rules out persisting mass unemployment.

This is just a sample of the methodological debates to be found in the history of economics. Their relevance has not diminished with time. The criticisms of mainstream economics have been made by some of the best minds in the discipline, as well as outside it. Mostly they have been parked into marginal fields, or taken up by other disciplines.

Piero Sraffa (1898–1983) has explained the strategy of assimilation through neglect and segregation:

> From time to time someone is unable any longer to resist the pressure of his doubts and express them openly; then, in order to prevent the scandal from spreading, he is promptly silenced, frequently with some concessions and partial admissions of his objections, which naturally, the theory had implicitly taken into account. And so, with the lapse of time, the qualifications, restrictions and the exceptions have piled up, and have eaten up, if not all, certainly the greater part of the theory. If their aggregate effect is not at once apparent, this is because they are scattered about in footnotes and articles and carefully segregated from one another.[11]

Paradigms and research programmes

The deep answer to the question of why the persistent sniping of the dissidents has had so little impact on the mainstream lies in the extraordinary power of persistence of intellectual paradigms and research programmes. The most important reason for the persistence of the mainstream methodology is that it is constructed in such a way that the conclusions deriving from it cannot easily be falsified (see Chapter 5). On this rock an almost invulnerable set of defences have been built to protect mainstream economics from its critics. Thomas Kuhn and Imre Lakatos have described how these defences work. In their view they are applicable to all sciences, but economics has benefited especially from these defensive strategies because of its claim to be like a natural science.

Persistence is partly inevitable in all sciences, as practitioners must be 'indoctrinated' before being allowed to practise, but it also provides a stable conceptual framework that can be scientifically useful and, perhaps most significantly, protects the positions of the established practitioners. The upshot is that once a 'normal' way of doing 'science' has been established, it develops strong staying power, however much its scientific claims are questioned. How much more is this likely to be the case in economics, when refutation is almost impossible and vested interests are rampant.

Let's start with Thomas Kuhn's explanation of paradigm persistence. A paradigm is a way of doing science which becomes hard-wired into the psychology and hierarchy of the scientific community, while simultaneously being open-ended enough on its own terms to leave all sorts of problems for the defined group of practitioners to practise their skills on. The paradigm directs the researcher to the problems to be investigated, and furnishes him or her with the conceptual tools and experimental methods to investigate them. This is the 'normal' way of doing science, necessary for any organised enquiry. Significant changes in the science do not occur within this framework, but instead represent changes in the framework, what Kuhn calls 'paradigm shifts'.

The threat to the paradigm comes not from empirical anomalies, which can usually be insulated as 'puzzles' to be worked on, but from changes in world-view, which make the puzzles seem intolerable. A mismatch develops between the institutional map of the science and the problem which needs to be solved. A crisis develops when more and more practitioners occupy themselves with the solution of the anomaly, which resists solution by means of the paradigm. Ultimately a new paradigm is suggested. This is resisted by other members of the community but slowly wins them over. The revolution is completed when a younger generation takes over.[12]

Two well-known examples in the natural sciences are the replacement of Ptolemaic astronomy by the Copernican revolution, and the replacement of phlogiston by gas as the agent of combustion. Has there been anything comparable in economics? Two candidates for paradigm shifts are the attack on the cost of production theory of value by subjective utility in the 1870s, and the assault on Walrasian general equilibrium theory by Keynesian economics in the 1930s. Both were partial shifts.

The shift to marginalism did not dislodge the central conception of the self-regulating market, but it did destroy the previous method of analysing economic life in terms of structures like classes and organisations. In the second case, although persistent mass unemployment was regarded by Keynes himself as a refutation of Walrasian general equilibrium, it came to be accepted by the orthodoxy as a special case of Walrasian general equilibrium, one in which wages and prices were sticky. In this form it could be co-opted into the mainstream. The marginalist revolution had a more durable effect on the way economics was done than did the Keynesian revolution.

Lakatos gives a less dramatic account of persistence and change than Kuhn, by distinguishing between the constant and variable elements in a 'research programme'. In such an enterprise the researchers will share a common set of basic axioms and assumptions; a set of accepted working practices for proposing and confirming theories (the heuristic); finally a 'protective belt' (the variable element) in which empirical research is done. Acknowledgement of 'frictions' is a typical strategy of the protective belt to preserve the core doctrine of equilibrium. Research programmes eventually degenerate if there are too many predictive failures in the protective belt.

The function of the protective belt is to prevent premature rejection of the core, like an organism which develops an immunity to infection. For example, when Copernicus developed a heliocentric model of the solar system, people suggested this should mean small movements in stars could be observed – parallax. They couldn't be found, but the theory wasn't thrown out over this one small error. These movements were later observed by more powerful telescopes. The protective belt is much more powerful in the social sciences than in the natural sciences, because of the weakness of the refutation procedure.[13]

The debates in orthodox economics have mainly taken place in the 'protective belt', to which economists have consigned puzzles, anomalies, and 'curiosa' for further work, leaving 'normal' science to proceed unaffected.

Perhaps the most important reason for the lack of theoretical shifts in economics (or indeed in any social science) is that these disciplines never developed hard paradigms in the full Kuhnian sense. Precisely because they are immune from refutation, social science paradigms have enjoyed greater latitude for assimilation and co-option. It is not so much that economic theories exist independently from each other as that different schools co-exist in a loose hierarchy, like the diversity of dialects within a single language.

John Bryan Davis (2016) has offered a persuasive account of the way an economic orthodoxy protects its dominant position. Traditional 'reflexive domains' for judging research quality – the theory-evidence nexus, the history and philosophy of economics – are pushed aside. Instead, research quality is assessed through journal ranking systems. This is highly biased towards the *status quo* and reinforces stratification: top journals feature articles by top academics at top institutions; top academics and institutions are those who feature heavily in top journals.

Because departmental funding is so dependent on journal scores, career advancement is often made on the basis of these rankings – they are not to be taken lightly. It is not that competition is lacking, but it is confined to those who slavishly accept the paradigm, as defined by the gatekeepers – the journal editors. In this self-referential system it is faithful adherence to a preconceived notion of 'good economics' that pushes one ahead. Some of the most important neoclassical economists today have also criticised the dominance of journal publications: it depresses quality by hindering basic research, development of innovative theories, and is often just a rudimentary follow-up of already published theories.

Nobel Laureate Lars Peter Hansen argues that 'this reliance on referees leads to a much more conservative strategy. I think it works against novel papers that cross subfield boundaries and that makes it all the more challenging. Basically it makes the simplest path to publication in the top 5 journals to be high quality follow up papers.'[14] The pressure to feature in those prestigious journals also pushes researchers to write journal articles rather than books. This constraint on space naturally favours partial accounts, which in turn promotes the use of *ceteris paribus* ('all else equal') conditions.

Economics shares with social science the existence of professional standards. This is not true (in general) of the arts. Of assertions or arguments in economics or sociology, it is possible to say 'you have made a mistake' in a way not possible, in say, fiction or painting, where what is conventional can always be challenged or overridden by 'creativity' or 'originality'. It is the existence of professional standards which helps explain why social sciences tend to be stable and resistant to change. But whether these internal standards are merely internal to the discourse or represent the most useful way of understanding reality is the point at issue.

Over the years, orthodox economics' tolerance for diversity has lessened. It may be that mathematics has so narrowed the scope of economics that it has at last become a real paradigm. This narrowing is connected with the political supremacy of the United States. The American school has largely obliterated the other schools: Marxism, Austrian economics, German economics, Keynesian economics, Swedish economics. American economics spread with American power; the decay of that power may finally open up a field which has seemed increasingly closed.

X

Absent from the training of today's economists, the dissenters nevertheless represent an unused, because neglected, arsenal of tools. The testimony of powerful forebears is particularly valuable. Current dissenters from established opinion need not feel lonely. One can recognise oneself in great thinkers of the past. To the extent that the existing research programme or paradigm in economics is coming to be seen as neglecting the problems of most interest to our own generation (stagnation, inequality, climate change, automation), the history of the discipline itself becomes a valuable intellectual tool.

The study of past debates has one great bonus. It is sometimes claimed that introducing students to too many conflicting ideas is going to muddle their heads. Better to thoroughly indoctrinate them in orthodox thinking before allowing them to dip their toes in the waters of dissenting ideas. In actual fact, historical debates have often been conducted in far more accessible language. Debate and disagreement, far from being off-putting, are really quite compelling. Especially when you can understand what is being said.

11

ECONOMIC HISTORY

> History doesn't repeat itself, but it often rhymes.
>
> Mark Twain (attr.)

Great economists like Adam Smith, Karl Marx, and John Maynard Keynes worked out their theories in the shadow of history, rather than aiming to perfect a mathematics suitable for conveying truths independent of history. They understood that states of affairs deemed permanent do not last for ever, or even for very long, and with each change in the state of the world comes a change in ideas about the world. Marshall said 'Every change in social conditions is likely to require a new development in economic doctrines.'[1]

In other words, the value of an economic theory does not depend on its place on the evolutionary tree, but on its place in the world. Economics should be a historically grounded social science. It's not only economic doctrines, but economic practices that need to be set in their time and place. In previous times the economy was not a separate domain but an order embedded in a complex of institutions and activities designed to ensure the survival of the population. 'Scientific economics' started off as a critique of the 'embedded' economy, but at the same time claimed that all people at all times were utility maximisers. This enabled the economists to argue for the existence of universal laws, valid at all times and in all places. History is a salutary warning against such effrontery.

There are two main reasons why economists should study the past. The first is to make economics better; the second is to make history better. Although economics has helped a bit with the second, my main focus is on the first. If history is the study of the particular, and economics of the general, the value of history to economists is to enable them to make their premises more concrete and admit their limits. History is an important source of the facts on which economists rely for their hypotheses.

Yet economic history has been almost entirely removed from the modern economics curriculum. As William Parker describes it:

> The institutional context, the social concepts, the moral zeal implicit in the training which economists used to be given through courses in economic history, economic institutions, and applied fields have been pushed aside, while those fields have been partially transformed into playgrounds for the imagination of the theorist.[2]

In short, orthodox economists have stopped listening to history, treating it rather as a source of numerical data for testing out their own theories. Equipped as they are with massive data banks, narrative history to economists is simply anecdote: where is the theory? Economists who turn to history are said to suffer from anecdotage, to which some may add: if economists are already in possession of universally valid laws, there is no point in turning to history to help discover them.

So economists are reluctant to find in history a useful intellectual resource for understanding the human condition. Indeed, their journey into the past is rather like a colonial expedition. Equipped, as they think, with their universal models, they can simply apply them to any topic, past or present, as hypotheses, using such data as available to test them. The hypotheses are almost always neoclassical hypotheses. The horse always maximises.

The consequence of this invasion is to empty economic history of its traditional content. Economic theory corrupts economic history by foisting on it ahistorical models and inappropriate testing strategy which merely confirms the model already in the economist's mind. 'Cliometrics', the application of statistical and mathematical techniques to past events, is the corruption of 'Clio', the ancient muse of history.

History as a source of statistics

The standard view is that history provides a field of observations to test economic hypotheses: a source of empirical evidence for testing theories, estimating relationships between variables, and forecasting future trends. A basic tool of economic history is the time-series, any statistical relationship recorded over a period of time. For example, Angus Maddison's historical estimates of national income, population, growth rates, and so on go back to AD 1, in certain territories (for the latest edition, see Bolt et al., 2018). The value of statistics, historical or otherwise, is that they provide a check on mere assertion. If somebody claims that the Romans were far richer than people today, Maddison's study of historical production and translation into modern equivalents provides conclusive rebuttal.

But one should not be bamboozled. Most of the time-series in Maddison were constructed long after the event. There were no national income statistics in 1800, let alone AD 1. So Maddison's are estimates based on such statistics as were available then, compiled for different purposes, and subject to a wide margin of error. They are useful for swatting away ludicrous assertions, but not for making precise comparisons of welfare between, say, ancient Athens and modern Ethiopia. The same is true of Thomas Piketty's statistics on economic inequality, and indeed all statistical time-series.[3]

Time-series analysis is also a core component of econometrics – the attempt to measure statistically the relationship between two or more economic variables over time in order to estimate their future relationship, or to test and validate those in the past. Historical data join comparative data as a source for econometric studies. There has been an enormous expansion of the data base for econometrics in recent years. Examples include the many attempts to establish an empirical basis for the quantity theory of money; the long time-series developed by Simon Kuznets (1901–1985) on national income and its components to test for the consumption function;

and E.F. Denison's use of time-series to estimate relationships of key inputs (labour, capital, education, efficiency) in the growth of output.[4]

But as we have already argued in Chapter 5, econometrics is vastly oversold as a way of testing theories: in addition to model specification problems, as soon as you get enough observations, too much time has passed to assume conditions are stationary. For example, do high taxes hinder economic growth? The evidence is inconclusive. Much of economics can never be 'proved'.

Robert Solow offers a devastating critique of the identification of economic history with econometrics. Econometrics, he says, is 'history blind'.

> The best and brightest in the profession proceed as if economics is the physics of society. There is a single universally valid model. It only needs to be applied. You could drop a modern economist from a time machine … at any time, in any place, along with his or her personal computer; he or she could set up in business without even bothering to ask what time and which place.[5]

In short, much of the modelling we do depends on assuming that people in the past had essentially the same values and motives as we do today.

A good example is from Peter Acton's recent book, *Poiesis: Manufacturing in Classical Athens* (2014), of which Michael Kulikowski has written:

> In case study after case study, Acton describes an Athens very unlike our post-industrial world, and still less like that of the 19th and 20th centuries. Yet all his case studies are couched in the language of classical microeconomic theory and a postwar competitive business and management theory that he spells out in great detail and with faith in its revealed truths … Acton presents his task reasonably, challenging readers to use classical microeconomics to ask whether Athenians 'might still have

operated in practice according to the same set of fundamental economic principles that we are familiar with today', even though they lacked the language or conceptual framework within which we articulate those principles. For Acton, there's never any question that 'the same economic laws prevailed despite the different context' because the microeconomic 'framework is timeless' and because 'irrespective of conscious motivation by ancient agents, elementary economic principles are heuristically effective and a source of important historical insight.'[6]

Fine studies of ancient economies, like those of Moses Finlay, show how remote all this is from good history. The rapacity of the upper classes, Finlay argues, was dictated by conventional expenditures for political and military careers, not by a 'maximising' logic.[7] Finlay's work brings out the fact that human societies are to a large extent constituted by their 'social imaginations'. This means that they cannot be understood in terms radically alien from those in which they understand themselves. If Ancient Greek craftsmen didn't think of themselves as maximising profit, who are we to say that was what they were 'really' doing?

In short, history should not surrender the uniqueness of its own vision to the econometricians. As Solow writes, in the new economic history you find 'the same integrals, the same regressions, the same substitution of t-values for thought' as you do in economics proper, but with worse data. Rather than widen the range of perceptions, the new economic historians and economists simply feed the same unilluminating stuff back and forth. Courses in econometrics are inescapably historical, but convey no sense of history, so we reach a point where 'economics has nothing to learn from economic history but the bad habits it has taught to economic history'.[8]

Can economics improve history?

But there is another side. Economics has improved history as well. A famous example is Fogel's *Time on the Cross* (1995 [1974]), which argued that, in contrast to the claims of nineteenth-century historians, slavery was economically efficient. It was morally reprehensible, but left to its own devices it could have rumbled on for much longer. This is an important insight, because it makes clear that the Civil War was necessary for ending slavery. Nick Crafts' work on the late-nineteenth-century British economy showed – with much more justification that Peter Acton's on ancient Athens – that British businessmen were making rational economic decisions, and not turning themselves into economically useless gentlemen.[9]

In a productive division between economics and economic history, economists should make various kinds of hypotheses based on stylised facts and economic historians should think about how and where different models and different kinds of evidence might apply. Economists should approach history in an enquiring, rather than a conquering, frame of mind.

'Cycles'

History shares the inbuilt bias of sociology towards conservatism. It is a record of what has happened, and there is strong temptation to say simply 'What is, is', and not what might be, still less of what should be. Reliance on history alone can be a fatal weakness for a statesman, because the historical imagination finds it very difficult to accommodate the idea of progress. The weakness of history as a school for statesmen comes out very clearly in the Treaty of Versailles in 1919, when the peacemakers fretted about frontiers and nationalities rather than with the need to reconstruct Europe economically. The much more durable results achieved after the Second World War stemmed from putting the economic rehabilitation of the war-shattered economies at the head of the peacemaking agenda – the task entrusted to the forward-looking economic technicians who devised the Bretton Woods system and Marshall Aid.

The idea that social and economic life oscillates round some, not necessarily static, point of equilibrium has been common to both economists and historians. But they have very different views of cycles. For economists cycles result from some 'shock' to otherwise smoothly functioning systems producing cycles of business activity. An example is the forty-year Kondratieff cycle, produced by a surge of technological innovation. Fluctuations may be steep as the economy adjusts to these changes, but they have never been sufficiently long-lasting to call into question the idea of progress itself. Cycles as conceived by historians are more like civilisational cycles. They may be triggered by business crisis, but their origin is existential, coming from the failure of society's central institutions.

Abstracting from technology, historians' cyclical theories have no built-in notion of progress. Technological progress is exogenous and unpredictable. History itself discloses no clear pattern of improvement: it swings backwards and forwards along familiar pathways. It does not repeat itself exactly, but it rhymes. In the typical historical cycle, societies are said to swing like pendulums between alternating phases of vigour and decay, progress and reaction, hedonism and puritanism. Each outward movement produces a crisis of excess which leads to a reaction. The equilibrium position is hard to achieve and always unstable. History cannot be used to predict the future, but it can indicate trends and inevitable reactions against them. Typically, the cycles are generational, with children reacting against the beliefs of their parents.

In his *Cycles of American History* (1986) Arthur Schlesinger Jr defined a 'political economy cycle' as 'a continuing shift in national involvement between public purpose and private interest'. Adapting his terms to European usage, the swing he identified was between 'liberal' and 'collectivist' epochs. Liberal periods (when private interests determine policy) succumb to the corruption of money; collectivist periods (dedicated to 'public purpose') succumb to the corruption of power. The cycle then repeats itself. This political economy oscillation fits the American historical narrative tolerably well. It also makes sense globally. The era of liberal economics opened with the publication of Adam Smith's *Wealth of Nations* in 1776. Despite the early intellectual ascendancy of free trade, it took a major crisis – the potato famine of the early 1840s – to produce an actual shift in policy: the 1846 repeal of the Corn Laws that ushered in the free trade era.

In the 1870s, the pendulum started to swing back to what the historian A. V. Dicey called the 'age of collectivism'. The major crisis that triggered this was the first great global depression, produced by a collapse in food prices. It was a severe enough shock to produce a major shift in political economy. This came in two waves. First, all industrial countries except Britain put up tariffs to protect employment in agriculture and industry. (Britain relied on mass emigration to eliminate rural unemployment.) Second, all industrial countries except the United States started schemes of social insurance to protect their citizens against life's hazards.

The great depression of 1929–32 produced a second wave of collectivism, whose virulent form was Nazism, but whose more enduring legacy was the 'Keynesian' use of fiscal and monetary policy to maintain full employment. Most capitalist countries nationalised key industries. Roosevelt's New Deal regulated banking and the power utilities, and belatedly embarked on the road of social security. International capital movements were severely controlled. The liberal instinct was not entirely extinguished, or else the West would have ended up split between communism and fascism.

What emerged from the Second World War was the victory of collectivism in the milder form of social democracy. However, even before the crisis of collectivism in the 1970s, a swing back to liberalism had started, as trade, after 1945, was progressively freed and capital movements liberalised. The rule was free trade abroad and social democracy at home. The Bretton Woods system, set up with Keynes's help in 1944, was the international expression of liberal/social democratic political economy. It aimed to free foreign trade after the freeze of the 1930s, by providing an environment that reduced incentives for economic nationalism. At its heart was a system of fixed exchange rates, subject to agreed adjustment, to avoid competitive currency depreciation.

The crisis of social democracy unfolded with stagflation and ungovernability in the 1970s. It broadly fits Schlesinger's notion of the 'corruption of power'. The Keynesian/social democratic policymakers succumbed to hubris, an intellectual corruption which convinced them that they possessed the knowledge and the tools to manage and control the economy and society from the top.

This was the malady against which Hayek inveighed in his classic *The Road to Serfdom* (1944). The attempt in the 1970s to control inflation by wage and price controls led directly to a 'crisis of governability', as trade unions, particularly in Britain, refused to accept them. Large state subsidies to producer groups, both public and private, fed the typical corruptions of behaviour identified by the new right: rent-seeking, moral hazard, free-riding. Palpable evidence of government failure obliterated memories of market failure.

The new generation of economists abandoned Keynes and, with the help of sophisticated mathematics, reinvented the classical economics of the self-regulating market. Battered by the inflationary crises of the 1970s, governments caved in to the 'inevitability' of free market forces. The swing back became world-wide with the collapse of communism. A conspicuous casualty of the swing back was the Bretton Woods system that succumbed in the 1970s to the refusal of the United States to curb its domestic spending. Currencies were set free to float and controls on international capital flows were lifted. This heralded a wholesale change of direction towards globalisation.

This was, in concept, not unattractive. The idea was that the nation state – which had been responsible for so much organised violence and wasteful spending – was on its way out, to be replaced by the global market. The Canadian philosopher, John Ralston Saul, described the promise of globalisation in a 2004 essay, with only modest parody:

> In the future, economics, not politics or arms, would determine the course of human events. Freed markets would quickly establish natural international balances, impervious to the old boom-and-bust cycles. The growth in international trade, as a result of lowering barriers, would unleash an economic-social tide that would raise all ships, whether of our western poor or of the developing world in general. Prosperous markets would turn dictatorships into democracies.[10]

Today we are living through a crisis of liberalism. The financial collapse has brought to a head a growing dissatisfaction with the corruption of money. Neoconservatism has sought to justify fabulous rewards to a financial plutocracy while median incomes stagnate or even fall; in the name of efficiency it has promoted the off-shoring of millions of jobs, the undermining of national communities, and the rape of nature. Such a system needs to be fabulously successful to command allegiance. Spectacular failure is bound to discredit it.

What this kind of history offers students of economics is the ability to situate themselves and their teaching in the flow of events. It helps explain why economic narratives, plausible in one epoch, lose their hold in others. It gives a historical dimension to the idea of 'crisis' which carries one beyond the notion of a 'shock' to an otherwise frictionless system.

'Stages of development' – *Kicking Away the Ladder*

A different kind of historical pattern is revealed by the so-called 'stages of development' literature. The standard story of the West's economic development is well-known: the Enlightenment unleashed the twin forces of science and market, giving both technology and the means to put it to use. But what happens if we start with the history?

Ha-Joon Chang's impressive *Kicking Away the Ladder* (2002) examines the history of industrialisation and discovers the rather visible hand of the state at every turn: protecting British mills from their competitors in France and Belgium, protecting German industry from the British, protecting new American industries from their rivals in Europe, protecting Japanese industries from America and Europe, and so on through the Asian Tigers of Hong Kong, Singapore, Taiwan, and South Korea and now the meteoric rise of China.

In each case government was directing and assisting targeted industries. It was only after each country had successfully industrialised that it perceived free trade and economic liberalisation to be in its interests. The narrative of their own success changed from state-led to market-led development, the visible hand of the state transformed into the invisible hand of the market.

Such essays in political economy are good examples of starting with historical facts rather than universalist premises. 'Why are some countries rich and others poor?' is a question that mainstream economists think should have a general answer, but no general theory will cover all cases. Great economic historians like David Landes (1924–2013) have emphasised the importance of cultural specifics, like the invention of spectacles and treatment of women, in the rise of Europe to economic and military supremacy. Economic history gives us the stories of the British Industrial Revolution, of German, American, and Japanese catch-up, of the stagnation and rise of Asia. It offers no general theory of economic development, but historically rich accounts, which can direct policy fruitfully to problems in the present.

The neoclassical growth story tells us that a universal precondition for economic development is a secure set of property rights, so that owners of land and business can reap private rewards from socially beneficial improvements and innovations. On this theory, enclosure of the 'commons' in eighteenth-century England led, via the agricultural revolution, to the Industrial Revolution. Applying this 'general theory' in the 1990s, the first generation of post-communist reformers in Russia and eastern Europe auctioned off most state property at a stroke. The results varied with the histories and resource-profiles of the countries concerned, and the amount of foreign help they received. But in Russia the results were disastrous. The economy collapsed, most of the state property was 'stolen' by the Soviet managers of the state companies, creating a class of fabulously wealthy 'oligarchs', and autocracy returned as the only barrier against social disintegration. Economists with a sense of history warned against 'shock therapy', but in the heyday of neoliberal economics, no one listened.

✕

Since the absorption of modern economics into mainstream intellectual life in the eighteenth century, economics has played a part in reshaping the motives and actions of economic agents (including governments). Rational economic calculation, which may be inherent in human beings as they struggle to make ends meet, has far greater scope for expression than it did in the Middle Ages, when custom was paramount. So how human beings behaved in the past is not necessarily a secure guide to how they behave today. But equally how they behave today is not a secure guide to how they will behave tomorrow.

History teaches that economies are path-dependent. Their present is 'inherited' from the past. So understanding a community's history can help one estimate its economic possibilities. The present and the future are connected to the past by the continuity of society's institutions. Economic policy is still different in German-speaking countries from the Anglo-Saxon world or from that in Latin America, even though nowadays economic research is widely connected, globalised, and easily accessible across countries.

It's not surprising that there has been a revival of Keynesian economics, as we ask ourselves whether the lessons we learned from the Great Depression of the 1930s can be fruitfully applied to the Great Recession of 2008 and after. To argue, as many economists have recently done, that the path to recovery lies in cutting government spending, seems a signal case of historical amnesia. As George Santayana famously wrote, 'those who cannot remember the past are condemned to repeat it'.

12

ETHICS AND ECONOMICS

> The fundamental problem ... is to find a social system
> which is efficient economically *and* morally.

> John Maynard Keynes

'There are no economic ends, only economical and uneconomical means for achieving given ends ... Economics deals with ascertainable facts; ethics with values and obligations. The only way to associate them is by juxtaposition.' They are 'not at the same place of discourse.'[1] With these words Lionel Robbins expelled ethics from economics. Nobel Laureate George Stigler (1911–1991) had the same idea when he wrote that economists needed arithmetic, not ethics, to correct 'social mistakes'.[2]

The older generation of economists had puzzled over such topics as the rationality of ends, the ethics of self-interest, and the morality of means. However attention to such questions was increasingly considered a hindrance to proper analytic work. Alfred Marshall, professor of political economy at Cambridge, took economics out of the moral sciences curriculum in 1903, convinced that 'metaphysics' was putting good people off studying economics. Economics, as Robbins said, became concerned purely with efficiency of means.

For example, there are more and less efficient ways of fighting a war. Whether the war ought to be fought, and the morality of the means by which it is fought (for example, the morality of using torture), are matters on which the economist may have private views, but they should not tamper with the 'scientific' advice he tenders. Even if he chooses not to be personally associated with a war, or the methods of fighting it, this is an ethical judgment from outside economics. Within the discipline, there is no moral or immoral behaviour, only efficient and inefficient behaviour. At best, moral maxims may be serviceable as tools of efficiency: 'honesty is the best policy'.

Evidently Adam Smith was disturbed by the selfish connotations of self-interest and equipped his agents with the separate motive of 'sympathy', something which his successors dropped, as complicating the logic of their deductive systems. Marx was concerned with the justice of distribution. John Stuart Mill raised the question 'how much is enough?' for a good life.[3] The Robbins terrain is stripped of such extraneous 'moral' clutter. His economics presents us with self-interested individuals, denuded of social ties, but with infinitely varied wants, facing budget constraints which prevent them satisfying all their wants simultaneously. Therefore they have to economise. Economics is about the logic of such economising.

Whether the model is intended to describe how people actually behave or how they should behave is beside the point here. Either way no ethics is involved, only arithmetic. If people's desires shift from wanting good goods to wanting bad goods this is simply taken to be a shift in demand schedules. And all economics asks of means is that they be fit for the purpose intended. The ethical value of means or purpose is irrelevant to economics.

All of this represented a considerable reversal of earlier thinking about the economy. Scientific economics grew, together with capitalism, out of a collapsing medieval order. At the heart of medieval thought stood the question of value, of what is worthy or unworthy of admiration or esteem, more simply, what is good and what is bad. Economics was part of this enquiry. But it had one decisive advantage in discussing goods and bads, which is that the value of material goods could be made commensurable – their costs and benefits could be precisely stated on the single scale of money. So questions of value, for this class of goods, were from the start stated in terms of money prices. Even so, the prices of economic goods were supposed to reflect the place of these goods in the moral order, and were explained by reference to it.

What we find as economics matures is that its moral content is dropped. Discussion about the relationship of value to price is collapsed into value-free arithmetic. The idea of property as stewardship disappears. The morality of means was subsumed in efficiency, and the morality of ends was outsourced to religion and ethics. The question today is whether we possess an ethical discourse powerful enough to overcome the social mistakes of economists.

The just price

Value theory in economics has a joint empirical-moral pedigree. On the one side, it is an explanation of why things cost what they do. On the other side, it is a theory of what things should cost: the just price. This is the price that does justice to the efforts of producers and the needs of consumers. It was based on a moral code designed to prevent people exploiting each other. Just price doctrines went back to Aristotle, and were elaborated by the medieval schoolmen. They were said to have their basis in divine or natural law. The just price is a measure of a fair transaction.

In pre-modern economic thinking the 'just price' was roughly equated with the 'customary price'. The customary price was a ready-reckoner of what societies believed was fair dealing. However, with the great inflation of the sixteenth and seventeenth centuries, and the spread of international commerce, market prices became seriously detached from customary prices: which is a way of saying that the moral economy shrank relative to the business economy.

The labour theory of value was a secular application of just price doctrine. The classical economists – the French Physiocrats and Adam Smith and his followers – distinguished productive from unproductive labour. The labour theory of value was intended to isolate that part of price which wasn't value, but represented rent. Economic rent was a price that had no basis in real cost but was purely a free lunch for the owners of land and money. The classic medieval unjust price was usury – taking interest on loans. Why was it unjust? Because it was seen as making money from money.

Lending out money for which you had no use cost nothing and was therefore not entitled to a reward.

Adam Smith and David Ricardo both accepted labour effort as an explanation of long-run or normal prices, in contradiction to 'market prices' which fluctuated round them: that is, they distinguished between the 'natural' price (the price of labour effort) and the market price. Smith posed the famous 'diamond-water paradox': why were diamonds so expensive and water so cheap, when diamonds were useless and water vital for life? Smith found the answer in 'the difficulty and expense of getting them from the mine', from which he concluded that 'what every thing really costs to the man who wishes to possess it is the toil and trouble of acquiring it.'[4]

Following Smith, the simple labour theory of value developed complications. Surely the labour of the capitalist also deserved to be rewarded? Ricardo incorporated the reward to the capitalist in the labour theory of value by treating capital as stored-up labour. Capital comes into existence through the abstinence or 'saving' of the capitalist. The saving of the capitalist adds value to the 'painful exertions' of labour.

In Ricardo's hands, the labour theory of value became a cost of production theory. It has one root in the medieval idea of the 'just' price. But it also seeks to give a certain moral grandeur to self-interest by investing it with a particular virtue – the sacrifice of present for future consumption. Thus profit could be seen as the just reward for sacrifice.[5] Much later came the idea that profit is the reward for risk-taking, or enterprise.

Karl Marx had a different agenda. He adopted the labour theory of value, not to justify the profits of the capitalist class, but to remove the capitalist class from the value equation. The capitalist's profit has nothing to do with his 'abstention' from consumption, everything to do with his abstention from labour. It arises from the capitalist being able to extract 'surplus value' from the worker. The worker is paid, say, five hours' worth of goods for eight hours' worth of work. This difference constitutes the capitalist 'rent': unearned income, or in Marxist terms the exploitation of labour. The exploitation is made possible by the capitalist owning all the machines, leaving the worker with nothing to sell but his labour power. So it's a classic unjust bargain, with the worker having to accept whatever wage the capitalist offers him, on pain of starvation.[6]

The problem facing all cost of production theories was that the prices which goods fetched in rapidly expanding and increasingly deregulated markets had little relation to the hours of labour spent in producing them. The long-run, or normal or 'natural' price obstinately failed to emerge from the ever-spreading web of exchange relations. The price system lacked a moral anchor. A theory of value which couldn't explain actual price behaviour was rather obviously deficient, and from the 1870s the cost of production theory was swept away by a supply and demand theory, in which market prices were jointly determined by scarcity and consumer demand.

Adam Smith had explained the high price of diamonds by the expense of getting them from the mines to the market. But, as an astute critic, Richard Whately pointed out at the time, with a different example, pearls don't fetch a high price because men dive for them; men dive for them because they fetch a high price.[7] Smith recognised this to some extent, maintaining a double perspective where scarcity and desire, as well as the cost of production, influenced price.[8]

The solution to the diamond-water paradox came in two bites known as the marginalist revolution. The first was the elimination of any distinction between needs and wants. Both were subsumed in the idea of subjective utility. Different goods gave people different intensities of pleasure; and their prices reflected the degree of pleasure, or utility, they afforded, and their relative scarcity. In ordinary language, what people pay for something depends on how much they want it and how scarce it is. People may want something but it has no price unless it is scarce. Water is normally a free good: it acquires a price in the desert; air is a free good if one is not suffocating.

The second step in the marginalist revolution was to say that prices are determined at the margin. It was Jevons who united the concept of subjective utility with the differential calculus: it was not total pleasure that needs to be measured, but the pleasure of having a little more. Utility is maximised when the pleasure of having a little more is equalised across alternative uses. Jevons predicted that numerical determination of the laws of utility would turn economics into a science on a par with the natural sciences.[9]

Marginalism knocked out the cost of production explanation of prices. Labour could not be regarded as the source of value, because the labour spent on producing a commodity was 'gone and lost forever'.[10] Wages were the effect not the cause of the value of the product; greater effort could theoretically increase supply, but would not do so unless the force of desire brought it forth.

Marginalism was a scientific, as well as political, triumph. It explained (or explained away) many puzzles in the older value theory, such as the high price of rare paintings – a prime example of labour 'gone and lost forever' – and it knocked away the foundations of Marxist exploitation theory. I leave to one side its own 'scientific' problems, such as its inability to measure intensities of pleasure.[11] More serious in the context of our discussion was the loss of the moral sense of value. Value depends entirely on individual anticipations of pleasure from goods in short supply. There is no appeal beyond the market price. Market prices can only be unjust if market competition is restricted by monopoly. The normative goal of mainstream economic policy follows: to make markets fully competitive.

The theory of subjective value marked a paradigm shift in method. So long as value was expounded in terms of costs, the subject matter of economics was seen as something social, and price phenomena purely a market relationship. Once it was realised that these market phenomena resulted from individual choice and that the very social phenomena by which they were explained were the reflex of individual choice, the social dimension of economics fell away. Mathematical economics formalised this shift.

Economics could not entirely shed its intellectual legacy. Its continued commitment to 'equilibrium' or 'natural' price models of economic life is unacknowledged homage to its earlier entanglement with the just price theory. The word 'natural' still runs through economics: concepts like the 'natural' rate of unemployment, the 'natural' rate of interest, are ghosts of earlier real-cost theories of value. But ghosts only: value has become whatever you can extract from the other fellow.

Property as stewardship

That private property is the moral Achilles heel of the capitalist system was recognised by Locke nearly 400 years ago. The medieval doctrine was that wealth must be put to reasonable use. In his *Two Treatises of Government* (1764 [1689]), Locke says that everyone has a natural right to property in his own labour, that is, to such fruits of the earth as his own labour brings forth. How can this be reconciled with the fact that most land is owned by a minority of proprietors? Locke argued that unequal property was the deserved reward of superior effort. Much later came the flowering of the utilitarian argument that inequality increases productivity. This was the core belief of the supply-side economics of Reagan and Thatcher.

Locke kept alive the connection to older concepts of just property holdings, by arguing that owners who left their land or capital idle should be dispossessed of it, since 'nothing was made by God for man to spoil or destroy'.[12] To own property was to hold it in trust for the general good. Good landlords were stewards. Thus private ownership, if used for the general good, need not abrogate people's 'natural' right to property in their own labour.

In the Industrial Age workers claimed a 'right to work' as an equivalent to a right to property ownership. Neoclassical economics evaded this claim by assuming full employment. Sufficiently flexible labour markets would guarantee everyone who wanted it a job. Unemployment was assumed to be a choice for leisure, carrying with it no right to income.

Workers also claimed a fair share of the surplus. Marx, as we have seen, denied this was possible under capitalism. Left-leaning neoclassical economists like Arthur Pigou (1877–1959) tried to establish a scientific case for income redistribution. The diminishing marginal utility of money to its possessor, Pigou argued, justified transferring money from the rich to the poor.[13] This effort foundered when Robbins pointed out the impossibility of measuring intensities of satisfaction (1938). It became accepted doctrine that no social welfare function could be derived from interpersonal comparisons of utility.

While heterodox economists insisted that the absence of a social welfare function didn't imply abandoning the goal of redistribution, mainstream economics simply gave up on the question of the justice of distribution.[14] Instead, proofs were supplied that in a perfectly competitive market all the factors of production received their marginal products. That took distribution off the economic, though not the political, agenda. In fact, the question of distribution dominated the political agenda for most of the twentieth century. It was argued by social democrats that citizenship entailed state responsibility for ensuring sufficient equality of material conditions for the exercise of democracy to be meaningful. Today, neoclassical economists and pessimistic sociologists find common cause in attacking the welfare state; to the former it undermines the incentive to work, to the latter it 'demoralises' society.

At present the question of the justice of property rights is much more discussed by philosophers than by economists. For example, John Rawls's (1921–2002) principle that inequality is justified to the extent that it improves the position of the least well-off owes something to Locke's idea that property ownership requires a moral justification. Outside mainstream economics there has been a revival of interest in the question of the moral responsibilities of ownership. Should companies have moral responsibilities in addition to their legal responsibility to maximise shareholder value? Ideas of 'corporate social responsibility' and 'stakeholder' capitalism are fruits of such discussion, though 'corporate social responsibility' is largely big business propaganda. There have been studies showing that firms which take seriously their responsibilities to their employees, suppliers, and neighbourhoods achieve better 'bottom lines' than companies which attend only to the interests of their owners and senior managers. But the concept of property as 'stewardship' has hardly an echo in mainstream economics, because it challenges not just the narrow concept of property rights but the deeply ingrained idea that markets in land, capital, and labour are, or can be made, perfectly 'just', in the sense of all producers being paid what their products are worth to the consumer.[15]

The moral debate is not one-sided. There is of course an efficiency argument for well-specified and legally enforceable property rights. Further, the insistence that property must be used for the public benefit undermines the classical liberal defence of private property as a barrier to arbitrary state confiscation. There is also a liberal argument for the state not interfering in the voluntary contracts made by employers and workers. Students of economics should not ignore such arguments. What one asks of them is that they be conscious of the moral – and political – choices implied by their analytic choices.

The costs of progress

A third aspect of the disappearance of morality from economics is found in the disappearance of the idea that progress has serious costs. Humans have always destroyed to build better, revolutions and wars being the main examples. Economic change is milder in method, but no less disruptive in effect. The shift from a static to dynamic economy in the nineteenth century was accompanied by furious denunciation of its moral cost, by no one more eloquently than Marx and Engels in the *Communist Manifesto*: 'Constant revolutionising of production, uninterrupted disturbance of all social conditions, everlasting uncertainty and agitation ... All fixed, fast frozen relations are swept away ... All that is solid melts into air.'

Duncan Foley has written: 'The moral fallacy of [Adam] Smith's position is that it urges us to accept direct and concrete evil in order that indirect and abstract good may come of it.'[16] He raises a question which shouldn't be evaded: does the end justify the means? Mainstream economics accepts that progress has a price, but nearly all economists will say that the price is worth paying: the future will be better than the past. If the critic points out the wrenching costs of continuous adjustment to new conditions, the economist will invite us to consider how much better most people live today than they did before the Industrial Revolution.

In the nineteenth century James Mill put the case in a way that would not seem out of place now: 'The free enterprise system has its hardships, but it is the price we pay for progress and the general good.'[17] His son, John Stuart Mill, unable so confidently to excuse the sufferings of others, added the proviso that this suffering would surely be temporary: as wealth advanced, suffering would ease. By contrast, Herbert Spencer took a tough social Darwinist stance: the sufferings of the poor were the mechanism through which society thrived. Only by rewarding the rich and punishing the poor would it continue do so.

Keynes agreed with the Mills. Capitalism's psychological main-spring, love of money, is ethically bad, but it is the means to the good. By creating abundance it will enable us 'to live wisely and agreeably and well'.[18] Capitalism was a passing phase, a view Keynes shared with Marx. Most economists cannot envisage a post-capitalist era, because they see scarcity as a permanent condition: the Robbins def-inition sets no limit to human wants. Scarcity continues to demand arithmetical – not moral – solutions. Further, capitalism has showed itself superior to communism as a growth engine, because central planning couldn't do the necessary social arithmetic – an argument we owe to Hayek (1937).

Then there was Joseph Schumpeter, whose views could be sum-marised as 'never let a recession go to waste'. He was the apostle of wealth-creation through 'creative destruction'. Progress was not a smooth evolutionary process but a chaotic one, in which mori-bund giants are constantly being replaced by agile upstarts through a succession of crises. This is a concept that modern-day Silicon Valley has embraced under the softer label of 'disruptive innova-tion'. For Schumpeter creative destruction is the way the capitalist system works. He would have said that it creates more 'value' than it destroys. The same reply is given by techno-enthusiasts. To be sure, they say, automation will destroy many existing jobs and ways of life, but in the long run all will benefit.

The 'costs of progress' literature was all about the costs to the current generation. It was assumed that future generations would benefit. The thought that future generations would pay the price of our profligate pursuit of growth was absent. Only recently has it started to be recognised that we are benefiting today at the expense of our children and grandchildren.

You will not find any serious discussion of the moral cost of progress in standard economic textbooks. The analytic language itself neutralises the enquiry: the costs of progress are segregated into a corner called 'the short run' or 'transition'; efficient markets and technological progress will ensure they are temporary. Economists with a more generous social imagination have argued that the 'compensation principle' was invented precisely to reduce the cost of progress. Provided the gainers can compensate the losers, markets will be 'Pareto efficient'. This assumes, wrongly, that gains and losses can be measured on a single money scale. It also abstracts from the problem of the politics needed to bring about the compensation in practice.

With rare exceptions, all those who concede that economic progress has a price tag beg the question of what economic growth is for. Is it to make us or our descendants richer, happier, or better? And what is the connection between these?

The 'growth of the cake [became] the object of true religion' (Keynes)

The defensible purpose of economics is not to enable people to satisfy their wants, but to help bring about the end of absolute poverty and disease. Once it has achieved that, it has done its main work. Philosophers, sociologists, historians, psychologists will have increasingly more to say as the non-measurable causes of ill-being and well-being move to the centre of the story. Economists will still be useful, because scarcities – not generalised scarcity – will still persist, requiring efficient allocation, especially of time.

This is certainly what Keynes thought. In the ironic summary quoted above, he claimed that the means – growth of the cake – had pre-empted the ethical question: what is economic growth for? The answer which most of us would give, on reflection, is to enable people to lead better lives. Economists are in tune with popular feeling in seeing material adequacy as necessary for 'well-being'.

But what is 'well-being'? A subjective state of mind or an objective state of affairs?

If we follow Lionel Robbins, individuals experience well-being when their needs are satisfied, as when their stomachs are full. This can be called an objective state of well-being. But the wants of the imagination are relative, so one cannot ever say how much is needed for the state of well-being. Scarcity will always exist. As long as people want more than they've got, economics has no purpose other than to show them how to get the cake to grow most efficiently. This is its only religion. Beyond this it has no gospel to preach.

We can identify three answers to the 'growth of the cake' question. The first is that the cake just needs to grow without end, since people are permanently dissatisfied with what they have. This dissatisfaction is independent of the level of wealth already achieved, or of income inequalities. Indeed, the smaller the income gaps between different sections of the population, the larger the impact of relative wants is likely to be, as envy will be more rampant, and competition for status more intense. The impossibility of satisfying relative wants is the bedrock of the scarcity perspective.

The second, left-wing, position holds the argument that with greater income equality the cake needs to grow less fast. People are dissatisfied with the *share* of the cake they are getting. What appears as insatiability is really the result of inequality. It is not so much the growth of the cake as its more equal division that is needed, though this may well be easier to achieve if the cake is growing at the same time. In Galbraith's language, what we need is less private and more public affluence. Perhaps the economy would not have to grow so fast if incomes were more equal and public services improved; perhaps it would not need to grow at all in rich countries. This introduces an explicit moral argument. It roots the feeling of dissatisfaction not in individual psychology (e.g. envy) but in the social demand for fairness.

A third, more recent, argument emphasising the long-term costs to the planet, and therefore to future generations, of our relentless pursuit of 'more and more', has led to demands for 'de-growth'.

However, these are differences within the circle of material adequacy; they do not discuss what the requisites are for. Thus we justify money spent on education and health as *means* to well-being, rather than treating them as part of well-being, and so intrinsically valuable. Since everyone has their own idea of well-being, economics must confine itself solely to means, and assume that people are efficient at converting physical resources into well-being. And so, economics stops at the frontier of gross national product (GNP) or GNP per head: we can at least measure that.

There have been fragmentary attempts to get policy to think beyond the growth of the cake. One inspiration comes from technical criticisms of what gross national product fails to measure. It is the sum of the annual market value of all final goods and services. But it excludes uncosted goods like volunteering, housework, and child-rearing and includes the costs of fighting crime, pollution, drug addiction, resource depletion, and so on. Even the father of national income statistics, Simon Kuznets, argued that 'the welfare of a nation can scarcely be inferred from a measure of national income'.[19]

Some economists have suggested making 'happiness' rather than GNP the goal of policy. Everyone can agree, surely, that making people happier, in the sense of improving their psychological well-being, is a laudable goal. This approach draws on surveys which show that happiness is not equated with quantity of income, a phenomenon known as the 'Easterlin Paradox'. The economist Richard Easterlin (b.1926) found that beyond a certain point, scales of reported happiness (e.g. 1 to 5) do not grow in line with the growth of GNP. They move together as income grows up to a certain point, and then happiness stays fixed as income continues to rise.[20]

This suggests that rather than pursuing income growth, policy should aim for happiness growth. This means enquiring into the causes which make people happy and unhappy, of which money is only one.[21] Correlating subjective measures of happiness and unhappiness with objective conditions is the name of the game. Surveys show what things make people happier: more time with family and friends, satisfying jobs, income security, and so on. Policy should seek to establish these objective correlates of happiness. It is the conception of happiness itself that is so feeble. For most researchers it means nothing more than psychological well-being or a pleasant sense of mind. Gurus preaching happiness, schools offering happiness courses, proliferate. British prime minister David Cameron, who took power in the aftermath of the 2008 crash, said he would measure the 'well-being' of the United Kingdom's citizens every three months, and 'hold himself accountable for the success or failure of his policies by changes in well-being'.[22] Little more was heard of this initiative. It seemed almost obscene to suggest measuring well-being while the economy was plunging.

At first blush, making happiness a goal of policy is an improvement on crude national income. It promises a way of getting off (or at least slowing down) the growth treadmill and concentrating on achieving instead something we can all agree is good.

But there is a terrible trap, even if we leave aside the thorny issue of how to measure happiness robustly. If happiness is taken to mean a permanently agreeable state of mind, it might be maximised by a free distribution of pleasure-enhancing drugs, leaving it to robots to produce the goods needed for survival, a kind of perpetual *dolce vita* or land of lotus eaters. This would be, literally, an 'opiate of the people'. Of course, happiness economists do not advocate this, though significantly the economist Richard Layard (b.1934) does include the use of both medical and recreational drugs in his happiness agenda.[23] They want policy to be directed to the conditions which make people less miserable, and believe these conditions can be discovered.

Less misery should certainly be taken seriously as an intermediate ethical goal, as making it possible for people to lead better lives. But happiness itself should not be taken as an end to be strived for. It is a result of living a good life, as the ancient Greeks recognised, not a separate goal, and is often the result of 'happenstance'.[24]

The economist Amartya Sen offers an argument for another set of measures. Sen, like Marshall, thinks that the aim of policy should be to increase 'well-being'. But well-being cannot be understood purely through material consumption. Instead, it is made up of multiple, overlapping 'capabilities' that cannot be reduced to each other, including material welfare, but also non-economic dimensions such as the freedom to make one's own plan. Consequently, economic development should be understood as expanding capabilities, and poverty should be understood as a deprivation of capabilities.[25] Making 'capability' the goal of policy avoids the trap of trying to define an ultimate goal. But it raises, and fails to answer, the question of 'capability for what?' Why should we care whether individuals are capable of being healthy or educated, and so forth? Surely what matters is that they are *actually* healthy and educated. But taking a public stance on what it means to be healthy and educated would be dictatorial. 'Capability' preserves the autonomy of individual choice.[26]

Sen realised that an alternative index was needed, so, with Mahbub ul Haq and others, he produced the Human Development Index, which includes indicators of a country's income, education, and health. Other indices include the OECD's Better Life Index, which contains eleven components, the King of Bhutan's 'Gross National Happiness' goal and the OPHI and UNDP's multidimensional poverty index.[27] The International Labour Organization (ILO) says that social justice – not growth – should be the goal, but acknowledges that there is 'no objective notion of social justice'. The ecological economist Herman Daly (b.1938) has suggested an index of 'sustainable development', which takes account of environmental degradation and depreciation of natural capital. Developed in 1989, Daly's three rules are: 1. Sustainable use of renewable resources, meaning that the pace of their depletion should not be faster than the rate at which they can regenerate. 2. Sustainable use of non-renewable resources, meaning that the pace of their depletion should not exceed the rate at which substitutes can be put in place. 3. Sustainable rate of pollution and waste, meaning that its growth should not be faster than the pace at which natural systems can absorb them, recycle them, or render them harmless.

All such hybrid indices are technically flawed. The first flaw is trying to measure non-measurables, like judging quality of social life by counting up quantity of friends. The second lies in the attempt to reduce incommensurable quantities to a single number, thus absolving policy-makers from making ethical choices.

As persuasive as these critiques of GNP are, the enduring factor in its popularity has been its simplicity: a single number with a clear meaning. A 'dashboard' approach that tries to look at everything can be immensely complicated: how is one supposed to compare an array of statistics on health, education, and so on to see which country is doing best at a glance?

How can ethics help economics?

The problem of reinserting ethics into economics, of planting within economic thinking itself an ethical foundation, is that contemporary moral theory is on stand-by. Over much of the western world, religion and custom have collapsed as the glue of a common morality. Systems of secular ethics are fragments of older religious beliefs, which lack the authority of divine law. Further, 'business' and 'business calculation' has become a much more important part of human activity, with business 'ethics' amounting to little more than the avoidance of fraud. Thus agreement on what constitutes moral behaviour is undermined from both sides: from the decline of religion and the spread of business values. As a result, ethics has become a matter of individual calculation. Individuals disagree on what is good. To try to revive a common idea of the good life, when its natural foundations in social life have been so eroded, smacks of paternalism, or worse, dictatorship. The default position is to produce and consume ever more material goods. Economics is the science that enables you to do this most efficiently. We are where we are.

On all the points at which economics might meet ethics, we find a weakness in ethics. Contemporary economics and contemporary ethics share the same individualist outlook. The main thrust of the ethical criticism of contemporary capitalism is that its power structure allows too few people the opportunity for making good choices. Justice in distribution may be seen as a form of empowerment. But the choices themselves should be left to suitably empowered individuals. Economics and ethics speak the same language of methodological individualism.

Keynes found a moral basis for economics in the prospect for the good life which economic (and especially technological) progress opened up. He had a very clear conception of what the good life was, and he thought it was grounded in universal moral intuitions. But he was referring back to the existence of a moral community, which in his youth was still taken for granted. Today we have small moral communities, which pursue their own visions of the good. But there is no moral consensus about what is good.

The collapse of an ethics of ends has transferred the weight of contemporary ethical argument to the morality of means, what we may call *procedural ethics*. The question of what constitutes a just distribution of income and life-chances has been vigorously debated among political philosophers, with the social democrat John Rawls (see above, p. 168) and the conservative Robert Nozick (1938–2002) being the most frequently cited. 'Natural' rights have morphed into 'human' rights. People have a 'right' not to be discriminated against on grounds of race, gender, and age. Reaching the conclusion by different routes, utilitarian and rights philosophies can agree that harm is bad. Preventing harm is evidently a minimalist moral programme; we can hope to agree on what is bad even though we can't agree on what is good.

Harm prevention builds on the idea that individuals should be free to pursue their own plans, on condition these do not harm others. For example, health and safety regulations are designed to prevent producers of goods and services harming their users; retailers are expected to provide honest information about their products; the world-wide web is increasingly subject to regulation to prevent the spread of harmful, abusive, and hateful material. The idea of preventing harm has been extended to robots. The first of three laws of robotics enunciated by biochemist and writer Isaac Asimov (1920–1992) is that 'a robot may not injure a human being or, through inaction, allow a human being to come to harm'.

Two branches of economics, environmental and ecological, have applied the harm principle to the survival of the human species. Given the threat posed by man-made climate change, economic activity must be made consistent with human survival. This is an entry point for the revival of the idea of stewardship. The current 'owners' of the planet have a duty to future owners to preserve the value of their inheritance. Economists, typically, work out what this duty will cost them.

One branch, 'environmental economics', argues that the environment is an important economic resource, and environmental damage represents a cost that is not borne by those who have caused it. This creates a problem of moral hazard, where companies can create pollution and leave others (in this case, future generations) to deal with the problems. This means that the costs of polluting the planet must be 'priced in' through carbon taxes.

The second, more radical approach is 'ecological economics'. This accepts the idea of protecting the environment, but rejects the claim that all aspects of environmental degradation can be correctly priced. The important thing is for people to understand how they fit into the global ecosystem, how economic activities are damaging this ecosystem, and how they might need to change to preserve it, a question first posed by the Club of Rome's classic *The Limits to Growth*.[28] Georgescu-Roegen went so far as to argue that the only way of preventing the entropy of the planet was through policies of 'de-growth'.

An important development of this line of argument is Kate Raworth's (b.1970) 'doughnut economics', which challenges economics to find a balance between the 'social foundation' and 'ecological ceiling'.[29] Economic activity must be set within the bounds of ecological possibility.

The diagram shows that ecological economics has the same imprecision in its core idea that we encountered in the economics of 'well-being'. What exactly does protecting the ecosystem entail? It lists a bunch of bad things outside the circle and good things inside it. While we may hope to measure the value of our own activities in terms of GNP, there is no accurate way of measuring the impact of GNP on the ecosystem. 'Climate change', which itself poses big measurement problems, is just one of the nine possible tears in the

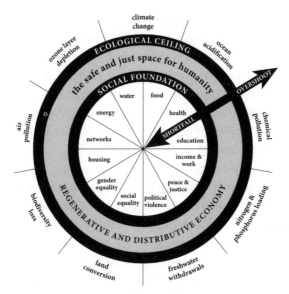

7. Raworth's Doughnut.

ecosystem's envelope. So 'doughnut economics' is a blanket term for a whole range of worthy goals like 'gender equality' and 'networks' which have no obvious connection with protecting the ecosystem. Probably its deepest appeal is to passionate haters of greed and luxury. Whether it is compatible with the western model of political and economic liberty is moot.[30]

Yet there is clearly a better ethical argument available, which is that to live in harmony with nature, and therefore within the bounds set by it, is part of the good life. This is irrespective of any measurably deleterious consequences to nature of our bad habits. But, sadly, such an argument depends on sufficient agreement on what constitutes the good life, which is lacking. So we fall back on pseudo-science and the hair shirt to rally support for the cause.[31]

There are two genuine ways of getting ethics back into economics. The first is to look more deeply into the 'mind of the horse' (see p. 81 on '*Homo economicus* in action'). This would show that although moral variety certainly exists it is less extensive than is generally supposed. It would reveal broad agreement on what might be called 'basic goods'. Health, respect, security, relationships of trust and love are recognised everywhere as part of a good human life; their absence is regarded everywhere as a misfortune. We have, then, the materials for a universal enquiry into the meaning of the good life, transcending time and place. We are not doomed to an endless clash of values, mediated only by the market, politics, and the law.

A second approach is that of the philosopher Michael Sandel. His starting point is that public discussion has been emptied of moral meaning by fear of paternalism. What he offers is not paternalism, but a public debate on the morality of the market. Should you be able to buy everything or are there some goods 'beyond price'? What are the consequences of buying a fast track in a queue? Of outsourcing wars and prisons to private contractors? Of offering cash rewards for good exam results? Of converting a market economy, which is a tool, into a market society in which money governs access to essential goods, and all social relations are squeezed into a cash nexus? His hope is that by raising such questions, we may recover the older idea of a common good.[32]

The Robbins programme of expelling ethics from economics so as to make it more 'scientific' was always a forlorn hope. It breaks down on the weakness of economics as a science. Given the near-impossibility of establishing empirically robust laws of human behaviour, its 'scientific core' has come to consist of logical/ mathematical deductions from tight, unrealistic priors. It cannot escape what Keynes called 'introspection' and 'judgments of value'; but it buries them in a logico-deductivist methodology. This makes large parts of economics useless as a picture of the world, and therefore seriously misleading as a guide of policy. Nevertheless, there is reason to doubt whether the moral resources which still exist in western societies are powerful enough to correct the social mistakes of economists.

13

RETREAT FROM OMNISCIENCE

> In the greater part of our concernment, God has afforded
> only the Twilight . . . of Probability, suitable, I presume, to
> the state of Mediocrity and Probationership He has been
> pleased to place us in here.
>
> John Locke, *An Essay Concerning*
> *Human Understanding*

Mainstream economics gets human behaviour wrong in two ways. It endows humans with excessive *power* to calculate; and ascribes to them an excessive *desire* to calculate. It ignores, that is, uncertainty and people's attachment to each other. These failures are rooted in a method of analysis whose major premise is individual maximisation. As Keynes well put it, the error of economics lies not in its logical inconsistency, but in the 'lack of . . . generality in its premises'.[1] There is a large gap between the account economics gives of human behaviour and behaviour as it is actually exhibited. This gap it hopes to close not by broadening its own premises, but by narrowing what it means to be human to the simple point of calculation, and empowering calculation by big data and accelerated computing power. The result is a growing disjunction between what economists think and what many people feel, which expresses itself in an explosion of social discontent. Mainstream economists have not looked deeply enough into the 'mind of the horse'.

In what follows I will try to draw together the book's two main threads of argument, those concerned with the epistemology of economics, and those concerned with its ontology.

Epistemology: risk and uncertainty

The first issue is about how much we do, or can, know about the future. Economics looks into people's minds and discovers utility maximisation. This then becomes the basis of its own theorising. A much more modest, and accurate, claim would be that people do the best they can under the circumstances. These circumstances include uncertainty.

We owe the distinction between risk and uncertainty to both Frank Knight (1885–1972) and John Maynard Keynes. 'Risk' applies to situations when the chance of a possible event is quantifiable; 'uncertainty' implies a lack of any quantifiable knowledge of the chance. (Equivalently, risk refers to all outcomes that can be insured against, uncertainty to those which cannot.) Mainstream economists do not recognise this distinction. They believe that individuals can accurately calculate the odds of any action turning out one way or the other. This is because they treat the economy as a closed system, like a game of draughts. The financial system is explicitly theorised this way by Chicago economists: the risks of all assets are said to be 'correctly priced on average'. The collapse of 2007–2008 was therefore impossible. Even economists who reject the full rigour of the Chicago school are professionally constrained to use the language of risk whenever they talk about forward-looking choices. People have 'risk profiles'; interest rates measure 'appetite for risk'; government bonds are 'risk-free' (except if they are Greek!), asset prices measure risk aversion and rational expectation and so on. Yet turn to the financial press, and we learn that the one thing businesses can't stand is 'uncertainty', that they are always calling on governments to 'end uncertainty' about this or that. Inflation-targeting was devised to 'end uncertainty' about the future course of prices. What on earth is going on?

The reason why 'Knightian uncertainty' has proved more acceptable to the profession than 'Keynesian uncertainty' is that Knight confined it to 'disequilibrium' situations, whereas for Keynes uncertainty determines the nature of the equilibrium itself. In his book *Risk, Uncertainty and Profit* (1921), Knight explains profit as a reward for entrepreneurship, or innovating a new product, and by definition there can be no probabilities attached to the success or failure of an innovation, because an innovation is a new event. So profit is a reward for a successful venture into the unknown. Such rewards of enterprise are to be distinguished from the 'normal' returns to capital; profit is a temporary monopoly phenomenon which will be competed away as the innovation is generally adopted. Economists are just about prepared to admit uncertainty on those terms. For Keynes, uncertainty contaminates the investment demand schedule as a whole, and not just enterprise. There is no 'normal' rate of return: there is simply an expected rate of return, governed by uncertainty.

There are two further reasons for the failure of Keynesian uncertainty to grip the mainstream. First, Keynes himself called his discussion of uncertainty in Chapter 13 of the *General Theory* a 'digression', and standard interpretations of the theory take him at his word. Second, his fragmentary account failed to distinguish clearly between those parts of an economic system which could be considered risky and those which were inescapably uncertain. This is why post-Keynesian attempts, like those of George Shackle (1903–1992), Hyman Minsky (1919–1996), and Paul Davidson (b.1930), to ground economics in epistemological uncertainty have made so little headway.

However, Keynes bequeathed another 'general theory', which does deserve serious consideration as a foundation for a reformed economics. This is his theory of probability, offered in his *Treatise on Probability*, a neglected masterpiece conceived before Keynes thought of himself as an economist, in which he expounds what Rod O'Donnell calls 'a general theory of rational belief and action'.[2] It was not published until 1921, the same year as Knight's *Risk, Uncertainty and Profit*, but the germ of the idea dates back to 1904, when Keynes was a student at Cambridge University.

Keynes, too, looked into the 'mind of the horse', but he didn't see maximisation, rather an attempt to behave reasonably under different degrees of certainty. His key move was to distinguish rational belief (or expectation) from true belief. Standard rational expectation theory identifies the two, because to have a rational expectation of an event is to have accurate knowledge of its probability.

Keynes claimed it was rational to believe that something would probably happen on the basis of the evidence supporting it, but that the evidence might be too sparse to deliver a numerical probability that it would happen.

Keynes recognised three classes of probability in descending order of certainty: a small class of cardinal probabilities, a much larger class of ordinal probabilities, and a third class to which no probability can be attached.

Cardinal probabilities are ratios, expressed as fractions. They are either known *a priori* (mathematically) or as a result of likeness to previous events. For example, if one smoker out of ten has died of lung cancer, the probability of smokers dying from cancer is 10 per cent. This second set of numerical probabilities is the standard domain of risk as recognised by actuaries: for example, all fire insurance premia are based on the number of houses which have burnt down in a district over a period of time relative to the total number of houses in it. At the opposite extreme is uncertainty, as both Keynes and Knight define it, but which the mainstream denies: a situation where we have no scientific basis for calculating a ratio. However, in between lie Keynes's 'orders of magnitude' which are orders of likelihood – 'more or less likely' – not exact ratios: we may say that one probability is greater than another, without knowing how much greater. He sums up as follows: 'The magnitudes of some pairs of probabilities we shall be able to compare numerically, others in respect of more and less only, and others not at all.' Keynes believed that it is in this middle ground of ordinal ranking that most of our rational choices have to be made.[3]

In the neoclassical epistemology, by contrast, all probabilities have numbers. They start off as odds you would give on, say, a horse winning a race. This requires no knowledge of past performance of the horse: rationality requires only that your bets should be internally consistent, such that nobody can construct a 'Dutch book' against you.[4] Subjective beliefs are transformed into objective probabilities by applying Bayes' theorem, a rule for updating subjective probabilities in the face of evidence.[5] If one assumes, as hardline rational expectation theorists do, that agents are fully equipped with up-to-date knowledge of the likelihood of any future event, then they are in a position accurately to price risks.

Keynes's 'general theory' of rationality is a big improvement on the neoclassical theory. It avoids the trap of calling behaviour 'irrational' where it does not conform to the neoclassical standard of rationality. It offers a way of distinguishing between closed, partly closed, and open systems. It challenges economics to think about human behaviour under varying conditions of knowledge, and not take the easy mathematical route to prediction. In doing so, it points the way to a unified social science methodology.

Ontology: what exists

The project of improving how to do economics cannot rely on a return to Keynes. Keynes's chief failing is an underdeveloped ontology – one which lacks a genuine sociological or historical perspective. He recognises that 'the atomic hypothesis which has worked so splendidly in physics breaks down in psychics', and gives examples like the 'fallacy of composition' and the 'paradox of thrift'. But he leaves it there.[6]

So an improved ontology – the study of what exists and of the basic constitution and nature of social phenomena – should be the second pillar of a reformed economics. The orthodox map of reality is peopled only with individuals; to the extent that they are recognised at all, groups and institutions exist only as instruments, tools like technology. This 'methodological individualist' approach cuts economics off from understanding a large part of human behaviour, as a consequence of which it often gives faulty advice. It fails to understand the hold of religious national and group loyalties, attachments, identities – all that Weber calls 'communal' associations – and the extent to which these modify its picture of the maximising individual; it fails to understand the power of self-understanding and the way social positions shape self-understanding; it fails to understand the role of ideas, power, technology in shaping choices, including its own; it fails to understand the historical contingency of some of its universal doctrines; and it is indifferent to its own history.

A more accurate map of social reality would feature at least three entities with 'agency': individuals, governments, and 'corporations', linked together through an intricate network of relationships. The meaning of the first two is clear enough: by 'corporations' I mean all those groups intermediate between the individual and the state which provide valued services to individuals, and to whom individuals relate: local governments, churches, universities, voluntary associations, firms, trade unions, banking systems, digital systems, social movements, and many others. A structure in which public goods (and bads) are provided by private bodies for reasons of prestige or duty or profit – as has been the case throughout history – cannot be fitted into a binary system of state and markets. One might think of the economy as a 'mesoeconomic' system, with the state administration at the top, the individual at the bottom, and a variety of intermediate institutions in between; the whole complex contributing to economic outputs. In the international system, the national state is itself an intermediate institution between the individual and supranational organisations.

The importance of structures is that they affect individual motives and thus shape individual behaviour. It's not behaviour *of* groups, but behaviour *in* groups which we should try to understand. Behaviour in groups cannot be understood as the outcome of individual calculations of self-interest, however hard the New Institutionalists try. Love, fear, courage, loyalty, greed, treachery, worship, and many other traits humans regularly display and admire or condemn can only be understood in a group context.

Proper understanding of both the roots and the logic of collective action leads us far from the neoclassical path. Cooperation did not start with the realisation that it could reduce transaction costs. Economists might say that this is just a precise way of talking about the costs of individual action. And there are such reasons for cooperation. But these do not lead to any deep understanding of sociability.

The weakness of the neoclassical perception is seen in the standard account of the origins of trade. In Paul Samuelson's words: 'A great debt of gratitude is owed to the first two ape-men who suddenly perceived that each could be made better off by giving up some of one good in exchange for some of another."[7] Most economists have favoured the bartering savage story because it leaves out society. The point is, though, that in order to enter into such transactions you have to be a social animal to start with, as Durkheim pointed out, though indeed a uniquely inventive one. Individuals don't voluntarily *choose* to be social; they are destined to be both social and socially inventive. Relative social instability is thereby built into the human condition. That is why it is impossible to freeze the frame, except temporarily and locally.

We are left with a conundrum which is hard to resolve. When economists 'look into the mind of a horse' do they really see what is there, or only the sermons they have already planted in it? In other words, is economics descriptive or prescriptive? This book suggests that it is intended to be both. Insofar as it is descriptive it is plainly inadequate; but is it not possible that description may, over time, come to resemble prescription? That people may actually behave more and more as economists tell them they do behave? This would be an ironic inversion of Bayes' theorem, with the objective reality coming increasingly to resemble the subjective bets economists place on humankind. To transform human nature, not just to describe it, has always been the dream of social engineers, as today it is that of the techno-utopians. It is the foundation of the doctrine of progress. But how far can it, or should it, be pressed, before humans cease to exist in a recognisable form? And is there something irreducibly human which will resist the ambitions of the engineers of the soul?

A better map

The two main problems we have identified in this book are related: insufficient generality of premises (epistemology) and lack of institutional mapping (ontology). We need a science which is more modest in its epistemology and richer in its ontology.

The parable of the blind men and the elephant (see above, p. 6) can be improved by constructing the following grid. On the vertical axis we plot ontology – the theory of what exists; on the horizontal axis, epistemology – the way true beliefs are generated.

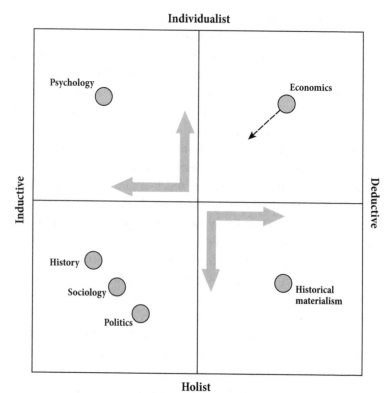

8. Different Approaches to Understanding.

Economics mainly occupies the top right-hand quadrant; sociology, politics, and history occupy the bottom left-hand one; psychology, the top left-hand quadrant. This leaves the bottom right-hand quadrant to historical materialism (Marxism). The argument of this book is that economics should move in the direction pointed to by the arrow, with less tight priors and looser deduction. It should be content, that is, with a logic of partial, rather than full, predictability.

The further task is to link ontology and epistemology in a broader understanding, in which the economy is seen not as a specialised activity, with its own logic of behaviour, but as an aspect of human life and human striving. Polanyi expressed this idea in the view of the market economy as an embedded system.

The standard objection to broadening the scope of economic analysis in the way I have suggested is that it will make the subject too vague to be useful. This is Professor Krugman's view. He gives two reasons: first, thinkers, however eloquent, who adopt a 'discursive, non-mathematical style' will not be listened to by other economists; second, that 'controlled, silly models' are the only way to get at useful truths. The first is simply a statement of current economic fashion; the second deserves more consideration. My argument is that the 'controlled, silly models' destroy old knowledge as much as they create new knowledge. This is because anything which can't be modelled in tight, silly ways is left out of the account. One can airily write off the destruction as the price of progress. But the resulting deficit in understanding may easily produce bad policy. In Krugman's own examples, the fact that economists couldn't model increasing returns to scale or oligopolistic competition till the 1970s (can they now?) meant they were stuck with the 'silly' model of the competitive economy.

I doubt if Krugman has realised the full import of saying that the methodology of economics prevents economists expressing 'sensible ideas'. His almost casual get-out is that in the long run these sensible ideas will be captured in 'fully worked-out models'.[8] But how long is the long run? How much useful knowledge is lost in the short run? And why on earth does he believe that even in the long run greater rigour will produce greater truth?

In the social sciences, formal modelling is unique to economics. Psychology, history, sociology, ethics do not rely on 'controlled, silly models' to get a better understanding of human behaviour. They aim at what Rosenberg has called 'qualitative', not 'quantitative', predictions. This is not a sacrifice mainstream economics has been prepared to make, for it would mean sacrificing its claim to be like a natural science. This would be fine if economics really were a natural science, if the policeman, decked out with his fancy equations, really did have the authority he claimed. But if economics is much like other social sciences, able to offer qualitative, not quantitative predictions, the claim that formal modelling is the only way to get at the truths which matter for economic life is a sign of hubris.

The radical question raised by Tony Lawson (see Chapter 7) is that if the material studied by economics is the same as the material studied by the other social sciences, what reason is there for the disciplinary divide between economics and the other social sciences, or indeed what would be the objection to a unified social science?

One answer is that the material of economics does exhibit 'closed worlds', absent from other social sciences, where quantitative predictions are to be had. These closed worlds are like the world of games, in which the aims are given, the rules are fixed, and there is only a limited number of moves. They have always existed and exist today. They are the stuff of microeconomics. But I doubt if closure is a good general presumption to make of modern economic life, especially one dominated by financial institutions. The question which needs to be asked is: to what worlds does the study of economics add unique value, to what worlds does it add about the same amount of value as do other social sciences, and to what worlds does it add no value at all, and even detract from it?

Finally, we must return to a question central to pre-modern thought, but pushed aside by 'scientific' economics: what is wealth for? Ethics should be reinserted onto the ground floor of economics. By taking wants as given, economics offers no critique whatsoever of the human hunger for accumulating wealth without limit. That this might sanction policies which lead to the destruction of the human species is not something that someone who is just an economist need concern himself with. But a well-educated economist will surely have to do better than that.

14

THE FUTURE OF ECONOMICS

The political purpose of economics

Economics delivers a great deal, but it promises more than it can deliver, and, by assuming a certain type of human being – the rational, forward-looking 'agent' – it underestimates the costs of its promises. This means that its path to re-engineering human behaviour is littered with broken societies. The spectre which haunted the first generation of sociologists, of rudderless masses coalescing under charismatic leaders promising them back their lost birthright, re-emerges.

The question of how to do economics has become particularly urgent today, because it is linked to the survival of a free society. Keynes posed the question in the 1930s thus:

> The authoritarian state systems of to-day seem to solve the problem of unemployment at the expense of efficiency and of freedom. It is certain that the world will not much longer tolerate the unemployment which is associated . . . with present day capitalistic individualism. But it may be possible by a right analysis of the problem to cure the disease while preserving efficiency and freedom.[1]

The problem of unemployment now appears in hydra-headed form – headline unemployment, underemployment, precarious employment – not all of them easy to define or measure, and is accompanied (and partly caused) by an 'arbitrary and inequitable distribution of wealth and incomes'.[2] As in the 1930s, these conditions give rise to dictatorial parties and regimes which promise to solve economic problems 'at the expense of efficiency and freedom'. In addition, there is popular anger at the hollowing out of community in the name of economic integration. Those whom President Macron of France described as the 'left-behinds' are full of both economic and social resentment at the elites who presume to manage affairs in their interest. So, good policy today requires not just a 'right analysis' of the economic problem, but a strong social imagination. Economics cannot do all this on its own. But anything it can do to help the economic system work better and more equitably will ease the strain of social resentment.

Keynes's attack on the orthodoxy of his day was an attack not on the competence of economists but on their methodology. This is the case for a radical rethinking of its methodology today. The neoclassical economist is a dangerous counsellor for turbulent times, because he promises things which unmanaged markets cannot deliver. The conclusions deriving from his closed worlds are seriously misleading if applied to open worlds, and can lead to large mistakes in policy. Specifically, the belief that competitive markets spontaneously deliver stability and equity ignores the need to make the market system stable and equitable by design: a truth which Keynes understood, but which neoclassical economics has resolutely ignored.

If economics is to be useful today it will need to modify its belief in the self-regulating market. That free markets contain a principle of order was a huge discovery. It meant that economic life could be set free from state, municipal, communal, and customary direction. But to maintain that market competition is a self-sufficient ordering principle is wrong. Markets are embedded in political institutions and moral beliefs. In today's world they are inescapably accountable to voters as well as to market transactors. Market integration across borders is a not unworthy goal. But it should be pressed only as far as, and by means which, the conditions of political consent allow. This is a matter of judgment, not of demonstrative proof. The only test of good policy should be the Polanyi test: how much disruption and inequality will societies tolerate for the sake of progress?

These considerations are relevant to the way economics should be taught. Economics started as microeconomics – the theory of relative prices as determined in barter markets. Keynes shifted the focus to the theory of money, and broadened monetary theory into macroeconomics. Macroeconomics has now been squeezed out, and macroeconomic relationships are viewed by the mainstream as the summed result of rational decisions taken by forward-looking producers and consumers in competitive markets.

My ideal textbook would reverse the causation. I would start with the institutions of the macroeconomy and show how they structure markets and shape individual choices within markets. This is what a properly sociological economics would do. Central topics would be the role of the state, the distribution of power, and the effect of both on the distribution of wealth and income. There would be no assumptions about individual behaviour except that individuals act as rationally as they can in the incomplete conditions of knowledge in which they find themselves. Further, my textbook would make clear that the only defensible purpose of economics is to lift humanity out of poverty. Beyond this, the lessons of economics end, and those of ethics, sociology, history, and politics take over. The mathematical requirements for this prospectus would be minimal, though proper understanding of the uses and limitations of statistics is essential. There will always be a place for clever puzzle-solvers, though they should not be taken too seriously.

In offering policies to improve the world, economists should pay much more attention than they have done to the conditions of political consent. Mainstream thinking on public choice is jejune. It leads much too quickly to the idea that, pending the invention of an omniscient computer, everything should be left to the market. Future historians, looking back, might well identify finance-led globalisation as the root cause of the tribulations of the twenty-first century. To allow the financial system to establish a phantom global hegemony while leaving political legitimacy to national governments was to court economic and political disaster. Economics was not the cause of these misfortunes, but it was complicit in them, because its method, as I have argued, offered no basis for robust counter-narratives.

Whatever the outcome of our current distempers, it does not seem that today's pretentious economics will be of much help. Its natural trajectory is towards the other social sciences. It will continue to provide indispensable tools for thinking about the human condition, but as a co-equal, not as a monarch.

NOTES

Preface

1. Marshall, 1890: 9
2. Harvey, 2016; Fischer et al., 2018

Chapter 1. Why Methodology?

1. Quoted in Robbins, 1935
2. Samuelson, 1992: 240
3. Hahn, 1992
4. Keynes, 2015 [1938]: 281
5. Bhaskar, 1975: 70
6. Christoph M. Schmidt, Chairman of the German Council of Economic Experts, 2017
7. Robbins, 1935: 84, 86
8. Lo, 2017: 6–7
9. Streeck, 2016: 242–6
10. Tetlock, 2005
11. Keynes, 2015 [1924]: 173–4

Chapter 2. The Basics: Wants and Means

1. Smith, 1904 [1776]: 4
2. Marshall, 1890: 1, 18
3. Robbins, 1935: 15–16
4. Ibid.: 13
5. McConnell, Brue and Flynn, 2009: 8
6. Robbins, 1935: 15
7. Sahlins, 1972
8. Robbins, 1935: 92–3
9. Smith, 1904 [1776]: 165
10. Menger, 2007 [1871]: 125
11. Ibid.: 125–7
12. Veblen, 1899
13. Galbraith, 1969; Packard, 1957
14. Hirsch, 1976; The positional good argument was anticipated by Roy Harrod (1900–1978) in his idea of 'oligarchic goods' and developed by Robert Frank (b.1945) in his notion of a 'positional arms race'.
15. Robbins, 1935: 76
16. Sen, 1981

17. Robbins, 1935: 85
18. Marshall, 1890: 1

Chapter 3. Economic Growth

1. Mokyr, 2016: 5–6
2. List, 1909 [1841]
3. Meadows et al., 1972: 45, 87
4. Ricardo, 1817
5. Ibid.
6. Chang, 2002; Amsden, 1992; Bairoch, 1993
7. Chang, 2008
8. Mazzucato, 2013
9. Mill, 1848: 804–5
10. Rosenstein-Rodan, 1943; Hirschman, 1958; Lewis, 1954
11. Prebisch, 1959
12. Johnson, 1977
13. Hirschman, 1958: 110
14. Frank, 1966
15. Krueger, 1974
16. Smith and Toye, 1979
17. Wolf and Wade, 2002

Chapter 4. Equilibrium

1. Schumpeter, 1954: 968
2. J.W. Goethe, 1808, *Faust: Prologue in Heaven* (translated by Bayard Taylor)
3. Walras, 1954 [1874]
4. Hayek, 1937
5. Backhouse, 1997: 32
6. Kornai, 2006: 174
7. Foley, 2016
8. Schumpeter, 1954: 963–4
9. Ibid.
10. For the best account of Marx as a cyclical theorist, see Desai, 2002
11. Arrow and Debreu, 1954; for a brief account, see Hahn, 1989

Chapter 5. Models and Laws

1. Quoted in Routh, 1984: 152
2. Samuelson, 1970: 1
3. Robbins, 1935: 66
4. Fleetwood, 2017
5. Jevons, Vol. 2, 1913 [1877]: 509
6. Phillips, 1958
7. Coase, 1999
8. Schelling, 2006 [1978]: 18
9. Paul Samuelson's more exact, but less playful, variant: 'In a sense, precisely because we are ourselves men, we have an advantage over the natural scientist. He cannot usefully say, "Suppose I were an H_2O molecule; what might I do in such a situation?". The social scientist often, knowingly or unknowingly, employs such introspective acts of *empathy*.' (Samuelson, 1970: 9).
10. Krugman, 1995
11. For this critique, see Albert, 1976

12. Kaldor, 1961: 177–8
13. In a celebrated book, *The Black Swan: The Impact of the Highly Improbable* (2007), Nassim Taleb accused conventional economics of ignoring the possibility of extreme events, which he called black swans. The fact that all swans were not white has long been known, as in the poet Samuel Taylor Coleridge imagining joining nineteenth-century British convicts being transported to Australia: 'Receive me, Lads! I'll go with you, Hunt the black swan and kangaroo.'
14. This is known as the Duhem-Quine theorem, which states that in order to test empirically an explicit hypothesis such as 'X is caused by Y', one must make additional implicit hypotheses such as 'this is a valid test of whether X is caused by Y', and 'the testing instruments are accurate'.
15. Popper, 2005[1959]: 65
16. Skoufias et al., 2001
17. Routh, 1984: 154
18. Alesina et al., 2019
19. Borjas, 2017
20. Hodgson, 1997
21. McCloskey, 1983
22. Mirowski, 1989
23. Rosenberg, 1995
24. Solow, 1985

Chapter 6. Economic Psychology

1. Mankiw, 2018: 6
2. There is no gender-neutral equivalent. Nevertheless, with its English translation 'Economic Man', it is too useful to discard.
3. Lazear, 2000
4. Haldar, 2018
5. Lucas, 1988
6. Stigler, 1982: 7,19
7. Sargent, 2015
8. Akerlof, 1970; Stiglitz and Rothschild, 1976
9. Wikipedia, Rational choice theory; Becker, 1968
10. For a classic nineteenth-century utilitarian approach to the problem of crime prevention, see Henry Sidgwick's discussion in *Elements of Politics* (1891), quoted in Skidelsky, 1993: 7–8.
11. Rampell, 2013
12. Anderson, 2011
13. Angner, 2012
14. Priest, 2016
15. Thaler and Sunstein, 2008
16. Schwartz, 2015: 29
17. Syll, 2018

Chapter 7. Sociology and Economics

1. Gorz, 2010
2. Harvey, 2016
3. Pareto, quoted in Fuller, 2006: 14
4. Samuels et al., 2003
5. Kant, 1784

6. Nisbet, 1993 [1966]: 13
7. Ibid.: 16
8. Marx and Engels, 2004 [1848]
9. Quoted in Nisbet, 1993 [1966]: 28
10. Tönnies, 1957 [1887]
11. Weber, 1930 [1905]
12. Habermas, 1981a; 1981b
13. Quoted in Nisbet, 1993 [1966]: 90
14. Durkheim, 2006[1897]
15. Eldridge, 1972: 93
16. Weber, 1930 [1905]
17. A follower of Weber, Werner Sombart, substituted Jews for Protestants as inventors of the spirit of capitalism. It was not Calvinism which made northern Europe the centre of economic development, but the expulsion of Jews from Spain and Portugal in the 1490s. See W. Sombart, 1913.
18. Polanyi, 2002 [1944]: 46–7
19. The breakdown of the relationship between the arm and the mind was amusingly portrayed in the film, *Dr. Strangelove or How I learned to stop worrying and love the bomb*, in which Dr. Strangelove (played by Peter Sellers) could not stop his arm shooting up in an involuntary Nazi salute.
20. Lawson, 1997
21. The 'theory of rational addiction' claims that 'addictions, even strong ones, are usually rational in the sense of involving forward-looking maximization with stable preferences' (Becker and Murphy, 1988). In a scathing critique, Ole Røgeberg suggested that this type of exercise is symptomatic of a wider problem in economics, writing that 'these theories show how a loose, unstructured approach to explaining and justifying a mathematical model allow one to hide problematic assumptions even when these are central to the argument made, while providing ad hoc illustrations that trigger feelings of understanding and insight though neither justifying the assumptions nor providing an adequate explanation in objectivistic terms.' (Røgeberg, 2004)

Chapter 8. Insitutional Economics

1. Simon, 1976: 218
2. Galbraith, 1967
3. Hodgson, 2000b, quoted in Hodgson, 2000a
4. Coase, 1937
5. Davis and North, 1971
6. North and Thomas, 1973: 16–17. The thought behind the idea that the enclosure of public land protected the peasant is that it removed the incentive for some to cheat by 'over-grazing'.
7. Ibid.: 4
8. There is much more to Olson than this. In his book *The Logic of Collective Action* (1971 [1965]), Olson explains the existence of public (or collectively provided) goods. Certain goods, like street lighting and defence systems, have to be provided through the tax system, because they have the property that non-contributors cannot be excluded from using them; therefore they will refrain from voluntary contribution to them ('free ride'). In Soviet Russia, the communist stationary bandit collapsed because it lost control over its

revenues. In the absence of private property, free-riding became endemic once the bandit's coercive power weakened.

9. Buchanan et al., 1978
10. Unger, 2019

Chapter 9. Economics and Power

1. Stiglitz, 1993
2. Varoufakis, 2017
3. Lukes, 2016
4. Hearn, 2012: 20
5. Gramsci, 1971 [1936]: 12
6. Marx and Engels, 2004 [1848]
7. Pareto, 1991 [1920]
8. Smith, 1904 [1776]: 131
9. Cooper, 2003
10. Tugendhat, 1972
11. The ability of cartels to keep prices stable may be an argument for cartels in an industry like oil, where natural conditions in the industry induce wild swings in price.
12. Robinson, 1969
13. Keynes, 2015 [1936]: 262
14. Robinson, 1962: 7
15. Cartwright, 1999: 2
16. In actual fact, no Nobel prize exists for economics either; it is properly called the Sveriges Riksbank Prize in Economic Sciences in Memory of Alfred Nobel. All the other prizes were established by Alfred Nobel's will in 1895, while the prize in economics was established by a donation from the Sveriges Riksbank (Swedish Central Bank).
17. Marx and Engels, 2004 [1848]
18. Streeck, 2016: 190
19. Skidelsky, 2018
20. Foucault, 1973 [1963]
21. Galbraith, 1983: 120
22. Ibid.: 105
23. Friedman, 1993, quoted in Cherrier, 2011
24. Earle et al., 2016

Chapter 10. Why Study the History of Economic Thought?

1. Hicks, 2008
2. Quoted in Gide and Rist, 1948: 10
3. Robbins, 1935: 69
4. Stigler, 1982
5. Krugman, 1995
6. Stigler, 1982
7. All quoted in Routh, 1975: 2–17
8. Leontief, 1970
9. Hahn, 1970
10. Johnson, 2013
11. Sraffa, 1926, quoted in Routh, 1975
12. Kuhn, 1962

13. Lakatos, 1978
14. Hansen, 2017

Chapter 11. Economic History

1. Marshall, 1890: 31
2. Parker, 1986
3. Piketty, 2014
4. Denison, 1962
5. Solow, 1985
6. Kulikowski, 2014
7. Finlay, 1973: 56
8. Solow, 1985
9. Crafts, 1987
10. Saul, 2004

Chapter 12. Ethics and Economics

1. Robbins, 1938: 148
2. Stigler, 1982: 8
3. Mill, 1848: 754
4. Smith, 1904[1776]: 32
5. Ricardo, 1817: 246
6. Marx, 1887[1867]
7. Whately, 1832
8. Anticipating Veblen, Smith wrote, 'The merit of the beauty [of diamonds] is greatly enhanced by their scarcity. With the greater part of rich people, the chief enjoyment of riches consists in the parade of riches, which in their eye is never so complete as when they appear to possess those decisive marks of opulence which nobody can possess but themselves.' (Smith, 1904 [1776]: 172–3)
9. Jevons, 1987 [1871]: 45
10. Ibid.: 164
11. Though neuroscientists are confident of cracking this problem: '[neuroscientists] can measure your emotional reaction to the things you see by simply monitoring the degree of your microsweating'. (Ramachandran, 2010: 95)
12. Locke, 1764 [1689]: 220
13. Pigou, 1932 [1920]
14. Kaldor, 1939
15. I vividly recall being at a debate in Moscow in the early 2000s between two Russian businessmen, Kakha Bendukidze and Mikhail Khodorkovsky. Bendukidze argued that a firm's duty to society was limited to maximising shareholder value; Khodorkovsky claimed that it had an additional duty to society. Bendukidze was simply echoing the view of neoclassical economics that firms should be seen as giant-sized profit-maximising individuals. This indeed became the standard doctrine of the 1980s: firms had no social obligation beyond maximising profits for their owners (shareholders). This overthrew the older 'stakeholder' view of the company expressed by Owen Young, CEO of General Electric between the wars: 'The stockholders are confined to a maximum return equivalent to a risk premium. The remaining profit stays in the enterprise, is paid out in higher wages, or is passed to the customer.' (quoted in Plender, 2019)

16. Foley, 2009
17. Quoted in Galbraith, 1987: 119
18. Keynes, 2015 [1930]: 82
19. Quoted in Chaves, 2003: 336
20. Easterlin, 1974
21. Layard, 2005
22. Quoted in Scull, 2019
23. Layard, 2005
24. For an expanded version of these arguments, see Skidelsky and Skidelsky, 2012: Ch. 4
25. Sen, 1999
26. For an expanded account, see Skidelsky and Skidelsky, 2012: 147–51
27. Alkire et al., 2015
28. Meadows et al., 1972
29. Raworth, 2017
30. See Oreskes and Conway, 2014.
31. For an extended version of this argument, see Skidelsky and Skidelsky, 2012: Ch. 5
32. Sandel, 2012

Chapter 13. Retreat from Omniscience

1. Keynes, 1964 [1936]: vii
2. O'Donnell, 1989: 3
3. Keynes: 1973 [1921]: 111
4. Suppose you go to a race with three horses, Red, Blue, and Yellow, and a book-maker offers you the following odds: evens (1–1) on Red, 2–1 on Blue, and 3–1 on Yellow (2–1 means if you win you have your initial stake returned, plus 2 times that). If you place $6 on Red, $4 on Blue, and $3 on Yellow, then you will win $12 no matter the outcome. But the initial outlay was $6+$4+$3=$13, so you will make a loss of $1 whatever happens. In this scenario you have allowed the bookmaker to make a 'Dutch book', because you bet on all three events, but the implied probability of all three adds up to more than 1 (events with lower odds have higher returns). This is analogous to the practice of arbitrage in financial markets.
5. Ramsey, 1931 [1926]. Notice that this procedure is identical to Friedman's rule for model construction: you can choose any premise you want, the test is the accuracy of the prediction.
6. Keynes, 1972 [1926]: 262
7. Quoted in Skidelsky, 2018: 24
8. Krugman, 1995

Chapter 14. The Future of Economics

1. Keynes, 2015 [1936]: 260
2. Ibid.: 252

BIBLIOGRAPHY

Preface

Harvey, John T. (2016). *Contending Perspectives in Economics: A Guide to Contemporary Schools of Thought*, Cheltenham: Edward Elgar.

Fischer, Liliann, Hasell, Joe, Proctor, J. Christopher, Uwakwe, David, Ward-Perkins, Zach and Watson, Catriona (2018). *Rethinking Economics: An Introduction to Pluralist Economics*, London: Routledge.

Marshall, Alfred (1890). *Principles of Economics*, London: Macmillan.

Chapter 1

Bhaskar, Roy (1975). *A Realist Theory of Science*, Leeds: Leeds Books.

Hahn, Frank (1992). 'Answer to Backhouse: Yes', *Royal Economic Society Newsletter*, 78: 3–5.

Harvey, John T. (2016). *Contending Perspectives in Economics: A Guide to Contemporary Schools of Thought*, Cheltenham: Edward Elgar.

Hodgson, Geoffrey (2019). *Is There a Future for Heterodox Economics? Institutions, Ideology and a Scientific Community*, Cheltenham: Edward Elgar.

Jensen, Michael C. (1978). 'Some Anomalous Evidence on the Efficient Market Hypothesis', *Journal of Financial Economics*, Vol. 6 (2/3): 95–101.

Joffe, Michael (2018). 'What's *Really* Wrong with Economics?', *Royal Economic Society Newsletter*, 183.

Keynes, John Maynard (2015 [1938, 1924]). 'Methodological Issues: Tinbergen, Harrod'; 'Alfred Marshall' in Robert Skidelsky (ed.), *The Essential Keynes*, Penguin Classics.

Kornai, János (2006). *By Force of Thought: Irregular Memoirs of an Intellectual Journey*, Cambridge, MA: MIT Press.

Lo, Andrew (2017). *Adaptive Markets: Financial Evolution at the Speed of Thought*, Princeton: Princeton University Press.

Robbins, Lionel (1935). *An Essay on the Nature and Significance of Economic Science*, 2nd ed., London: Macmillan.

Samuelson, Paul (1992). 'My Life Philosophy: Policy Credos and Working Ways', in Michael Szenberg (ed.), *Eminent Economists: Their Life Philosophies*, Cambridge: Cambridge University Press.

Schmidt, Christoph M. (2017). 'The Art of the Surplus', Project Syndicate.

Streeck, Wolfgang (2016). *How Capitalism Will End: Essays on a Failing System*, London: Verso.

Tetlock, P.E. (2005). *Expert Political Judgement: How Good Is It? How Can We Know?*, Princeton University Press. Tetlock's research is reported by David Epstein in 'The Peculiar Blindness of Experts', *The Atlantic*, June 2019.

Chapter 2

Frank, Robert (1985). *Choosing the Right Pond: Human Behaviour and the Quest for Status*, Oxford: Oxford University Press.

Galbraith, John Kenneth (1958). *The Affluent Society*, Houghton Mifflin Harcourt.

Georgescu-Roegen, Nicholas (1971). *The Entropy Law and the Economic Process*, Princeton: Princeton University Press.

Harrod, Roy (1958). 'The Possibility of Economic Satiety', in *Problems of US Economic Development*, Vol. 1, New York: Washington Committee for Economic Development.

Hirsch, Fred (1976). *Social Limits to Growth*, Cambridge, MA: Harvard University Press.

Keynes, John Maynard (2015 [1930]). 'Economic Possibilities for our Grandchildren', in Robert Skidelsky (ed.), *The Essential Keynes*, Penguin Classics.

Marshall, Alfred (1890). *Principles of Economics*, London: Macmillan.

McConnell, Campbell, Brue, Stanley and Flynn, Sean (2009). *Macroeconomics*, New York: McGraw-Hill.

Menger, Carl (2007 [1871]). *Principles of Economics*, Online: Mises Institute.

Packard, Vance (1957). *The Hidden Persuaders*, New York: D. McKay Co.

Robbins, Lionel (1935). *An Essay on the Nature and Significance of Economic Science*, 2nd ed., London: Macmillan.

Sahlins, Marshall (1972). *Stone Age Economics*, New York: de Gruyter.

Sen, Amartya (1981). *Poverty and Famines: An Essay on Entitlement and Deprivation*, Oxford: Oxford University Press.

Smith, Adam (1904 [1776]). *An Inquiry into the Nature and Causes of the Wealth of Nations*, London: Methuen.

Veblen, Thorstein (1899). *The Theory of the Leisure Class*, New York: Macmillan.

Chapter 3

Acemoglu, Daron, Johnson, Simon and Robinson, James (2001). 'The Colonial Origins of Comparative Development: An Empirical Investigation', *American Economic Review*, Vol. 91 (5): 1369–1401.

Amsden, Alice (1992). *Asia's Next Giant: South Korea and Late Industrialization*, Oxford: Oxford University Press.

Bairoch, Paul (1993). *Economics and World History: Myths and Paradoxes*, Hemel Hempstead: Harvester Wheatsheaf.

Chang, Ha-Joon (2008). *Bad Samaritans: Rich Nations, Poor Policies and the Threat to the Developing World*, London: Random House Business.

Chang, Ha-Joon (2002). *Kicking Away the Ladder: Development Strategy in Historical Perspective*, London: Anthem Press.

Frank, Andre Gunder (1966). *The Development of Underdevelopment*, Boston: New England Free Press.

Hirschman, Albert (1958). *The Strategy of Economic Development*, New Haven: Yale University Press.

Johnson, Harry (1977). 'Keynes and the Developing World', in Robert Skidelsky (ed.), *The End of the Keynesian Era: Essays on the Disintegration of the Keynesian Political Economy*, London: Macmillan.

Krueger, Anne (1974). 'The Political Economy of the Rent-Seeking Society', *American Economic Review*, Vol. 64 (3): 291–303.

Krugman, Paul (1987). 'Is Free Trade Passé?', *Journal of Economic Perspectives*, Vol. 1 (2): 131–44.

Lewis, W. Arthur (1954). 'Economic Development with Unlimited Supplies of Labour', *The Manchester School*, Vol. 22 (2): 129–91.

List, Friedrich (1909 [1841]). *The National System of Political Economy*, London: Longmans, Green and Co.

Malthus, Thomas (1798). *An Essay on the Principle of Population*, London: J. Johnson.

Malthus, Thomas (1803). *An Essay on the Principle of Population* (2nd ed.), London: J. Johnson.

Mazzucato, Mariana (2013). *The Entrepreneurial State*, London: Anthem Press.

Meadows, Donella H., Meadows, Dennis L., Randers, Jørgen and Behrens, William W. III (1972). *The Limits to Growth*, New York: Universe Books.

Mill, John Stuart (1848). *Principles of Political Economy*, London: John W. Parker.

Mokyr, Joel (2016). *A Culture of Growth: The Origins of the Modern Economy*, Princeton: Princeton University Press.

Prebisch, Raúl (1959). 'Commercial Policy in the Underdeveloped Countries', *American Economic Review*, Vol. 49 (2): 251–73.

Ricardo, David (1817). *On the Principles of Political Economy and Taxation*, London: John Murray.

Rosenstein-Rodan, Paul (1943). 'Problems of Industrialization of Eastern and South-Eastern Europe', *Economic Journal* Vol. 53 (210/211): 202–11.

Smith, Sheila and Toye, John (1979). 'Introduction: Three Stories about Trade and Poor Economies', *Journal of Development Studies*, Vol. 15 (3): 1–18.

Wolf, Martin and Wade, Robert (2002). 'Are Global Poverty and Inequality Getting Worse?', *Prospect Magazine*. https://www.prospectmagazine.co.uk/magazine/areglobalpovertyandinequalitygettingworse

Chapter 4

Arrow, Kenneth and Debreu, Gerard (1954). 'Existence of an Equilibrium for a Competitive Economy', *Econometrica*, Vol. 22 (3): 265–90.

Backhouse, Roger E. (2004). 'History and Equilibrium: A Partial Defense of Equilibrium Economics', *Journal of Economic Methodology*, Vol. 11 (3): 291–305.

Backhouse, Roger E. (1997). 'The Rhetoric and Methodology of Modern Macroeconomics', in Brian Snowdon and Howard Vane (eds.), *Reflections in the Development of Modern Macroeconomics*, Cheltenham: Edward Elgar.

Desai, Meghad (2002). *Marx's Revenge*, London: Verso.

Foley, Duncan (2016). 'Crisis and Theoretical Methods: Equilibrium and Disequilibrium Once Again', in *Conference Paper Presented at the International Conference on Economics, Economic Policies and Sustainable Growth in the Wake of the Crisis*, Ancona.

Hahn, Frank (1989). 'The Emergence of the New Right', in Robert Skidelsky (ed.), *Thatcherism*, Oxford: Basil Blackwell.

Hayek, Friedrich (1937). 'Economics and Knowledge', *Economica*, New Series, Vol. 4 (13): 33–54.

Kornai, János (2006). *By Force of Thought: Irregular Memoirs of an Intellectual Journey*, Cambridge, MA: MIT Press.

Lazear, Edward P. (2000). 'Economic Imperialism', *Quarterly Journal of Economics*, Vol. 115 (1): 99–146.

Robinson, Joan (1978). *Contributions to Modern Economics*, Oxford: B. Blackwell.

Schumpeter, Joseph A. (1954). *History of Economic Analysis*, London: Allen & Unwin.

Walras, Léon (1954 [1874]). *Elements of Pure Economics*, London: Allen & Unwin.

Chapter 5

Albert, Hans (1976). 'Science and the Search for Truth: Critical Rationality and the Methods of Science', in Robert S. Cohen and Marx Wartofsky (eds.), *Boston Studies in the Philosophy of Science*, Vol. LVIII.

Alesina, Alberto, Favero, Carlo and Giavazzi, Francesco (2019). *Austerity: When it Works and When It Doesn't*, Princeton: Princeton University Press.

Borjas, George (2017). 'The Wage Impact of the Marielitos: A Reappraisal', *Industrial and Labor Relations Review* 70 (5): 1077–110.

Coase, Ronald (1999). 'Speech to the ISNIE: The Task of Economics', *Opening Address to the Annual Conference of the International Society of New Institutional Economics*, Washington, DC.

Fleetwood, Steven (2017). 'The Critical Realist Conception of Open and Closed Systems', *Journal of Economic Methodology*, 24 (1).

Forrester, Jay W. (1971). 'Counterintuitive Behavior of Social Systems', *Theory and Decision*, Vol. 2 (2): 109–40.

Friedman, Milton (1953). 'The Methodology of Positive Economics', in Milton Friedman, *Essays in Positive Economics,* Chicago: University of Chicago Press.

Friedman, Milton (1968). 'The Role of Monetary Policy', *American Economic Review*, Vol. 58 (1): 1–17.

Hodgson, Geoffrey M. (1997). 'The Ubiquity of Habits and Rules', *Cambridge Journal of Economics*, Vol. 21 (6): 663–84.

Jevons, William Stanley (1913 [1877]). *The Principles of Science: A Treatise on Logic and Scientific Method,* London: Macmillan.

Kaldor, Nicholas (1961). 'Capital Accumulation and Economic Growth', in Friedrich Lutz (ed.) *The Theory of Capital,* London: MacMillan.

Krugman, Paul (1995). 'The Fall and Rise of Development Economics', in Paul Krugman, *Development, Geography and Economic Theory,* Cambridge, MA: MIT Press.

Mankiw, N. Gregory (2018). *Principles of Economics*, Mason, OH: Cengage Learning.

McCloskey, Deirdre (1983). 'The Rhetoric of Economics', *Journal of Economic Literature*, Vol. 21 (2): 481–517.

Mirowski, Philip (1989). *More Heat than Light: Economics as Social Physics, Physics as Nature's Economics*, Cambridge: Cambridge University Press.

Phelps, Edmund (1967). 'Phillips Curves, Expectations of Inflation and Optimal Unemployment Over Time', *Economica*, Vol. 34 (135): 254–81.

Phillips, A.W. (1958). 'The Relation Between Unemployment and the Rate of Change of Money Wage Rates in the United Kingdom, 1861–1957', *Economica*, Vol. 25 (100): 283–99.

Popper, Karl (2005 [1959]). *The Logic of Scientific Discovery,* London: Routledge.

Robbins, Lionel (1935). *An Essay on the Nature and Significance of Economic Science*, 2nd ed., London: Macmillan.

Roscoe, Philip (2014). *I Spend Therefore I Am,* London: Viking.

Rosenberg, Alexander (1995). *The Philosophy of Social Science,* Boulder: Westview Press.

Routh, Guy (1984). *Economics: An Alternative Text,* London: Macmillan.

Samuelson, Paul (1970). *Economics* (8th ed.), New York: McGraw-Hill.

Samuelson, Paul and Solow, Robert M. (1960). 'Analytical Aspects of Anti-Inflation Policy', *American Economic Review*, 50 (2): 177–94.

Schelling, Thomas (2006 [1978]). *Micromotives and Macrobehavior,* New York: W.W. Norton.

Skoufias, Emmanuel, Parker, Susan W., Behrman, Jere R. and Pessino, Carola (2001). 'Conditional Cash Transfers and Their Impact on Child Work and Schooling: Evidence from the PROGRESA Program in Mexico', *Economía*, Vol. 2 (1): 45–96.

Solow, Robert (1985). 'Economic History and Economics', *American Economic Review*, Vol. 75 (2): 328–31.

Chapter 6

Akerlof, George (1970). 'The Market for Lemons: Quality, Uncertainty, and the Market Mechanism', *Quarterly Journal of Economics*, Vol. 84 (3): 488–500.

Akerlof, George and Shiller, Robert (2015). *Phishing for Phools: The Economics of Manipulation and Deception*, Princeton: Princeton University Press.

Anderson, Jenny (2011). Economists in Love: Betsey Stevenson and Justin Wolfers, *It's not you, it's the dishes.* (http://www.itsthedishes.com/2343/2011/03/economists-in-love-betsey-stevenson-and-justin-wolfers/)

Angner, Erik (2012). *A Course in Behavioural Economics*, London: Palgrave.

Becker, Gary (1968). 'Crime and Punishment: An Economic Approach', *Journal of Political Economy*, Vol. 76 (2): 169–217.

Becker, Gary (1974). 'A Theory of Marriage', in Theodore William Schultz (ed.), *Economics of the Family: Marriage, Children, and Human Capital*, Chicago: University of Chicago Press.

Haldar, Antara (2018). 'Intrinsic Goodness: Why We Might Behave Better Than We Think', *Times Literary Supplement*, No. 6031.

Kahneman, Daniel (2011). *Thinking, Fast and Slow*, London: Allen Lane.

Lazear, Edward P. (2000). 'Economic Imperialism', *Quarterly Journal of Economics*, Vol. 115 (1): 99–146.

Lucas, Robert E. (1988). 'On the Mechanics of Economic Development', *Journal of Monetary Economics*, Vol. 22 (1): 3–42.

Priest, George L. (2016). 'Something Smells Phishy', *Claremont Review of Books*, Vol. XVI (4).

Rampell, Catherine (2013). 'Outsource Your Way to Success', *New York Times Magazine*, 10 November.

Sargent, Thomas (2015). 'Computational Challenges in Economics', podcast, Platform for Advanced Scientific Computing Conference, Zurich, 1–3 June.

Schwartz, Barry (2015). *Why We Work*, London: Red Books–Simon & Schuster.

Skidelsky, Robert (1993). *Interests and Obsessions*, London: Macmillan.

Stigler, George (1982). *The Economist as Preacher, and Other Essays*, Chicago: University of Chicago Press.

Stiglitz, Joseph and Rothschild, Michael (1976). 'Equilibrium in Competitive Insurance Markets: An Essay on the Economics of Imperfect Competition', *Quarterly Journal of Economics*, Vol. 90 (4): 629–649.

Syll, Lars Pålsson (2018). 'On Randomness and Probability in Economics', *Real-World Economics Review* Blog. https://rwer.wordpress.com/2018/06/18/on-randomness-and-probability-in-economics/

Thaler, Richard H. and Sunstein, Cass R. (2008). *Nudge: Improving Decisions about Health, Wealth, and Happiness*, New Haven: Yale University Press.

Chapter 7

Arrow, Kenneth J. (1994). 'Methodological Individualism and Social Knowledge' (Richard T. Ely Lecture), *American Economic Review, special issue: Papers and*

Proceedings of the Hundred and Sixth Annual Meeting of the American Economic Association, American Economic Association, 84 (2): 1–9.

Becker, Gary S. and Murphy, Kevin M. (1988). 'A Theory of Rational Addiction', *Journal of Political Economy,* Vol. 96 (4): 675–700.

Dawkins, Richard (1976). *The Selfish Gene,* Oxford: Oxford University Press.

Durkheim, Émile (2006 [1897]). *On Suicide,* London: Penguin.

Eldridge, J.E.T. (ed.) (1972). *Max Weber: The Interpretation of Social Reality,* London: Nelson.

Fuller, Steve (2006). *The Philosophy of Science and Technology Studies,* London: Routledge.

Gorz, André (2010). *Ecologica,* London: Seagull Books.

Habermas, Jürgen (1981). *The Theory of Communicative Action,* Vols I & II, Boston: Beacon Press.

Harvey, John T. (2016). *Contending Perspectives in Economics: A Guide to Contemporary Schools of Thought,* Cheltenham: Edward Elgar.

Hawthorn, Geoffrey (1987). *Enlightenment and Despair: A History of Social Theory,* Cambridge: Cambridge University Press.

Kant, Immanuel (1784). 'What is Enlightenment?', in *Foundations of the Metaphysics of Morals and What is Enlightenment,* New York: Liberal Arts Press.

Lawson, Tony (1997). *Economics and Reality,* London: Routledge.

Marx, Karl and Engels, Friedrich (2004 [1848]). *Manifesto of the Communist Party.* Online: Marxists Internet Archive. https://www.marxists.org/archive/marx/works/1848/communist-manifesto/index.htm

Nisbet, Robert (1993 [1966]). *The Sociological Tradition,* New Brunswick: Transaction Publishers.

Polanyi, Karl (2002 [1944]). *The Great Transformation: The Political and Economic Origins of Our Time,* Boston: Beacon Press.

Røgeberg, Ole (2004). 'Taking Absurd Theories Seriously: Economics and the Case of Rational Addiction Theories', *Philosophy of Science,* Vol. 71 (3): 263–85.

Samuels, Warren J., Biddle, Jeff E. and Davis, John B. (2003). *A Companion to the History of Economic Thought,* Oxford: Oxford University Press.

Sombart, Werner (1913). *The Jews and Modern Capitalism,* New Brunswick: Transaction Publishers.

Tocqueville, Alexis (2017 [1835]). *Democracy in America,* Mineola, NY: Dover.

Tönnies, Ferdinand (1957 [1887]). *Community and Society [Gemeinschaft und Gesellschaft],* Oxford: Michigan State University Press.

Weber, Max (1930 [1905]). *The Protestant Ethic and the Spirit of Capitalism,* London: Allen & Unwin. https://www.marxists.org/reference/archive/weber/protestant-ethic.

Williamson, Oliver (1975). *Markets and Hierarchies, Analysis and Antitrust Implications,* New York: Free Press.

Chapter 8

Buchanan, James M., Rowley, Charles K., Breton, Albert, Wiseman, Jack, Frey, Bruno, Peacock, A. T., Grimond, Jo, Niskanen, W.A. and Ricketts, Martin (1978). *The Economics of Politics,* London: Institute of Economic Affairs.

Chang, Ha-Joon (2011). 'Institutions and Economic Development: Theory, Policy and History', *Journal of Institutional Economics,* Vol. 7 (4): 473–98.

Coase, Ronald (1937). 'The Nature of the Firm', *Economica,* Vol. 4 (16): 386–405.

Coase, Ronald (1960). 'The Problem of Social Cost', *Journal of Law and Economics*, Vol. 3: 1–44.

Davis, Lance and North, Douglass C. (1971). *Institutional Change and American Economic Growth*, Cambridge: Cambridge University Press.

Galbraith, John Kenneth (1967). *The New Industrial State*, London: Hamish Hamilton.

Hodgson, Geoffrey (2000a). 'What Is the Essence of Institutional Economics?', *Journal of Economic Issues*, Vol. 34 (2): 317–29.

Hodgson, Geoffrey (2000b). 'Structures and Institutions: Reflections on Institutionalism, Structuration Theory and Critical Realism', unpublished mimeo, University of Hertfordshire.

North, Douglass and Thomas, Robert (1973). *The Rise of the Western World: A New Economic History*, Cambridge: Cambridge University Press.

Olson, Mancur (1971 [1965]). *The Logic of Collective Action: Public Goods and the Theory of Groups* (Revised ed.), Cambridge, MA: Harvard University Press.

Simon, Herbert (1976). *Administrative Behavior: A Study of Decision-making Processes in Administrative Organization*, New York: Free Press.

Simon, Herbert (1991). 'Organizations and Markets', *Journal of Economic Perspectives*, Vol. 5 (2): 25–44.

Standing, Guy (2014 [2011]). *The Precariat: The New Dangerous Class*, London: Bloomsbury Academic.

Unger, Roberto Mangabeira (2019). *The Knowledge Economy*, London: Verso.

Chapter 9

Cartwright, Nancy (1999). *The Dappled World: A Study of the Boundaries of Science*, Cambridge: Cambridge University Press.

Cherrier, Beatrice (2011). 'The Lucky Consistency of Milton Friedman's Science and Politics, 1933–1963', in R. Van Horn, P. Mirowski and T. Stapleford (eds.), *Building Chicago Economics: New Perspectives on the History of America's Most Powerful Economics Program* (Historical Perspectives on Modern Economics), Cambridge: Cambridge University Press.

Collini, Stefan (2009). 'Impact on Humanities', *Times Literary Supplement*, 13 November.

Cooper, Robert (2003). *Is "Economic Power" a Useful and Operational Concept?* ms. version.

Earle, Joe, Moran, Cahal and Ward-Perkins, Zach (2016). *The Econocracy: The Perils of Leaving Economics to the Experts*, Manchester: Manchester University Press.

Foucault, Michel (1973 [1963]). *The Birth of the Clinic: An Archaeology of Medical Perception*, London: Tavistock Publications.

Friedman, Milton (1993). 'Postface', in Marc Lavoie and Mario Seccareccia (eds.), *Milton Friedman et son œuvre*, Montreal: Les presses de l'Université de Montréal.

Galbraith, John Kenneth (1983). *The Anatomy of Power*, New York: Houghton Mifflin.

Gramsci, Antonio (1971 [1936]). *Selections from Prison Notebooks*, London: Lawrence & Wishart.

Hearn, Jonathan (2016). 'Power and Economics', in Robert Skidelsky and Nan Craig (eds.), *Who Runs the Economy?: The Role of Power in Economics*, London: Palgrave Macmillan.

Hearn, Jonathan (2012). *Theorizing Power*, Basingstoke: Palgrave Macmillan.

Keynes, John Maynard (2015 [1936]). 'The General Theory of Interest, Unemployment and Money', in Robert Skidelsky (ed.), *The Essential Keynes*, Penguin Classics.

Lukes, Steven (2016). 'Power and Economics', in Robert Skidelsky and Nan Craig (eds.), *Who Runs the Economy?: The Role of Power in Economics*, London: Palgrave Macmillan.

Lukes, Steven (2004). *Power: A Radical View*, London: Palgrave Macmillan.

Marx, Karl and Engels, Friedrich (2004 [1848]). *Manifesto of the Communist Party*. Online: Marxists Internet Archive. https://www.marxists.org/archive/marx/works/1848/communist-manifesto/index.htm

Mill, John Stuart (1869). *On Liberty*, London: Longmans, Green, Reader and Dyer.

Packard, Vance (1957). *The Hidden Persuaders*, New York: McKay.

Pareto, Vilfredo (1991 [1920]). *The Rise and Fall of Elites: An Application of Theoretical Sociology*, New Jersey: Transaction Publishers.

Robinson, Joan (1962). *Economic Philosophy*, London: Watts.

Robinson, Joan (1969). *The Economics of Imperfect Competition* (2nd ed.), London: Palgrave Macmillan.

Russell, Bertrand (1938). *Power: A New Social Analysis*, London: Allen & Unwin.

Skidelsky, Robert (2018). *Money and Government*, London: Allen Lane; New Haven: Yale University Press.

Skidelsky, Robert (2005). 'Keynes, Globalization and the Bretton Woods Institutions in the Light of Changing Ideas about Markets', *World Economics*, Vol. 6 (1): 1–16.

Skidelsky, Robert and Craig, Nan (eds.) (2016). *Who Runs the Economy?: The Role of Power in Economics*, London: Palgrave Macmillan.

Smith, Adam (1904 [1776]). *An Inquiry into the Nature and Causes of the Wealth of Nations*, London: Methuen.

Stiglitz, Joseph E. (1993). 'Post Walrasian and Post Marxian Economics', *Journal of Economic Perspectives*, Vol. 7 (1): 109–114.

Streeck, Wolfgang (2016). *How Will Capitalism End? Essays on a Failing System*, London: Verso.

Tugendhat, Christopher (1972). *The Multinationals*, New York: Random House.

Varoufakis, Yanis (2017). *Adults in the Room*, London: The Bodley Head.

Chapter 10

Blaug, Mark (2001). 'No History of Ideas, Please, We're Economists', *Journal of Economic Perspectives*, Vol. 15 (1): 145–64.

Dasgupta, A.K. (1985). *Epochs of Economic Theory*, Oxford: Basil Blackwell.

Davis, John Bryan (2016). 'Economics as Science', in Robert Skidelsky and Nan Craig (eds.), *Who Runs the Economy?: The Role of Power in Economics*, London: Palgrave Macmillan.

Galbraith, John Kenneth (1987). *A History of Economics: The Past as Present*, London: Penguin.

Gide, Charles and Rist, Charles (1948). *A History of Economic Doctrines, from the Time of the Physiocrats to the Present Day*, London: George G. Harrap.

Hahn, Frank (1970). 'Some Adjustment Problems', *Econometrica*, Vol. 38 (1): 1–17.

Hansen, Lars Peter (2017). 'Publishing and Promotion in Economics: The Curse of the Top Five (Panel Discussion)', 2017 American Economic Association Annual Meeting, 7 January, Chicago, Illinois.

Hicks, John (2008). '"Revolutions" in Economics', in Spiro Latsis (ed.), *Methods and Appraisal in Economics*, Cambridge: Cambridge University Press.

Johnson, Harry (2013). 'The Keynesian Revolution and the Monetarist Counter-Revolution', in *Selected Essays in Monetary Economics (Collected Works of Harry Johnson)*, London: Routledge.

Krugman, Paul (1995). 'The Fall and Rise of Development Economics', in Paul Krugman, *Development, Geography and Economic Theory*, Cambridge, MA: MIT Press.

Kuhn, Thomas (1962). *The Structure of Scientific Revolutions*, Chicago: University of Chicago Press.

Lakatos, Imre (1978). *The Methodology of Scientific Research Programmes: Philosophical Papers*, Vol. 1, Cambridge: Cambridge University Press.

Leontief, Wassily (1970). 'Presidential Address', *Eighty-third Meeting of the American Economic Association*, 29 December, Detroit, Michigan.

Robbins, Lionel (1935). *An Essay on the Nature and Significance of Economic Science*, 2nd ed., London: Macmillan.

Routh, Guy (1975). *The Origin of Economic Ideas*, London: Macmillan.

Schumpeter, Josef (1981 [1954]). *The History of Economic Analysis*, London: Allen & Unwin.

Sraffa, Piero (1926). 'The Laws of Returns under Competitive Conditions', *The Economic Journal*, Vol. 36 (144): 535–50.

Stigler, George (1982). 'Does Economics Have a Useful Past?', in George Stigler, *The Economist as Preacher and Other Essays*, Chicago: University of Chicago Press.

Chapter 11

Acton, Peter (2014). *Poiesis: Manufacturing in Classical Athens*, New York: Oxford University Press.

Bolt, Jutta, Inklaar, Robert, de Jong, Herman and Luiten van Zanden, Jan (2018). 'Rebasing "Maddison": New Income Comparisons and the Shape of Long-run Economic Development', *Maddison Project Working Paper* 10, Maddison Project Database.

Boulding, Kenneth E. (1971). 'After Samuelson Who Needs Adam Smith?', *History of Political Economy*, Vol. 3 (2): 225–37.

Chang, Ha-Joon (2002). *Kicking Away the Ladder: Development Strategy in Historical Perspective*, London: Anthem.

Crafts, Nick (1987). 'Economic History', in John Eatwell, Murray Milgate and Peter K. Newman (eds.), *The New Palgrave: A Dictionary of Economics*, London: Palgrave.

Dasgupta, A.K. (1985). *Epochs of Economic Theory*, Oxford: Basil Blackwell.

Denison, Edward F. (1962). *The Sources of Economic Growth in the United States and the Alternatives Before Us*, New York: Committee for Economic Development.

Finlay, Moses (1973). *The Ancient Economy*, Berkeley: University of California Press.

Fogel, Robert W. and Engerman, Stanley L. (1995 [1974]). *Time on the Cross*, New York: W.W. Norton.

Hayek, Friedrich (1944). *The Road to Serfdom*, Chicago: University of Chicago Press.

Kulikowski, Michael (2014). 'The Glorious Free Market', *London Review of Books*, Vol. 38 (12): 37–8.

Landes, David (1998). *The Wealth and Poverty of Nations: Why Some Are So Rich and Others So Poor*, New York: W.W. Norton.

Marshall, Alfred (1890). *Principles of Economics*, London: Macmillan.

Parker, William Nelson (1986). *Economic History and the Modern Economist*, Oxford: Basil Blackwell.

Piketty, Thomas (2014). *Capital in the 21st Century*, Cambridge, MA: Harvard University Press.

Saul, John Ralston (2004). 'The Collapse of Globalism', *Harper's Magazine*, March.

Schlesinger, Arthur M. (1986). *The Cycles of American History*, London: Penguin.

Schumpeter, Joseph (1983 [1934]). *The Theory of Economic Development: An Inquiry into Profits, Capital, Credit, Interest, and the Business Cycle*, New Brunswick: Transaction Publishers.

Solow, Robert (1985). 'Economic History and Economics', *American Economic Review*, Vol. 75 (2): 328–31.

Chapter 12

Alkire, Sabina, Foster, James E., Seth, Suman, Santos, Maria Emma, Roche, Jose M. and Ballon, Paola (2015). *Multidimensional Poverty Measurement and Analysis*, Oxford: Oxford University Press.

Arrow, Kenneth (1951). *Social Choice and Individual Values*, London: Chapman & Hall.

Chaves, Emilio José (2003). 'Toward a Centre-Periphery Model of Global Accounting', in Gernot Kohler and Emilio José Chaves (eds.), *Globalization: Critical Perspectives*, New York: Nova Science.

Daly, Herman E. (1996). *Beyond Growth: The Economics of Sustainable Development*, Boston: Beacon Press.

Easterlin, Richard (1974). 'Does Economic Growth Improve the Human Lot?', in P.A. David and M.W. Reder (eds.), *Nations and Households in Economic Growth: Essays in Honour of Moses Abramovitz*, New York: Academic Press.

Foley, Duncan K. (2009). *Adam's Fallacy: A Guide to Economic Theology*, Cambridge, MA: Harvard University Press.

Galbraith, John Kenneth (1987). *A History of Economics: The Past as Present*, London: Penguin.

Hayek, Friedrich (1937). 'Economics and Knowledge', *Economica*, New Series, Vol. 4 (13): 33–54.

Jevons, W. Stanley (1987 [1871]). *The Theory of Political Economy*, London: Macmillan.

Kaldor, Nicholas (1939). 'Welfare Proposition of Economics and Interpersonal Comparisons of Utility', *The Economic Journal*, Vol. 49 (195): 549–52.

Keynes, John Maynard (2015 [1930]). 'Economic Possibilities for Our Grandchildren', in Robert Skidelsky (ed.), *The Essential Keynes*, Penguin Classics.

Layard, Richard (2005). *Happiness: Lessons from a New Science*, London: Penguin.

Locke, John (1764 [1689]). *Two Treatises of Government*, London: A. Millar et al.

Marx, Karl (1887 [1867]). *Capital*, Vol. 1, Moscow: Progress Publishers.

Marx, Karl and Engels, Friedrich (2004 [1848]). *Manifesto of the Communist Party*. Online: Marxists Internet Archive. https://www.marxists.org/archive/marx/works/1848/communist-manifesto/index.htm

Meadows, Donella H., Meadows, Dennis L., Randers, Jørgen and Behrens, William W. III (1972). *The Limits to Growth*, New York: Universe Books.

Mill, John Stuart (1848). *Principles of Political Economy*, London: John W. Parker.

Nozick, Robert (1974). *Anarchy, State, and Utopia*, New York: Basic Books.

Oreskes, Naomi and Conway, Erik M. (2014). *The Collapse of Western Civilization: A View from the Future*, New York: Columbia University Press.

Pigou, C. Arthur (1932 [1920]). *The Economics of Welfare* (4th ed.), London: Macmillan.

Plender, John (2019). 'Shareholders Are Being Dethroned as Rulers of Value', *The Financial Times*, 3 January.

Ramachandran, V.S. (2010). *The Tell-Tale Brain*, India: Random House.

Rawls, John (1999 [1971]). *A Theory of Justice*, Cambridge, MA: Harvard University Press.

Raworth, Kate (2017). *Doughnut Economics: Seven Ways to Think Like a 21st-Century Economist*, London: Random House.

Ricardo, David (1817). *On the Principles of Political Economy and Taxation*, London: John Murray.

Robbins, Lionel (1938). 'Interpersonal Comparisons of Utility: A Comment', *The Economic Journal*, Vol. 48 (192): 635–41.

Sandel, Michael J. (2012). *What Money Can't Buy: The Moral Limits of Markets*, New York: Farrar, Strauss and Giroux.

Scull, Andrew (2019). 'Egos and Experiments', *Times Literary Supplement*, 18 January.

Sen, Amartya (1999). *Development as Freedom*, Oxford: Oxford University Press.

Skidelsky, Robert and Skidelsky, Edward (2012). *How Much is Enough?*, London: Allen Lane.

Smith, Adam (1904 [1776]). *An Inquiry into the Nature and Causes of the Wealth of Nations*, London: Methuen.

Stigler, George (1982). *The Economist as Preacher, and Other Essays*, Chicago: University of Chicago Press.

Whately, Richard (1832). 'Lecture IX' in *Introductory Lectures on Political Economy*, London: B. Fellowes.

Chapter 13

Davidson, Paul (1994). *Post-Keynesian Macroeconomic Theory: A Foundation for Successful Economic Policies for the Twenty-first Century*, Aldershot: Edward Elgar.

Hayek, Friedrich (1944). *The Road to Serfdom*, London: Routledge.

Hollis, Martin (1987). *The Cunning of Reason*, Cambridge: Cambridge University Press.

Keynes, John Maynard (1921) [*Collected Writings of, Vol. 8*, 1973]. *A Treatise on Probability*, London: Macmillan. (available at: http://www.gutenberg.org/files/32625/32625-pdf.pdf)

Keynes, John Maynard (1964 [1936]). *The General Theory of Employment, Interest and Money*, San Diego: Harcourt.

Keynes, John Maynard (1926) [*Collected Writings of, Vol. 10*]. 'Francis Ysidro Edgeworth, 1845–1926: A Memoir', in *The Collected Writings of John Maynard Keynes, Vol. 10: Essays in Biography*, London: Macmillan.

Keynes, John Maynard (1936) [*Collected Writings of, Vol. 7*, 1972]. 'The General Theory of Interest, Unemployment and Money', in Robert Skidelsky (ed.), *The Essential Keynes*, Penguin Classics.

Krugman, Paul (1995). 'The Fall and Rise of Development Economics', in Paul Krugman, *Development, Geography and Economic Theory*, Cambridge, MA: MIT Press.

Minsky, H. (1986). *Stabilizing an Unstable Economy*, New York: McGraw-Hill.

Neumann, John von and Morgenstern, Oskar (1944). *Theory of Games and Economic Behavior*, Princeton: Princeton University Press.

O'Donnell, Rod (1989). *Keynes: Philosophy, Economics and Politics*, London: Macmillan.

Ramsey, Frank P. (1931 [1926]). 'Truth and Probability', in Frank P. Ramsey (1931), *The Foundations of Mathematics and Other Logical Essays*, Ch. VII, ed. R.B. Braithwaite, London: Kegan, Paul.

Shackle, G.L.S. (1955). *Uncertainty in Economics and Other Reflections*, Cambridge: Cambridge University Press.

Skidelsky, Robert (2018). *Money and Government*, London: Allen Lane.

Skidelsky, Robert (1994). *John Maynard Keynes: The Economist as Saviour, 1920–1937*, New York: Allen Lane.

Chapter 14

Keynes, John Maynard (2015 [1936]). 'The General Theory of Interest, Unemployment and Money', in Robert Skidelsky (ed.), *The Essential Keynes*, Penguin Classics.

Additional Reading

Feynman, Richard P. (2011 [1965]). *Six Easy Pieces: Essentials of Physics Explained by Its Most Brilliant Teacher*, New York: Basic Books.

Fischer, Liliann, Hasell, Joe, Proctor, J. Christopher, Uwakwe, David, Ward-Perkins,, Zach and Watson, Catriona (2018). *Rethinking Economics: An Introduction to Pluralist Economics*, London: Routledge.

Graeber, David (2011). *Debt: The First 5,000 Years*, London: Verso.

Heidegger, Martin (1977). *The Question Concerning Technology and Other Essays*, New York: Harper Torchbooks.

Kay, John and King, Mervin (2020). *Radical Uncertainty: Decision-making Beyond the Numbers*, New York: W.W. Norton.

Spengler, Oswald (1932). *Man and Technics*, London: Allen & Unwin.

INDEX